W. F. Clocksin   C. S. Mellish

Programming in Prolog

Third, Revised and Extended Edition

Springer-Verlag
Berlin Heidelberg New York
London Paris Tokyo

William F. Clocksin

Computer Laboratory, University of Cambridge
Corn Exchange Street
Cambridge CB2 3QG/England

Christopher S. Mellish

Cognitive Studies Programme, University of Sussex
Arts Building, Falmer
Brighton BN1 9QN/England

ISBN 3-540-17539-3 Springer-Verlag Berlin Heidelberg New York
ISBN 0-387-17539-3 Springer-Verlag New York Berlin Heidelberg

ISBN 3-540-15011-0 2. Auflage Springer-Verlag Berlin Heidelberg New York
ISBN 0-387-15011-0 2nd Edition Springer-Verlag New York Berlin Heidelberg

Printed and bound by Arcata Graphics/Halliday, West Hanover, Massachusetts.

PREFACE TO THE THIRD EDITION

We have added new material to Chapter 3 to give an account of up-to-date programming techniques using accumulators and difference structures. Chapter 8 contains some new information on syntax errors. Operator precedences are now compatible with the most widely-used implementations. We have made further reorganisations and improvements in presentation, and have corrected a number of minor errors. We thank the many people who brought typographical errors in the previous edition to our attention, and we thank A.R.C. for careful proofreading.

Cambridge, England   W.F.C.
January, 1987   C.S.M.

PREFACE TO THE SECOND EDITION (1984)

Since the first publishing of *Programming in Prolog* in 1981, Prolog has continued to attract an unexpectedly great deal of interest in the computer science community and is now seen as a potential basis for an important new generation of programming languages and systems. We hope that *Programming in Prolog* has partially satisfied the increasing need for an easy, yet comprehensive introduction to the language as a tool for practical programming. In this second edition we have taken the opportunity to improve the presentation and to correct various minor errors in the original. We thank the many people who have given us suggestions for corrections and improvement.

Cambridge, England   W.F.C.
August, 1984   C.S.M.

PREFACE TO THE FIRST EDITION (1981)

The computer programming language *Prolog* is quickly gaining popularity throughout the world. Since its beginnings around 1970, Prolog has been chosen by many programmers for applications of symbolic computation, including:

- [ ] relational databases

- [ ] mathematical logic

- [ ] abstract problem solving

- [ ] understanding natural language

- [ ] design automation

- [ ] symbolic equation solving

- [ ] biochemical structure analysis

- [ ] many areas of artificial intelligence

Until now, there has been no textbook with the aim of teaching Prolog as a practical programming language. It is perhaps a tribute to Prolog that so many people have been motivated to learn it by referring to the necessarily concise reference manuals, a few published papers, and by the orally transmitted "folklore" of the modern computing community. However, as Prolog is beginning to be introduced to large numbers of undergraduate and postgraduate students, many of our colleagues have expressed a great need for a tutorial guide to learning Prolog. We hope this little book will go some way towards meeting this need.

Many newcomers to Prolog find that the task of writing a Prolog program is not like specifying an algorithm in the same way as in a conventional programming language. Instead, the Prolog programmer asks more what formal relationships and objects occur in his problem, and what relationships are "true" about the desired solution. So, Prolog can be viewed as a *descriptive* language as well as a *prescriptive* one. The Prolog approach is rather to describe known facts and relationships about a problem, than to prescribe the sequence of steps taken by a computer to solve the problem. When a computer is programmed in Prolog, the actual way the computer carries out the computation is specified partly by the logical declarative semantics of Prolog, partly by what new facts Prolog can "infer" from the given ones, and only partly by explicit control information supplied by the programmer.

Prolog is a practical and efficient implementation of many aspects of "intelligent" program execution, such as non-determinism, parallelism, and pattern-directed procedure call. Prolog provides a uniform data structure, called the *term*, out of which all data, as well as Prolog programs, are constructed. A Prolog program consists of a set of clauses, where each clause is either a fact about the given information or a rule about how the solution may relate to or be inferred from the given facts. Thus, Prolog can be seen as a first step towards the ultimate goal of programming in logic. In this book we shall not be concerned greatly with the wider implications of logic programming or with why Prolog is not the ultimate logic programming language. Instead, we will be concerned with showing how useful programs can be written using the Prolog systems that exist today.

This book can serve several purposes. The aim of this book is not to teach the art of programming as such. We feel that programming cannot be learned simply by reading a book or by listening to a lecturer. You've got to <u>do</u> programming to learn it. We hope that beginners without a mathematical background can learn Prolog from this book, although in this case we would recommend that the beginner is taught by a programmer who knows Prolog, as part of a course that introduces the student to programming as such. It is assumed that the beginner can obtain the use of a computer that has a Prolog system installed, and that he has been instructed in the use of a computer terminal. The experienced programmer should not require extra assistance, but we hope he will not dismay at our efforts to restrain mathematical affectation. We have used draft versions of this book to teach university graduates who did little mathematics as schoolchildren, and who specialised in philosophy and psychology whilst at university.

In our experience, novice programmers find that Prolog programs seem to be more comprehensible than equivalent programs in conventional languages. However, the same people tend not to appreciate the limitations that conventional languages place on their use of computing resources. On the other hand, the programmer experienced in conventional languages is better prepared to deal with abstract concepts such as variables and control flow. But, in spite of his prior experience, he may find Prolog difficult to adapt to, and he may need a lot of convincing before he considers Prolog a useful programming tool. Of course, we know of many highly experienced programmers who have taken up Prolog with much enthusiasm. However, the aim of this book is not to convert, but to teach.

Like most other programming languages, Prolog exists in a number of different implementations, each with its own semantic and syntactic peculiarities. In this book we have adopted a "core Prolog", and all of our examples conform to a standard version that corresponds to the implementations, developed mainly at Edinburgh, for several different computer systems: the DECsystem-10 running TOPS-10, the DEC VAX and

PDP-11 running Unix, the DEC LSI-11 running RT-11, and the ICL 2980 running EMAS. The implementations for the DEC computers are probably the most widespead. All the examples in this book will run on all of the implementations. In the appendices, we list some of the existing Prolog implementations, indicating how they diverge from the standard. The reader will appreciate that most of the deviations are of a purely cosmetic nature.

This book was designed to be read sequentially, although it will prove helpful to read Chapter 8 at the time the reader begins to write Prolog programs consisting of more than about ten clauses. Furthermore, it is wise to read the appropriate appendix that describes the particular implementation of Prolog. Appendices tell how to enter clauses, what debugging facilities are available, and other practical matters. It shouldn't hurt to browse through the book, but do take care not to skip over the earlier chapters.

Each chapter is divided into several sections, and we advise the reader to attempt the exercises that are at the end of many sections. The solutions to some of the exercises appear at the end of the book. Chapter 1 is a tutorial introduction that is intended to give the reader a "feel" for what is required to program in Prolog. The fundamental ideas of Prolog are introduced, and the reader is advised to study them carefully. Chapter 2 presents a more complete discussion of points that are introduced in Chapter 1. Chapter 3 deals with data structures and derives some small example programs. Chapter 4 treats the subject of backtracking in more detail, and introduces the "cut" symbol, which is used to control backtracking. Chapter 5 introduces the facilities that are available for input and output. Chapter 6 describes each built-in predicate in the standard "core" of Prolog. Chapter 7 is a potpourri of example programs collected from many sources, together with an explanation of how they are written. Chapter 8 offers some advice on debugging Prolog programs. Chapter 9 introduces the Grammar Rule syntax, and examines the design decisions for some aspects of analysing natural language by using Grammar Rules. Chapter 10 describes the relation of Prolog to its origins in mathematical theorem proving and logic programming. Chapter 11 specifies a number of projects on which interested readers may wish to practise their programming ability.

Acknowledgements. We express our gratitude to our teachers who have influenced the way we think about programming: Rod Burstall, Peter Scott Langston, and Robin Popplestone. We thank those friends who have collaborated in the development of Prolog as a practical and useful programming tool, and who encouraged us in the preparation of this book: Alan Bundy, Lawrence Byrd, Robert Kowalski, Fernando Pereira, and David Warren. In particular, Lawrence Byrd supported the development of this book from its inception by suggesting programs, exercises, some of the projects listed in Chapter 11, and many ideas. We also thank our friends who contributed to this book by providing helpful comments and advice on earlier drafts of this book: Jon Cunningham, Richard O'Keefe, Helen Pain, Fernando Pereira, Gordon Plotkin, Robert Rae, Peter Ross, Maxwell Shorter, Aaron Sloman and David Warren. In this regard, W.F.C. especially thanks his postgraduate students of the School of Epistemics, and of the Department of Artificial Intelligence, who were obliged to be the subjects of many experiments in teaching programming. For our examples, we have been free in adapting and developing programs from the general Prolog folklore. We tender our apologies to anyone who feels slighted or plagiarized by this. This book was prepared while the authors were employed at the Department of Artificial Intelligence, University of Edinburgh. We thank Jim Howe, Head of the Department, who provided the necessary opportunities and facilities with which to carry out this project.

Edinburgh, Scotland   W.F.C.

June, 1981   C.S.M.

TABLE OF CONTENTS

By this point, the reader will be able to write reasonable programs, and so the problem of debugging will be relevant. Flow of control model, hints about common bugs, techniques of debugging.

Applications of existing techniques. Using Grammar Rules. Examining the design decisions for some aspects of analysing natural language with Grammar Rules.

Predicate Calculus, clausal form, resolution theorem proving, logic programming.

A selection of suggested exercises, projects, and problems.

APPENDICES

Chapter 1
Tutorial Introduction

Prolog is a computer programming language that is used for solving problems that involve *objects* and the *relationships* between objects. In this chapter we shall show the essential elements of the language in real programs, but without becoming diverted by details, formal rules, and exceptions. At this point, we are not trying to be complete or precise. We want to bring you quickly to the point where you can write useful programs, so to do that we must concentrate on the basics: facts, questions, variables, conjunctions, and rules. Other features of Prolog, such as lists and recursion, will be treated in later chapters.

We use Prolog when we wish the computer to solve problems that can be expressed in the form of objects and their relationships. For example, when we say "John owns the book", we are declaring that a relationship, ownership, exists between one object "John" and another individual object "the book". Furthermore, the relationship has a specific order: John owns the book, but the book doesn't own John! When we ask the question "Does John own the book?", we are trying to find out about a relationship.

Some relationships don't always mention all the objects that are involved. For example, when we say "The jewel is valuable", we mean that there is a relationship, called "being valuable", which involves a jewel. We did not mention who finds the jewel valuable, or why. It all depends on what you want to say. In Prolog, when you will be programming the computer about relationships like these, the amount of detail you provide also depends on what you want the computer to accomplish.

There is one more point of philosophy to mention, then we shall begin programming. We are all familiar with using rules to describe relationships between objects. For example, the rule "Two people are sisters if they are both female and have the same parents" tells us something about what it means to be sisters. It also tells us how to find out if two people are sisters: simply check to see if they are both female and have the same parents. What is important to notice about rules is that they are usually oversimplified, but they are acceptable as *definitions*. After all, one cannot expect a definition to tell us everything about something.

For example, most people would agree there is much more to "being sisters" in real life than the above rule implies. However, when we are solving a particular problem, we need to concentrate on just those rules that help to solve the problem. So, we ought to consider an imaginary and simplified definition if it is sufficient for our purposes.

Computer programming in Prolog consists of:

- declaring some *facts* about objects and their relationships,
- defining some *rules* about objects and their relationships, and
- asking *questions* about objects and their relationships.

For example, suppose we told a Prolog system our rule about sisters. We could then ask the question whether Mary and Jane are sisters. Prolog would search through what we told it about Mary and Jane, and come back with the answer **yes** or **no**, depending on what we told it earlier. So, we can consider Prolog as a storehouse of facts and rules, and it uses the facts and rules to answer questions. Programming in Prolog consists of supplying all these facts and rules. The Prolog system enables a computer to be used as a storehouse of facts and rules, and it provides ways to make inferences from one fact to another.

Prolog is a conversational language, which means that you and the computer carry out a kind of conversation. Assume that you are seated at a computer terminal and have asked to use Prolog. The computer terminal you use has a *keyboard* and a *display*. You use the keyboard to type characters into the computer, and the computer uses the display (either a screen or paper) to type results back to you. Prolog will wait for you to type in the facts and rules that pertain to the problem you want to solve. Then, if you ask the right kind of questions, Prolog will work out the answers and show them on the display.

We shall now introduce each of the fundamentals of Prolog one by one. Don't worry about not having the complete story about each feature of Prolog straight away. There will be complete summaries and more examples worked out in later chapters.

1.1 Facts

We first discuss *facts* about objects. Suppose we want to tell Prolog the fact that "John likes Mary". This fact consists of two objects, called "Mary" and "John", and a relationship, called "likes". In Prolog, we need to write facts in a standard form, like this:

likes(john,mary).

The following things are important:

- The names of all relationships and objects must begin with a lower-case letter. For example, likes, john, mary.

- The relationship is written first, and the objects are written separated by commas, and the objects are enclosed by a pair of round brackets.

- The full stop character ". " must come at the end of a fact.

When defining relationships between objects using facts, you should pay attention to what order the objects are written between the round brackets. In fact, the order is arbitrary, but you must decide on some order and be consistent about it. For example, in the above fact, we have put the "liker" in as the first of the two objects in round brackets, and we have but the object that is liked in the second slot. So, the fact likes(john,mary) is not the same thing as likes(mary,john). The first fact says that John likes Mary, and the second fact says that Mary likes John, according to our current arbitrary convention. If we want to say that Mary likes John, then we must explicitly say so:

likes(mary,john).

Look at the following examples of facts, together with possible interpretations in English:

valuable(gold).	Gold is valuable.
female(jane).	Jane is female.
owns(john,gold).	John owns gold.
father(john,mary).	John is the father of Mary.
gives(john,book,mary).	John gives the book to Mary.

Each time a name is used, the name refers to a particular individual object. Because of our familiarity with English, it is fairly clear that the names john and jane refer to individuals. But, in some other facts, we have used the names gold and valuable and it is not necessarily obvious what they mean. This sort of name is called a "non-count word" by logicians. When using names, we must decide on how to *interpret* the name.

For example, the name gold could refer to an object. In this case we think of the object as some particular lump of gold that we denote by the name gold. And when we say in Prolog valuable(gold), we would mean that this particular lump of gold, which we have named gold, is valuable. On the other hand, we could interpret the name gold to be a word standing for the chemical element Gold having atomic number 79, and when we say valuable(gold), we would mean that the chemical element Gold is valuable. So, there is more than one way to interpret a name, and it is you, the programmer, who decides on the interpretation. There should be no problem as long as you interpret names consistently. It is important to bring out the distinctions between different interpretations early, so that we are quite certain what names mean.

Now for some terminology. The names of the objects that are enclosed within the round brackets in each fact are called the *arguments*. Note that computer programmers use the word "argument" in a technical sense which bears none of the common connotations of dispute, debate, discussion, theme, or topic. The name of the relationship, which comes just before the round brackets, is called the *predicate*. So, valuable is a predicate having one argument, and likes is a predicate having two arguments.

The names of the objects and relationships are completely arbitrary. Instead of a term such as likes(john,mary), we could just as well represent this as a(b,c), and remember that a means *likes*, b means *John*, and c means *Mary*. However, we normally select names that help us to remember what they represent. So, we must decide in advance what our names mean, and what the order of arguments shall be. Thereafter we must remain consistent.

Relationships can have an arbitrary number of arguments. If we want to define a predicate called play, where we mention two players and a game they play with each other, we need three arguments. Here are two examples of this:

    play(john,mary,football).

    play(jane,jim,badminton).

Using many arguments is important for representing complicated interactions between relationships, as we shall see later.

We may also declare facts that are not true in the real world. We could write king(john,france) to specify that *John is the king of France*. In the real world this is obviously false, especially because the monarchy was abolished in France sometime around 1792. But Prolog does not know, and does not care. Facts in Prolog simply allow you to express arbitrary relationships between objects.

In Prolog, a collection of facts is called a *database*. We shall use the word *database* whenever we have collected together some facts (and later, rules) that are used to solve a particular problem.

1.2 Questions

Once we have some facts, we can ask some questions about them. In Prolog, a question looks just like a fact, except that we put a special symbol before it. The special symbol is written as a question mark and a hyphen. Consider the question:

```
?- owns(mary,book).
```

If we interpret mary to be *a person called Mary*, and book to be some particular book, this question is asking *Does Mary own the book?*, or *Is it a fact that Mary owns the book?* We are not asking whether she owns all books, or books in general.

When a question is asked of Prolog, it will search through the database you typed in before. It looks for facts that *match* the fact in the question. Two facts *match* if their predicates are the same (spelled the same way), and if their corresponding arguments each are the same. If Prolog finds a fact that matches the question, Prolog will respond yes. If no such fact exists in the database, Prolog will respond no. The response from Prolog is printed on on the display of your computer terminal on the line just below your question. Consider the following database:

```
likes(joe,fish).
likes(joe,mary).
likes(mary,book).
likes(john,book).
```

If we typed in all those facts to the Prolog system, we could ask the following questions, and Prolog would give the answers (shown from now on in bold type) on the line just after the question:

```
?- likes(joe,money).
```
no
```
?- likes(mary,joe).
```
no
```
?- likes(mary,book).
```
yes
```
?- king(john,france).
```
no

The answers to the first three questions should be clear to you. Prolog also answered no to the question of whether John was the king of France. This is because there were no facts about royal relationships in the list of four likes relationships above. In Prolog, the answer no is used to mean *nothing matches the question*. It is important to remember that no is not the same as *is false.* For example, suppose a database about some famous Greeks contains only the following three facts:

```
human(socrates).
human(aristotle).

athenian(socrates).
```

We can ask some questions:

```
?- athenian(socrates).
```
yes
```
?- athenian(aristotle).
```
no
```
?- greek(socrates).
```
no

Although it may be true in real history that Aristotle once lived in Athens, we cannot *prove* it simply from the facts shown in the database. Furthermore, although it is shown in the database that Socrates is an Athenian, this does not *prove* he is a Greek unless more information is in the database. So, when Prolog answers no to a question, it means *not provable.*

In the above database, both John and Mary like the same object. We know they like the same object because the same name, book appears in both facts.

The facts and questions we have discussed so far are not particularly interesting. All we can do is get back the same information we put in. It would be more useful to ask question such as, *What objects does Mary like?* and, *Who lives in Athens?* This is what *variables* are for.

1.3 Variables

If you want to find out what things that John likes, it is tiresome to ask *Does John like books?*, *Does John like Mary?*, and so forth, with Prolog giving a yes-or-no answer each time. It is more sensible to ask Prolog to tell you something that he likes. We could phrase a question of this form as, *Does John like X?*. When we ask a question, we do not know what the object is that X could *stand for*. We would like Prolog to tell us what the possibilities are. In Prolog we can not only name particular objects, but we can also use names like X to stand for objects to be determined by Prolog. Names of this second kind are called *variables*. When Prolog uses a variable, the variable can be either *instantiated* or *not instantiated*. A variable is instantiated when there is an object that the variable stands for.

A variable is not instantiated when what the variable stands for is not yet known. Prolog can distinguish variables from names of particular objects because *any* name beginning with a capital letter is taken to be a variable.

When Prolog is asked a question containing a variable, Prolog searches through all its facts to find an object that the variable could stand for. So when we ask *Does John like X?*, Prolog searches through all its facts to find things that John likes.

A variable, such as X, does not name a particular object in itself, but it can be used to stand for objects that we cannot name. For example, we cannot name *something that John likes* as an object, so Prolog adopts a way of saying this. Instead of asking a question like:

```
?- likes(john, something that John likes).
```

Prolog lets us use variables, like this:

```
?- likes(john,X).
```

Variables can have longer names if we wish. This question is acceptable to Prolog:

```
?- likes(john,Somethingthatjohnlikes).
```

Why? Because a variable can be any name that begins with a capital letter. Consider the following database of facts, followed by a question:

```
likes(john,flowers).
likes(john,mary).
likes(paul,mary).

?- likes(john,X).
```

The question asks, *Is there anything that John likes?* When asked the question, Prolog will respond:

X=flowers

and then wait for further instructions, which we will talk about shortly. How does this work? When Prolog is asked this question, the variable X is initially not instantiated. Prolog searches though the database, looking for a fact that *matches* the question. Now if an uninstantiated variable appears as an argument, Prolog will allow that argument to match *any* other argument in the same position in the fact. What happens here is that Prolog searches for any fact where the predicate is likes, and the first argument is john. The second argument in this case may be anything, because the question was asked with an uninstantiated variable as the second argument. When such a fact is found, then the variable X now stands for the second argument in the fact, whatever it may be. Prolog searches through the database in the order it was typed in (or top-to-bottom on the printed page) so the fact likes(john,flowers) is found first. Variable X now stands for the object flowers. Or, we say that X is *instantiated* to flowers. Prolog now *marks the place* in the database where a match is found. The place-marker is used for reasons we discuss shortly.

Once Prolog finds a fact that matches a question, it prints out the objects that the variables now stand for. In this case, the only variable was X, and it matched the object flowers. Now Prolog waits for further instructions, as we said above. If you type the computer terminal's RETURN key, meaning you are satisfied with just one answer, then Prolog will stop searching for more. If instead you type the ';' key (followed by RETURN), Prolog will resume its search through the database as before, *starting from where it left the place-marker*. When Prolog begins searching from a place-marker, instead of from the beginning of the database, we say that Prolog is attempting to *re-satisfy* the question.

Suppose in response to Prolog's first answer (X=flowers) we asked it to carry on (by typing ';'). This means we want to satisfy the question in another way; we want to find another object that X could stand for. This means that Prolog must 'forget' that X stands for flowers, and resume searching with X uninstantiated again. Because we are searching for an alternative solution, the search is continued from the place-marker. The next matching fact found is likes(john,mary). The variable X is now *instantiated* to mary, and Prolog puts a place-marker at the fact likes(john,mary). Prolog will print X=mary, and wait for further commands. If we relentlessly type another semicolon, Prolog will continue the search. In this example there is nothing more that John likes. So, Prolog will stop its search, and allow us to ask more questions or declare more facts.

What happens if, given the same facts above, we ask the question:

```
?-likes(X,mary).
```

This question asks, *Is there an object that likes Mary?* By now you should see that the objects in the example that like Mary are john and paul. Again, if we wanted to see all of them, we would type ';' after Prolog types out each one of the answers:

```
?- likes(X,mary).        our question.

X=john;                  first answer. We type ';' in reply.

X=paul;                  second answer. Again we type ';'.

no                       no more answers.
```

1.4 Conjunctions

Suppose we wish to answer questions about more complicated relationships, such as, *Do John and Mary like each other?* One way to do this would be first to ask if John likes Mary, and if Prolog tells us yes, then we ask if Mary likes John. So, this problem consists of two separate *goals* that the Prolog system must try to satisfy. Because a combination like this is frequently used by

Prolog programmers, there is a special notation for it. Suppose we have the following database:

```
likes(mary,food).
likes(mary,wine).
likes(john,wine).
likes(john,mary).
```

We want to ask if John and Mary like each other. To do this, we ask, *Does John like Mary?* **and** *does Mary like John?* The *and* expresses the idea that we are interested in the *conjunction* of the two goals – we want to satisfy them both one after the other. We represent this by putting a comma between the goals:

```
?- likes(john,mary), likes(mary,john).
```

The comma is pronounced "and", and it serves to separate any number of different goals that have to be satisfied in order to answer a question. When a sequence of goals (separated by commas) is given to Prolog, Prolog attempts to satisfy each goal in turn by searching for a matching goal in the database. All goals have to be satisfied in order for the sequence to be satisfied. Using the above list of facts, what should Prolog print out when given the above question? The answer is no. It is a fact that John likes Mary, so the first goal is true. However, the second goal cannot be proved, since there is nowhere in the list of facts where likes(mary,john) occurs. Since we wanted to know if they *both* like each other, the whole question is answered no.

Conjunctions and the use of variables can be combined to ask quite interesting questions. Now that we know that it cannot be shown that John and Mary like each other, we ask: *Is there anything that John and Mary both like?* This question also consists of two goals:

- First, find out if there is some X that Mary likes.
- Then, find out if John likes whatever X is.

In Prolog the two goals would be written as a conjunction like this:

```
?- likes(mary,X), likes(john,X).
```

Prolog answers the question by attempting to satisfy the first goal. If the first goal is in the database, then Prolog will mark the place in the database, and attempt to satisfy the second goal. If the second goal is satisfied, then Prolog marks *that goal's* place in the database, and we have found a solution that satisfies both goals.

It is most important to remember that each goal keeps its own place-marker. If, however, the second goal is not satisfied, then Prolog will attempt to re-satisfy the previous goal (in this case the first goal). Remember that Prolog searches the database completely for each goal. If a fact in the database happens to match, satisfying the goal, then Prolog will mark the place in the database in case it has to re-satisfy the goal at a later time. But when a goal needs to be re-satisfied, Prolog will begin the search from the goal's own place-marker, rather than from the start of the database. Our above question *is anything liked by Mary also liked by John?* illustrates an example of this "backtracking" behaviour in the following way:

1. The database is searched for the first goal. As the second argument (X) is uninstantiated, it may match anything. The first such matching fact in our above database is likes(mary,food). So, now X is instantiated to food *everywhere* in the question where X appears. Prolog marks the place in the database where it found the fact, so it can return to this point in case it needs to re-satisfy the goal. Furthermore, we need to remember that X became instantiated here, so Prolog can "forget" X if it needs to re-satisfy this goal.

2. Now, the database is searched for likes(john,food). This is because the next goal is likes(john,X), and X currently stands for food. As you can see, no such fact exists, so the goal fails. Now when a goal fails, we must try to re-satisfy the previous goal, so Prolog attempts to re-satisfy likes(mary,X), but this time starting from the place that was marked in the database. But first we need to make X uninstantiated once more, so X may match against anything.

3. The marked place is likes(mary,food), so Prolog begins searching from after that fact. Because we have not reached the end of the database yet, we have not exhausted the possibilities of what Mary likes, and the next matching fact is likes(mary,wine). The variable X is now instantiated to wine, and Prolog marks the place in case it must re-satisfy what mary likes.

4. As before, Prolog now tries the second goal, searching this time for likes(john,wine). Prolog is not trying to re-satisfy this goal. It is entering the goal again (from the left-hand side, as it were), so it must start searching from the beginning of the database. After not too much searching, the matching fact is found, and Prolog notifies you. Since this goal was satisfied, Prolog also marks *its* place in the database, in case you want to re-satisfy the goal. There is a place-marker in the database for each goal that Prolog is attempting to satisfy.

5. At this point, both goals have been satisfied. Variable X stands for the name wine. The first goal has a place-marker in the database at the fact likes(mary,wine), and the second goal has a place-marker in the database at the fact likes(john,wine).

As with any other question, as soon as Prolog finds one answer, it stops and waits for futher instructions. If we type ';', Prolog will search for more things that both John and Mary like. We know now that this amounts to re-satisfying both goals starting from the place-markers they left behind.

To sum up, we can imagine a conjunction of goals to be arranged from left to right, separated by commas. Each goal may have a left-hand neighbour and a right-hand neighbour. Clearly, the left-most goal does not have a left-hand neighbour, and the right-most goal does not have a right-hand neighbour. When handling a conjunction of goals, Prolog attempts to satisfy each goal in turn, working from left to right. If a goal becomes satisfied, Prolog leaves a place-marker in the database that is associated with the goal. Think of this as drawing an arrow from the goal to the place in the database where the solution is. Furthermore, any variables previously uninstantiated might now be instantiated. This happened above at Step 1. If a variable becomes instantiated, all occurrences of the variable in the question become instantiated. Prolog then attempts to satisfy the goal's right-hand neighbour, starting from the top of the database.

As each goal in turn becomes satisfied, it leaves behind a place-marker in the database (draws another arrow from the goal to the matching fact), in case the goal needs to be re-satisfied at a later time. Any time a goal fails (cannot find a matching fact), Prolog goes back and attempts to satisfy its left-hand neighbour, starting from its place-marker. Furthermore, Prolog must "uninstantiate" any variables that became instantiated at this goal. In other words, Prolog must "undo" all the variables when it re-satisfies a goal. If each goal, upon being entered from its right, cannot be re-satisfied, then the failures will cause Prolog to gradually creep to the left as each goal fails. If the first goal (the left-most goal) fails, then it does not have a left-hand neighbour it can attempt to re-satisfy. In this case, the entire conjunction fails. This behaviour, where Prolog repeatedly attempts to satisfy and re-satisfy goals in a conjunction, is called *backtracking*. Backtracking is summarised in the next chapter, and is given a more complete and sophisticated treatment in Chapter 4.

When following the examples, you may find it helpful to write, below each variable in a goal, the object that has been instantiated by the success of the goal. You should also write in an arrow from the goal to its place-marker in the database. An example of this pencil-and-paper aid is shown below at four "snapshots" during the evaluation of the above example. In each snapshot, the complete database and question is shown, together with a numbered commentary. Goals which have been satisfied are outlined in their own little box:

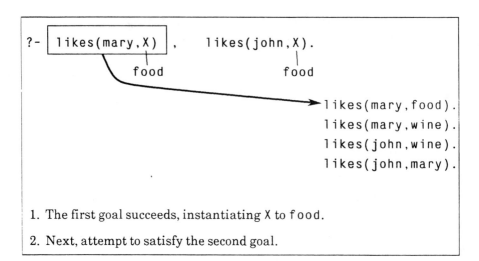

1. The first goal succeeds, instantiating X to food.

2. Next, attempt to satisfy the second goal.

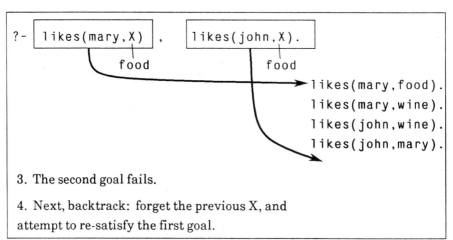

3. The second goal fails.

4. Next, backtrack: forget the previous X, and
attempt to re-satisfy the first goal.

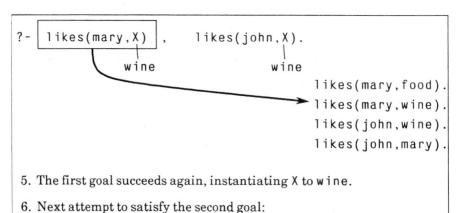

5. The first goal succeeds again, instantiating X to wine.

6. Next attempt to satisfy the second goal:

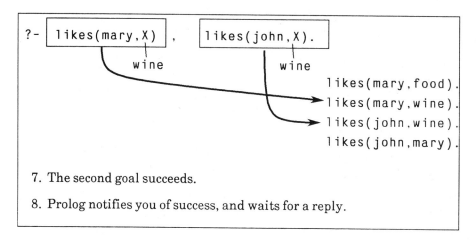

7. The second goal succeeds.

8. Prolog notifies you of success, and waits for a reply.

Throughout this book we will endeavour to show where backtracking occurs in the examples, and what effect it has on solving the problems. Backtracking is so important that the whole of Chapter 4 is devoted to it.

Exercise 1.1: Continue the pencil-and-paper simulation of the example given above, assuming that you have just typed a semicolon to initiate backtracking in order to find out if John and Mary both like anything else.

1.5 Rules

Suppose we wanted to state the fact that John likes all people. One way to do this would be to write down separate facts, like this:

```
likes(john,alfred).
likes(john,bertrand).
likes(john,charles).
likes(john,david).
          .
          .
          .
```

for every person in our database. This could become tedious, especially if there are hundreds of people in our Prolog program. Another way to say that John likes all people is to say, *John likes any object provided it is a person.* This fact is in the form of a *rule* about what John likes, instead of listing all the people John likes. In a world where John could like every person, the rule is much more compact than a list of facts.

In Prolog, rules are used when you want to say that a fact *depends* on a group of other facts. In English, we use the word "if" to express a rule. For example,

I use an umbrella if there is rain.
John buys the wine if it is less expensive than the beer.

Rules are also used to express definitions, for example:

X is a bird if:
 X is an animal, and
 X has feathers.

or

X is a sister of Y if:
 X is female, and
 X and Y have the same parents.

In the above English definitions, we have used variables X and Y. It is important to remember that a variable stands for the same object wherever it occurs in a rule. Otherwise we would be violating the spirit of the definition. For example, in the bird rule above, we could not show that Fred is a bird because Fido is an animal and Mary has feathers. The same principle of consistent interpretation of variables is true also for rules in Prolog.

A rule is a *general statement about objects and their relationships.* For example, we can say that Fred is a bird if Fred is an animal and Fred has feathers, and we can also say that Bertram is a bird if Bertram is an animal and Bertram has feathers. So, we can allow a variable to stand for a different object in each different *use* of the rule. Within a use of a rule, of course, variables are interpreted consistently as pointed out above.

Let us consider several examples, beginning with a rule using one variable and a conjunction.
 John likes anyone who likes wine,
or, in other words,
 John likes anything if it likes wine,
or, with variables,
 John likes X if X likes wine.

In Prolog, a rule consists of a *head* and a *body*. The head and body are connected by the symbol ':-', which is made up of a colon and a hyphen. The ':-' is pronounced *if*. The above example is written in Prolog as:

```
likes(john,X) :- likes(X,wine).
```

Notice that rules also are ended with a dot. The head of this rule is `likes(john,X)`. The head of the rule describes what fact the rule is intended to define. The body, in this case `likes(X,wine)`, describes the conjunction of goals that must be satisfied, one after the other, for the head to be true. For example, we can make John more choosy about whom he likes, simply by adding more goals onto the body, separated by commas:

```
likes(john,X) :- likes(X,wine), likes(X,food).
```

or, in words, *John likes anyone who likes wine and food*. Or, suppose John
likes any female who likes wine:

```
likes(john,X) :- female(X), likes(X,wine).
```

Whenever we look at a Prolog rule, we should take notice of where the
variables are. In the above rule, the variable X is used three times. Whenever
X becomes instantiated to some object, all X's are instantiated *within the scope
of* X. For some particular use of a rule, the scope of X is the whole rule,
including the head, and extending to the dot '.' at the end of the rule. So, in
the above rule, if X happens to be instantiated to mary, then Prolog will try to
satisfy the goals female(mary) and likes(mary,wine).

Next, as an example of a rule that uses more than one variable, consider a
database consisting of facts about some of the family of Queen Victoria. We
shall use the predicate parents having three arguments such that:
parents(X,Y,Z) means *The parents of X are Y and Z*. The second argument
is for the mother, and the third argument is for the father. We shall also use
the predicates female and male in the obvious way. One part of the
database might look like this:

```
male(albert).
male(edward).

female(alice).
female(victoria).

parents(edward,victoria,albert).
parents(alice,victoria,albert).
```

Now we shall use the rule about *sister of* described earlier. The rule defines
the predicate sister_of, having two arguments such that sister_of(X,Y)
is a fact if X is a sister of Y. Notice that we have used the underscore character
'_' in the predicate name. Although we have not yet given the complete rules
for how to construct names, it is permitted to include underscores in a name,
and we shall summarise the rules in the next chapter. Now X is a sister of Y if:

- X is female,
- X has mother M and father F, and
- Y has the same mother and father as X does.

This can be written as the following Prolog rule.

```
sister_of(X,Y) :-
    female(X),
    parents(X,M,F),
    parents(Y,M,F).
```

We use the variable names M and F to indicate mother and father, although
we could have used Mother and Father had we been so inclined. Notice that

we are using variables that do not appear in the head of the rule. These variables, M and F, are treated in the same way as any other variable. When Prolog uses the rule, variables M and F will initially be uninstantiated, so they will match against anything when it becomes time to satisfy the goal parents(X,M,F). However, as soon as they are instantiated, then *all* the M's and F's in this use of the rule will become instantiated. The following example should help to explain how these variables are used.

Let us ask the question:

    ?- sister_of(alice,edward).

When asked this question given the above database and rule for sister_of, Prolog proceeds as follows:

1. First, the question matches the head of the only sister_of rule above, so X in the rule becomes instantiated to alice, and Y becomes instantiated to edward. The place marker for the question is put against this rule. Now Prolog attempts to satisfy the three goals in the body, one by one.

2. The first goal is female(alice) because X was instantiated to alice in the previous step. This goal is true from the list of facts, so the goal succeeds. As it succeeds, Prolog marks the goal's place in the database (the third entry in the database). No new variables were instantiated, so no other note is made. Prolog now attempts to satisfy the next goal.

3. Now Prolog searches for parents(alice,M,F), where M and F will match against any arguments because they are uninstantiated. A matching fact is parents(alice,victoria,albert), so the goal succeeds. Prolog marks the place in the database (sixth down from the top) and records that M became instantiated to victoria, and F to albert. (You may write these under the goal in the rule if you like). Prolog now attempts to satisfy the next goal.

4. Now Prolog searches for parents(edward,victoria,albert) because Y is known as edward from the question, and M and F were known to stand for victoria and albert from the previous goal. The goal succeeds, because a matching fact is found (fifth down from the top). Since it is the last goal in the conjunction, the entire goal succeeds, and the fact sister_of(alice,edward) is established as true. Prolog answers yes.

Suppose we want to know if Alice is the sister of anyone. The appropriate question in Prolog is

    ?- sister_of(alice,X).

For this question, Prolog proceeds as follows:

1. The question matches the head of the only `sister_of` rule. Variable X in the rule becomes instantiated to `alice`. As variable X in the question is uninstantiated, then variable Y in the question will also be uninstantiated. However, these variables now become *shared*. As soon as one of the variables becomes instantiated to an object, the other variable becomes instantiated to the same object. At the moment, as we said, they are not instantiated.

2. The first goal is `female(alice)`, which succeeds as before.

3. The second goal is `parents(alice,M,F)`, and it matches against `parents(alice,victoria,albert)`. Variables M and F are now known.

4. As Y is not yet known, the third goal is therefore `parents(Y,victoria,albert)`. This goal matches against the fact `parents(edward,victoria,albert)`. Variable Y is now known to be `edward`.

5. Since all goals succeed, the entire rule succeeds, with X known to be `alice` (given in the question), and Y as `edward`. Since Y (in the rule) is shared with X (in the question), then X is also instantiated to `edward`. Prolog prints out **X=edward**.

As usual, Prolog waits for you to tell it if you want to find all the solutions to the question. As it turns out, this question has more than one solution. How Prolog finds the remaining solution[s] is set as an exercise at the end of this chapter.

As we have seen thus far, there are two ways to give Prolog information about a given predicate such as `likes`. We can provide both facts and rules. In general, a predicate will be defined by a mixture of facts and rules. These are called the *clauses* for a predicate. We shall use the word *clause* whenever we refer to either a fact or a rule.

As a further example, this time not dealing with monarchs, consider the rule: A person may steal something if the person is a thief and the person likes the thing and the thing is valuable. In Prolog, this is written:

```
may_steal(P,T) :- thief(P), likes(P,T), valuable(T).
```

Here we use the predicate `may_steal`, which has two arguments P and T to represent some person P may steal thing T. This rule depends on clauses for `thief`, `likes`, and `valuable`. These could be represented as a mixture of facts and rules, whatever is most appropriate. For example, consider the following Prolog database, which has been made up from clauses discussed earlier. We have added some clause numbers enclosed between `/*...*/` brackets. This is how we write a *comment*. Comments are ignored by Prolog, but we may add them to our programs for convenience. In the discussion that follows, we shall refer to the clause number comments.

```
/*1*/   thief(john).
/*2*/   likes(mary,food).
/*3*/   likes(mary,wine).
/*4*/   likes(john,X) :- likes(X,wine).
/*5*/   may_steal(X,Y) :-
              thief(X), likes(X,Y), valuable(Y).
```

Notice that the definition of likes has three separate clauses: two facts and a rule. Let us follow what happens when the question *What may John steal?* is asked. First, this question translates into Prolog as:

```
?- may_steal(john,X).
```

To answer this question, Prolog searches as follows:

1. First, Prolog searches in the database for a clause about may_steal, and finds one in the form of a rule at clause number 5. Prolog marks the place in the database. Since it is a rule, its body must be satisfied to establish whether the head is true. So the X in the rule is instantiated to john from the question. Again we find that we have to match two uninstantiated variables (X in the question and Y in the rule), so they will share. The goals of a rule must succeed for the rule to succeed: the first goal, thief(john) is now searched for.

2. The goal succeeds, since thief(john) is in the database (clause 1). Prolog marks the place in the database, and no variables have become newly instantiated. Prolog then attempts to satisfy the second goal using clause 5. Since X still stands for john, Prolog now searches for for likes(john,Y). Notice that Y is still instantiated at this point.

3. The goal likes(john,Y) matches with the head of the rule (at clause 4). The Y in the goal shares with the X in the head, and both remain uninstantiated. To satisfy this rule, likes(X,wine) is now searched for.

4. The goal succeeds, because it matches with likes(mary,wine), the fact at clause 3. So, X now stands for mary.

5. Since the goal in clause 4 succeeds, the whole rule succeeds. The fact likes(john,mary) is established from clause 4 because Y in clause 5 shares with X; it is also instantiated to mary.

6. Clause 5 now succeeds, with Y instantiated to mary. As Y was shared with the second argument of the original question, X in the question is now instantiated to mary.

We chose this example to show how easy it is to generate unexpected answers, such as "John may steal Mary". The reasoning behind establishing that John may steal Mary is:

False unless valuable(Mary)

In order to steal something, first John must be a thief. From clause 1, this is a fact. Next John must like the thing. From clause 4, we see that John likes anything that likes wine. From clause 3, we see that Mary likes wine. Therefore, John likes Mary. Therefore, both conditions for stealing something can be satisfied, so John may steal Mary.

Notice that the fact (clause 2) that Mary likes food, is irrelevant to this particular question.

In this example we have repeatedly used the variables X and Y in different clauses. For example, in the may_steal rule, X stands for the object that can steal something. But in the likes rule, X stands for the object that is liked. In order for this program to make sense, Prolog must be able to tell that X can stand for two different things in two different uses of the clauses. Remember that knowing the scope of a variable can resolve any confusion. We could have used more mnemonic names to attempt to prevent any confusion, but we use simple names such as X to demonstrate the scoping principle.

1.6 Summary and Exercises

At this point we have covered most of the basic core of Prolog. In particular, we have looked at

- Asserting facts about objects.
- Asking questions about the facts.
- Using variables and what their scopes are.
- Conjunction as a way of saying "and".
- Representing relationships in the form of rules.
- An introduction to backtracking.

With this small number of building blocks, it is possible to write useful programs for manipulating simple databases, and it would probably be a good idea if you did so by working out the exercises below.

To see how to use this book, you should read the Preface if you have not already done so. Also, when you begin to write programs for a Prolog system that is available to you, you should consult the appropriate Appendix to see what a sample programming session looks like. You will also find some practical tips in Chapter 8.

After you have this much of Prolog under your control, you should carry on into the next chapter, which makes clear some of the points we did not mention in this chapter. Also, we shall show how to work with numbers in Prolog. The features covered in the next few chapters are where the expressiveness and convenience of Prolog become apparent.

Exercise 1.2. When the sister_of rule is applied to the database of part of Queen Victoria's family discussed previously, more than one answer can be obtained. Explain how all the answers can be obtained, and what they are.

Exercise 1.3 This exercise has been inspired by one in Robert Kowalski's book *Logic for Problem Solving*, published by North Holland in 1979. Suppose someone has already written Prolog clauses that define the following relationships:

```
father(X,Y)        /* X is the father of Y */
mother(X,Y)        /* X is the mother of Y */
male(X)            /* X is male  */
female(X)          /* X is female */
parent(X,Y)        /* X is a parent of Y */
diff(X,Y)          /* X and Y are different */
```

The problem is to write Prolog clauses to define the following relationships:

```
is_mother(X)       /* X is a mother */
is_father(X)       /* X is a father */
is_son(X)          /* X is a son */
sister_of(X,Y)     /* X is a sister of Y */
granpa_of(X,Y)     /* X is a grandfather of Y */
sibling(X,Y)       /* X is a sibling of Y */
```

For example, we could write a rule for aunt, provided we were supplied with (or wrote) rules for female, sibling, and parent.

```
aunt(X,Y) :-  female(X), sibling(X,Z), parent(Z,Y).
```

This could also be written:

```
aunt(X,Y) :-  sister_of(X,Z), parent(Z,Y).
```

provided that we wrote the sister_of rule.

Exercise 1.4. Using the sister_of rule defined in the text, explain why it is possible for some object to be her own sister. How would you change the rule if you did not want this property? Hint: assume that the predicate diff of Exercise 1.3 is already defined.

Chapter 2
A Closer Look

In this chapter we provide a more complete discussion of the parts of Prolog that were introduced in the previous chapter. Prolog provides ways to structure data as well as ways to structure the order in which attempts are made to satisfy goals. Structuring data involves knowing the syntax by which we can denote data. Structuring the order in which goals are solved involves knowing about backtracking.

2.1 Syntax

The syntax of a language describes how we are allowed to fit words together. In English, the syntax of the sentence "I see a zebra" is correct, but the syntax of "zebra see I a" is not correct. In the first chapter, we did not discuss the syntax of Prolog explicitly, but we simply showed what some parts of Prolog looked like. Here we will summarise the syntax of those parts of Prolog we have seen thus far.

Prolog programs are built from *terms*. A term is either a *constant*, a *variable*, or a *structure*. We saw each of these terms in the previous chapter, but we did not know them by these names. Each term is written as a sequence of *characters*. Characters are divided into four categories as follows:

```
A B C D E F G H I J K L M N O P Q R S T U V W X Y Z

a b c d e f g h i j k l m n o p q r s t u v w x y z

0 1 2 3 4 5 6 7 8 9

+ - * / \ ~ ^ < > : . ? @ # $ &
```

The first row consists of upper-case letters. The second row consists of lower-case letters. The third row consists of digits. The fourth row consists of sign characters. There are actually more sign characters than those shown in the fourth row, but others have special uses discussed below. Each kind of term, whether it is a constant, variable, or structure, has different rules for how characters are put together to form its name. Now we shall summarise each kind of term.

2.1.1 Constants

Constants *name* specific objects or specific relationships. There are two kinds of constants: atoms, and integers. Examples of atoms are the names that were given in the last chapter:

likes   mary   john   book   wine   owns   jewels   can_steal

The special symbols that Prolog uses to denote questions "?-" and rules ":-" are also atoms. There are two kinds of atoms: those made up of letters and digits, and those made up from signs. The first kind must normally begin with a lower-case letter, as did all the ones we saw in the previous chapter. Those atoms made from signs normally are made up from signs only. Sometimes it may be necessary to have an atom beginning with a capital letter or a digit. If an atom is enclosed in single quotes "'", then the atom may have *any* characters in its name. Finally, the underline character "_" may be inserted in the middle of an atom to improve legibility. The following are further examples of atoms:

a void   =   'george-smith'   -->   george_smith   ieh2304

The following are *not* examples of atoms:

2304ieh   george-smith   Void   _alpha

Integers, the other kind of constant, are used to represent numbers, so that arithmetic operations can be carried out. We have not discussed how to do arithmetic in Prolog, but this will be introduced later in this chapter. Integers are whole numbers consisting only of digits and may not contain a decimal point. In this book, only fairly small positive integers will be used, for example:

0   1   999   512   8192   14765   6224

Prolog is available on several different computers, and depending on what computer you use, you may not be able to use large numbers or negative numbers. However, in this book we will only give examples that will work on any Prolog you are likely to find. It is safe to say that you will be allowed to use any integer ranging from 0 to 16383. Depending on what computer you use, you may be allowed to use larger numbers or negative numbers, but we will not depend on them here. It is perhaps surprising that the applications for which Prolog is useful tend not to demand the ability to calculate with very large integers, fractions, or negative numbers. However, as Prolog is an extensible language, the resourceful programmer can add predicates to define such features without too much difficulty. For example, some Prolog systems provide library programs that define operations on rational numbers and numbers of arbitrary precision.

2.1.2 Variables

The second kind of term used in Prolog is the variable. Variables look like atoms, except they have names beginning with a capital letter or an underline sign "_". A variable should be thought of as standing for some object that we may not be able to name. This corresponds roughly to the use of a pronoun in English. In the example Prolog clauses we have seen so far, we have used variables with names such as X, Y, and Z. However, the names can be as long as you like, for example:

```
Answer    Input    Gross_Pay    _3_blind_mice
```

Sometimes one needs to use a variable, but its name will never be used. For example, if we want to find out if anyone likes John, but we do not need to know just who, we can use the "anonymous variable". The anonymous variable is written as a single underline character. Our example is written in Prolog as:

```
?- likes(_,john).
```

Several anonymous variables in the same clause need not be given consistent interpretations. This is a characteristic peculiar to the anonymous variable. It is used to save having to dream up different variable names when they will not be used elsewhere in the clause.

2.1.3 Structures

The third kind of term with which Prolog programs are written is the structure. A structure is a single object which consists of a collection of other objects, called components. The components are grouped together into a single structure for convenience in handling them. Structures are sometimes called "compound terms" or "complex terms". Of these two alternatives, we prefer the name "compound term".

One example of a structure in real life is an index card for a library book. The index card will contain several components: the author's name, the title of the book, the date when it was published, the location where it can be found in the library, and so forth. Some of the components can be broken down into further components. For example, the author's name consists of some initials and a surname.

Structures help to organise the data in a program because they permit a group of related information to be treated as a single object (a library card) instead of as separate entities. The way that you decompose data into components depends on what problem you want to solve, and later on we will give advice on how to do this.

Structures are also useful when there is a common kind of object, of
which many may exist. Books, for example. In Chapter 1 we discussed the
fact

```
owns(john,book).
```

to denote that John owns some particular book. If we later said

```
owns(mary,book).
```

this means that Mary owns the same object that John owns, because it has
the same name. There is no other way of telling objects apart, except by their
name. We could say:

```
owns(john,wuthering_heights).
owns(mary,moby_dick).
```

to specify more carefully what books John and Mary own. However, in large
programs, it may become confusing to have many different constants with no
context to tell what they mean. Someone reading this Prolog program may
not know that we meant wuthering_heights to be the name of the book
written by the author Emily Brontë who flourished in Yorkshire, England
during the 19th Century. Perhaps they will think that John has named his
pet rabbit "wuthering_heights", say. Structures can help to provide this
context.

A structure is written in Prolog by specifying its *functor*, and its
components. The functor names the general kind of structure, and
corresponds to a datatype in an ordinary programming language. The
components are enclosed in round brackets and separated by commas. The
functor is written just before the opening round bracket. Consider the
following fact, that John owns the book called *Wuthering Heights*, by Emily
Brontë:

```
owns(john,book(wuthering_heights,bronte)).
```

Inside the owns fact we have a structure by the name of book, which has two
components, a title and an author. Since the book structure appears *inside*
the fact as one of the fact's arguments, it is acting as an object, taking part in
a relationship. If we like, we can also have another structure for the author's
name, because there were three Brontë writers we wish to distinguish:

```
owns(john,book(wuthering_heights,author(emily,bronte))).
```

Structures may participate in the process of question-answering using
variables. For example, we may ask if John owns any book by any of the
Bronte sisters:

```
?- owns(john,book(X,author(Y,bronte))).
```

If this is true, X will then be instantiated to the title that was found, and Y will be instantiated to the first name of the author. Or, we may not need to use the variables, so we can use anonymous ones:

```
?- owns(john,book(_,author(_,bronte))).
```

Remember that the anonymous variables do not "share" with each other.

We could improve the book structure by adding another argument indicating *which copy* the book was. For example, a third argument, where we would insert an integer, would provide a way of uniquely identifying a book:

```
owns(john,book(ulysses,author(james,joyce),3129)).
```

which we could use to represent *John owns the 3,129th copy of Ulysses, by James Joyce.*

If you have guessed that the syntax for structures is the same as for Prolog facts, you are correct. A predicate (used in facts and rules) is actually the functor of a structure. The arguments of a fact or rule are actually the components of a structure. There are many advantages to representing Prolog programs themselves as structures. It is not important to know why just now, but do keep in mind that all parts of Prolog, even Prolog programs themselves, are made up of constants, variables, and structures.

2.2 Characters

The names of constants and variables are built up from strings of characters. Although each kind of name (atom, integer, variable) has special rules about what characters may make it up, it is helpful to know what all the characters are that Prolog recognises. This is because a character can be treated as an item of data in its own right. Now that we know about integers, it is appropriate to describe how characters are represented as small integers. It is most common to use "input" and "output" operations on characters; this will be discussed in Chapter 5.

Prolog recognises two kinds of characters: printing characters and non-printing characters. Printing characters cause a mark to appear on your computer terminal's display. Non-printing characters do not cause a mark to appear, but cause an action to be carried out. Such actions include printing a blank space, beginning new lines of text, and perhaps ringing a bell. The following are all the printing characters that can be used

```
A B C D E F G H I J K L M N O P Q R S T U V W X Y Z
a b c d e f g h i j k l m n o p q r s t u v w x y z
```

```
 0  1  2  3  4  5  6  7  8  9
 !  "  #  $  %  &  '  (  )  =  -  ~  ^  |  \  {  }  [  ]  _  `  @  +  ;  *  :
 <  >  ,  .  ?  /
```

You should recognise this as a more complete set than the one given at the beginning of this chapter. Some of the characters have special meanings. For example, the round brackets are used to enclose the components of a structure. However, we shall see in later chapters that all the characters may be treated as information by Prolog programs. Characters may be printed, read from the keyboard, compared, and take part in arithmetic operations.

Characters are actually treated as small integers between 0 and 127. Each character has an integer associated with it, called its ASCII code The term "ASCII" means "American Standard Code for Information Interchange", and it is the code which is used by many computers and computer languages in the world. A table of the ASCII code can be found in various computer reference manuals. The letters are arranged in alphabetical order, so comparing alphabetic order of characters means simply comparing ASCII codes using the relational operators described later in this chapter. The printing characters all have ASCII codes that are greater than 32.

Although the ASCII code may not seem useful at the moment, the next places we mention it are in Section 3.2 and 3.5.

2.3 Operators

Sometimes it is convenient to write some functors as *operators*. This is a form of syntax that makes some structures easier to read. For example, arithmetic operations are commonly written as operators. When we write the arithmetic expression "x + y * z", we call the "plus sign" and the "multiply" sign *operators*. If we had to write the arithmetic expression "x + y * z" in the normal way for structures, it would look like this: +(x,*(y,z)), and this would be a legal Prolog term. The operators are sometimes easier to use, however, because we have grown accustomed to using them in arithmetic expressions ever since our schooldays. Also, the structure form requires that round brackets be placed around the functor's components, which may seem awkward at times.

It is important to note that the operators do not "cause" any arithmetic to be carried out. So in Prolog, 3+4 does not mean the same thing as 7. The term 3+4 is another way to write the term +(3,4), which is a data structure. Later we shall explain a way in which structures can be interpreted as though they represent arithmetic expressions, and evaluated according to the rules of arithmetic.

First we need to know how to read arithmetic expressions that have operators in them. To do this, we need to know three things about each operator: its position, its precedence, and its associativity. In this section we will describe how to use Prolog operators with these three things in mind, but we will not go into very much detail at this point. Although many different kinds of operators can be made up, we shall deal only with the familiar atoms +, -, *, and /.

The syntax of a term with operators depends in part on the position of the operator. Operators like plus (+), hyphen (-), asterisk (*), and slash (/) are written between their arguments, so we call them *infix* operators. It is also possible to put operators before their arguments, as in "- x + y", where the hyphen before the x is used in arithmetic to denote negation. Operators that come before their arguments are called *prefix* operators. Finally, some operators may come after their argument. For example, the factorial operator, used by mathematicians, comes after the number you want to find the factorial of. In mathematical notation, the factorial of x is written "x!", where the exclamation sign is used to denote factorial. Operators that are written after their arguments are called *postfix* operators. So, the position of an operator tells where it is written with relationship to its arguments. It turns out that the operators that we will use in the next section are all *infix* operators.

Now precedence. When we see the term "x + y * z", and assume that it can be interpreted as an arithmetic expression, we know that to evaluate it, we must multiply y and z first, then add x. This is because we were taught in school that mutiplications and divisions are done before additions and subtractions, except where brackets are used for grouping. On the other hand, the structure form +(x , *(y , z)) makes explicit the rule that the multiplication is done before the addition. This is because the "*" structure is an argument of the "+" structure, so if we actually wanted the computer to carry out the calculation, the "*" has to be carried out first in order for "+" to know what its arguments are. So when using operators, we need rules that tell us the order in which operations are carried out. This is what *precedence* tells us about.

The precedence of an operator is used to indicate which operation is carried out first. Each operator that is used in Prolog has a *precedence class* associated with it. The precedence class is an integer which is associated with an operator. The exact value of the integer depends on the particular version of Prolog you are using. However, it is always true that an operator with a higher precedence has a precedence class which is closer to 1. If precedence classes range from 1 to 255, then an operator in the first precedence class is carried out first, before operators belonging to the 129th (say) precedence class. In Prolog the multiplication and division operators are in a higher precedence class than addition and subtraction, so the term a-b/c is the same as the term -(a,/(b,c)). The exact association of operators to precedence classes is not important at the moment, but it is worth remembering the relative order in which operations are carried out.

Finally, consider how different operators associate. How they associate comes to our attention when we have several operators of the same precedence. When we see the expression "8/2/2", does this mean "(8/2)/2" or "8/(2/2)"? In the first case, the expression could be interpreted to mean 2, and in the second case, 8. To be able to distinguish between these two cases, we must be able to tell whether an operator is *left associative* or *right associative*. A left associative operator must have the same or lower precedence operations on the left, and lower precedence operations on the right. For example, all the arithmetic operations (add, subtract, multiply, and divide) are left associative. This means that expressions like "8/4/4" are treated as "(8/4)/4". Also, "5+8/2/2" means "5+((8/2)/2)".

In practice, people tend to use round brackets for expressions that may be difficult to understand because of the precedence and associativity rules. In this book we will also try to make it as clear as possible by using lots of round brackets, but it is still important to know the syntax rules for operators so your understanding of operators is complete.

Remember that a structure made up of arithmetic operators is like any other structure. No arithmetic is actually carried out until commanded by the "is" predicate described in Section 2.5.

2.4 Equality and Matching

One noteworthy predicate is equality, which is an infix operator written as "=". When an attempt is made to satisfy the goal

    ?- X = Y.

(pronounced "X equals Y"), Prolog attempts to *match* X and Y, and the goal succeeds if they match. We can think of this act as *trying to make X and Y equal*. The equality predicate is *built-in*, which means that it is already defined in the Prolog system. The equality predicate works as though it were defined by the following fact:

```
X = X.
```

Within a use of some clause, X always equals X, and we exploit this property when defining the equality predicate in the way shown.

Given a goal of the form X = Y, where X and Y are any two terms which are permitted to contain uninstantiated variables, the rules for deciding whether X and Y are equal are as follows:

- If X is an uninstantiated variable, and if Y is instantiated to any term, then X and Y are equal. Also, X will become instantiated to whatever Y is. For example, the following question succeeds, causing X to be instantiated to the structure `rides(clergyman,bicycle)`:

  ```
  ?- rides(clergyman, bicycle) = X.
  ```

- Integers and atoms are always equal to themselves. For example, the following goals have the behaviour shown:

  ```
  policeman = policeman   succeeds
  paper = pencil          fails
  1066 = 1066             succeeds
  1206 = 1583             fails
  ```

- Two structures are equal if they have the same functor and number of components, and all the corresponding components are equal. For example, the following goal succeeds, and causes X to be instantiated to b i cyc l e:

  ```
  rides(clergyman,bicycle) = rides(clergyman,X)
  ```

Structures can be "nested" one inside another to any depth. If such nested structures are tested for equality, the test may take more time to carry out, because there is more structure to test. The following goal

```
a(b,C,d(e,F,g(h,i,J))) = a(B,c,d(E,f,g(H,i,j)))
```

would succeed, and cause B to be instantiated to b, C to c, E to e, F to f, H to h, and J to j. What happens when we attempt to make two uninstantiated variables equal? This is just a special case of the first rule above. The goal succeeds, and the two variables *share*. If two variables share, then whenever one of them becomes instantiated to some term, the other one automatically is instantiated to the same term. The variables "co-refer", or refer to the same thing. So, in the following rule, the second argument will be instantiated to whatever the first argument is:

```
equal(X,Y) :-  X=Y.
```

An X = Y goal will always succeed if either argument is uninstantiated. An easier way to write such a rule is to take advantage of the fact that a variable equals itself, and write:

```
equal(X,X).
```

Prolog also provides a predicate "\=", pronounced "not equal". The goal X \= Y succeeds if X = Y fails, and it fails if X = Y succeeds. So, X \= Y means X *cannot be made equal to* Y.

Exercise 2.1: Say whether the following goals would succeed, and which variables, if any, would be instantiated to what values:

```
pilots(A,london) = pilots(london,paris)
point(X,Y,Z) = point(X1,Y1,Z1)
letter(C) = word(letter)
noun(alpha) = alpha
'vicar' = vicar
f(X,X) = f(a,b)
f(X,a(b,c)) = f(Z,a(Z,c))
```

2.5 Arithmetic

Many people use computers to do operations on numbers. Arithmetic operations are useful for comparing numbers and for calculating results. In this section we will see examples of each kind.

First, consider comparing numbers. Given two numbers, we can tell whether one number is equal to the other, or less than the other, or greater than the other. Prolog provides certain "built-in" predicates for comparing numbers. The predicates "=" and "\=" as discussed in Section 2.4 can be used for comparing numbers. The arguments could be variables instantiated to integers, or they could be integers written as constants. There are several other predicates for comparing numbers, and we can summarise all of them here. Note that we are allowed to write them as infix operators:

X = Y   X and Y stand for the same number

X \= Y   X and Y stand for different numbers

X < Y   X is less than Y

X > Y   X is greater than Y

X =< Y   X is less than or equal to Y

X >= Y   X is greater than or equal to Y

Note that the "less than or equal to" symbol is *not* written as < = as in many programming languages. This is done so that the Prolog programmer is free to use the < = atom, which looks like an arrow, for other purposes of his own devising.

As these comparison operators are predicates, one might think it possible to write a Prolog fact as follows,

```
2 > 3.
```

in order to assert that 2 is actually greater than 3. A fact like this one is perfectly well-formed Prolog. However, Prolog will not allow further facts to be added to predicates that are "built in" to Prolog. This prevents you from changing the meaning of built-in predicates in unexpected ways. In Chapter 6 we shall describe all of the built-in predicates, including all those we have met thus far.

As a first example of using numbers, suppose we have a database of the reigns of the Sovereign Princes of Wales in the 9th and 10th Centuries. The predicate reigns is defined such that the goal reigns(X,Y,Z) is true if the prince named X reigned from year Y to year Z. The list of facts in the database looks like this:

```
reigns(rhodri,844,878).
reigns(anarawd,878,916).
reigns(hywel_dda,916,950).
reigns(Iago_ap_idwal,950,979).
reigns(hywel_ap_ieuaf,979,985).
reigns(cadwallon,985,986).
reigns(maredudd,986,999).
```

Now suppose we want to ask who was on the Welsh throne during a particular year. We could define a rule, which given a name and a date, would search the database, and compare the given date aginst the dates of the reign. Let us define the predicate prince(X,Y), which is true if the prince named X was on the throne during year Y:

X was a prince during year Y if:
>X reigned between years A and B, and
>Y is between A and B, inclusive.

Now the first goal will be satisfied by using the reigns database above. The second goal is satisfied if Y is equal to A, or Y is equal to B, or Y lies between A and B. You can test for this by testing if Y > = A and Y = < B. Translating all this into Prolog, we obtain:

```
prince(X,Y) :-
    reigns(X,A,B),
    Y >= A,
    Y =< B.
```

Here are some questions one might ask, with the answers that Prolog gives:

```
?- prince(cadwallon,986).
yes
?- prince(rhodri,1979).
no
?- prince(X,900).
X=anarawd
yes
?- prince(X,979).
X=lago_ap_idwal ;
X=hywel_ap_ieuaf
yes
```

Notice the use of variables in the latter examples. Make sure you know how Prolog's searching mechanism allows questions like these to be answered.

Arithmetic can also be used for calculating. For example, if we know the population and ground area of a country, we can calculate the population density of the country. The population density tells us how crowded the country would be if all the people were evenly spread throughout the country. Consider the following database about the population and area of various countries in 1976. We will use the predicate pop to represent the relationship between a country and its population. Nowadays, the populations of countries are generally quite large numbers. Depending on what computer you use, Prolog may not be able to use such large numbers. So, we will represent population figures in millions: pop(X,Y) means the population of country X is about "Y million" people. The predicate area will denote the relationship between a country and its area (in millions of square miles):

```
pop(usa,203).
pop(india,548).
pop(china,800).
pop(brazil,108).

area(usa,3).
area(india,1).
area(china,4).
area(brazil,3).
```

Now to find the population density of a country, we must use the rule that the density is the population divided by the area. This can be represented as the predicate density, where the goal density(X,Y) succeeds for country X having Y as the population density of that country. A Prolog rule for this is:

```
density(X,Y) :-
    pop(X,P),
    area(X,A),
    Y is P/A.
```

The rule is read as follows:

> The population density of country X is Y, if:
>   The population of X is P, and
>   The area of X is A, and
>   Y is calculated by dividing P by A.

This rule uses the divide operator "/", which was introduced in the previous section. The divide operation is actually integer division, which gives only the integer part of the quotient of the result.

The "is" operator is new. The "is" operator is an infix operator. Its right-hand argument is a term which is interpreted as an arithmetic expression. To satisfy an "is", Prolog first evaluates its right-hand argument according to the rules of arithmetic. The answer is matched with the left-hand argument to determine whether the goal succeeds. In the above example, Y is unknown when the "is" is encountered, and it is up to the "is" to evaluate the expression, and let Y stand for the value. This means that the values of all the variables on the right of an "is" must be known.

We need to use the "is" predicate any time we require to evaluate an arithmetic expression. Remember that something like P/A is just an ordinary Prolog structure like author(emily,bronte). But if we interpret a structure as an arithmetic expression, there is a special operation that can be applied to the structure: that of actually carrying out the bits of arithmetic and calculating the result. This is called *evaluating* the arithmetic expression. Not all structures can be evaluated as arithmetic expressions. Clearly we cannot evaluate structures such as the author one, because author is not defined here as an arithmetic operation.

Getting back to the population density example, it is not hard now to see that typical questions and their answers are:

```
?- density(china,X).
X=200
yes
?- density(turkey,X).
no
```

In the first question, the **X=200** is Prolog's answer, meaning 200 people per square mile. The second question failed, because the population of Turkey could not be found in our example database.

Depending on what computer you use, various arithmetic operators can be used on the right-hand side of the "is" operator. All Prolog systems, however, will have:

        X + Y   the sum of X and Y

        X - Y   the difference of X and Y

        X * Y   the product of X and Y

        X / Y   the quotient of X divided by Y

        X mod Y the remainder of X divided by Y.

This list together with the above list of comparison operators should tell you nearly all you need for doing simple arithmetic problems. Of course, Prolog is mainly intended for non-numerical purposes, so arithmetic facilities are not as important as in other computer languages.

2.6 Summary of Satisfying Goals

Prolog performs a task in response to a *question* from the programmer (you). A question provides a *conjunction* of goals to be *satisfied*. Prolog uses the known *clauses* to satisfy the goals. A fact can cause a goal to be satisfied immediately, whereas a rule can only reduce the task to that of satisfying a conjunction of *subgoals*. However, a clause can only be used if it *matches* the goal under consideration. If a goal cannot be satisfied, *backtracking* will be initiated. Backtracking consists of reviewing what has been done, attempting to *re-satisfy* the goals by finding an alternative way to satisfying them. Furthermore, if you are not content with an answer to your question, you can initiate backtracking yourself by typing a semicolon when Prolog informs you of a solution. In this section, we present a diagrammatic notation for showing how and when Prolog attempts to satisfy and re-satisfy goals.

2.6.1 Successful satisfaction of a conjunction of goals

Prolog attempts to satisfy the goals in a conjunction, whether they appear in a rule body or in a question, in the order they are written (left to right). This means that Prolog will not attempt to satisfy a goal until its neighbour on the left has been satisfied. And, when it has been satisfied, Prolog will attempt to satisfy its neighbour on the right. Consider the following simple program about family relations:

```
parent(C,M,F) :- mother(C,M), father(C,F).

mother(john,ann).
mother(mary,ann).

father(mary,fred).
father(john,fred).
```

Let us look at the sequence of events that leads to the question:

```
?- female(mary), parent(mary,M,F), parent(john,M,F).
```

being answered. This question is to ascertain whether mary is a sister of john. To do this Prolog needs to satisfy the following sequence of subgoals shown in Figure 2.1. We represent goals as boxes distributed down the page. An arrow starting from the top of the page indicates which goals have already been satisfied. Boxes that the arrow has passed through indicate goals that have been satisfied. Boxes that lie below the arrowhead represent goals that Prolog has not yet considered. As a program runs, the arrow moves up and down the page as Prolog turns its attention to the various goals. We call this the *flow of satisfaction*. In the example, the arrow starts at the top of the page, as shown above. It will extend downwards, moving

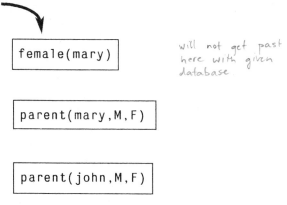

will not get past here with given database

Figure 2.1   A sequence of subgoals not yet satisfied.

through the three boxes as the three goals are satisfied. So the final situation will be as shown in Figure 2.2. Notice that values have now been found for the variables M and F. This diagram shows the coarse structure of what has happened, but it fails to show *how* these three goals were satisfied. We can show this by putting more detail inside the boxes. Let us concentrate on how the second goal is satisfied. Satisfying a goal involves searching the database for a *matching* clause, then marking the place in the database, and then satisfying any subgoals.

We can show this for the second goal by indicating in the parent box which clause was chosen and which subgoals had to be satisfied. The clause chosen is shown by a number in brackets, here (1). This number indicates which clause *out of the set of clauses for the appropriate predicate* has been chosen. So the number 1 indicates that the first clause for the predicate has been chosen. This is enough information to mark the place in the database. The subgoals are shown in small boxes inside the box for the goal. At the point when the parent clause has been chosen, the situation looks like Figure 2.3.

The arrow has entered the parent box and passed through the brackets indicating that a clause has been chosen. The clause has introduced two subgoals, involving mother and father. At this point, the arrow must pass through these two smaller boxes, emerge from the current parent box and then pass through the second parent box in order for the question to succeed. When the arrow passes through the smaller boxes, the same steps of choosing a clause and satisfying the clause's subgoals must be performed. In this example, both of these goals succeed by finding facts in the database. So

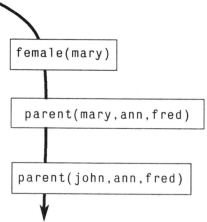

Figure 2.2   The sequence of subgoals has been satisfied. Note that variables have been instantiated.

Figure 2.4 shows a more detailed picture of the situation when the question
succeeds

Note that to be precise we should have shown the details of how the
goals female(mary) and parent(john,ann,fred)were satisfied.
However, this would have been too much detail to fit onto one page. This
example shows the general pattern of how Prolog attempts to satisfy goals in
a case where the conjunction of goals succeeds. The arrow moves down the
page, passing through the boxes in turn. When it enters a box, a clause is
chosen and its position marked. If the clause matches the goal and the clause
is a fact, then the arrow can leave the box (this happened for the mother and
father goals. On the other hand, if the clause matches the goal and the
clause is a rule then new boxes are created for the subgoals and the arrow
must then pass through all of these before it can leave the original box.

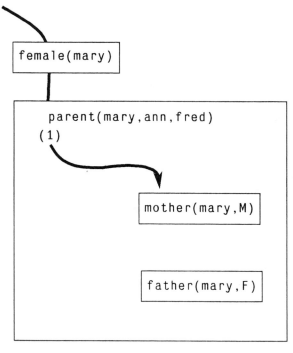

Figure 2.3 The number (1) indicates that the first clause for the
predicate has been chosen. The subgoals are shown in small boxes
inside the box for the goal.

2.6.2 Consideration of goals in backtracking

When a failure is generated (because all the alternative clauses for a goal have been tried, or because you type a semicolon), the "flow of satisfaction" passes *back* along the way it has come. This involves retreating back into boxes that have previously been left in order to *re-satisfy* the goals. When the arrow gets back to a place where a clause was chosen (represented by a number in brackets), Prolog attempts to find an alternative clause for the appropriate goal. First, it makes uninstantiated all variables that had been instantiated in the course of satisfying the goal. Then, it searches on in the database from where the place-marker was put. If it finds another matching possibility, it marks the place, and things continue as in Section 2.6.1 above.

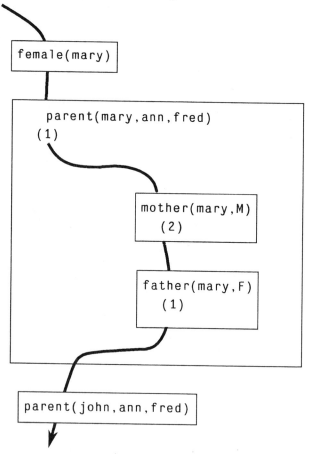

Figure 2.4 The question has succeeded.

Note that work on any goals "below" this (even if such goals were tackled under the previous alternative) will always start from scratch. Prolog will try to satisfy, and not to re-satisfy them. If no other matching possibility can be found, the goal fails, and the arrow retreats further until it comes to another place-marker.

In our example, if the goal parent(john,ann,fred) failed, the arrow would retreat upwards from the parent(john,ann,fred) box and re-enter the parent(mary,ann,fred) box from below, attempting to re-satisfy this goal. It would then retreat further, re-entering the father(mary,fred) box and trying to re-satisfy this goal, as shown in Figure 2.5.

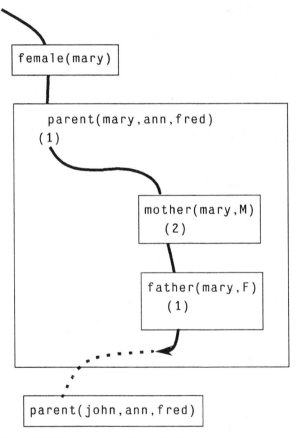

Figure 2.5 What happens if a goal fails.

Retreating further, the arrow reaches the place where the clause for the
father goal was chosen. First of all, all variables that became instantiated
as the result of using this clause are set back to uninstantiated. This means
that F becomes uninstantiated again. Then Prolog looks through the
database, starting after the first father clause (the one marked), trying to
find an alternative clause for this goal. Assuming that mary has only one
father, this will not succeed. So the arrow will have to retreat further. It
retreats upwards, out of the father(mary,F) box (this goal has failed) and
back into the mother(mary,ann) box (to attempt to re-satisfy this goal).
We get the situation shown in Figure 2.6.

    We can see from these examples the general pattern of how goals are
reconsidered in backtracking. When a goal fails, the arrow retreats upwards

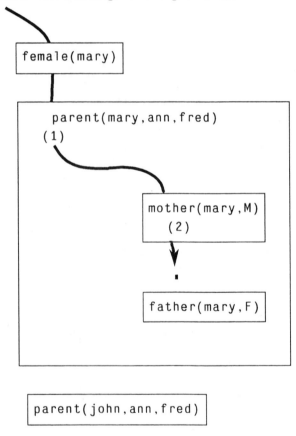

Figure 2.6 Attempting to re-satisfy a goal.

out of the box for the failing goal and back into the box for the goal above. The arrow continues retreating until it reaches a place marker. All variables that were instantiated as a result of the previous choice of clause are reset to uninstantiated. Then Prolog searches the database for a clause after the place marker. If it finds a clause that matches the goal, then a new place mark is recorded, boxes for the subgoals are created and the arrow starts moving downwards again. Otherwise, the arrow continues to retreat upwards, in search of another place marker.

2.6.3 Matching

The rules for deciding whether a goal matches the head of a use of a clause are as follows. Note that in the use of a clause, all variables are initially uninstantiated.

- An uninstantiated variable will match any object. As a result, that object will be what the variable stands for.

- Otherwise, an integer or atom will match only itself.

- Otherwise, a structure will match another structure with the same functor and number of arguments, and all the corresponding arguments must match.

A noteworthy case in matching is one in which two uninstantiated variables are matched together. In this case, we say that these variables *share*. Two sharing variables are such that as soon as one is instantiated, so is the other (with the same value). If you have noticed a similarity between matching and making arguments equal (Section 2.4), then you are correct. This is because the "=" predicate attempts to make its arguments equal by matching them. Now we can bring together what we have discussed about operators, arithmetic, and matching. Suppose the following facts are in the database:

```
sum(5).
sum(3).
sum(X+Y).
```

Consider the question

```
?- sum(2+3).
```

Now, which one of the facts above will match with the question? If you think it is the first one, then you should go back and read about structures and operators. In the question the argument of the sum structure is a structure having the plus sign as its functor, and having the 2 and 3 as its components. In fact, the goal shown will match with the third fact, instantiating X to 2, and Y to 3. On the other hand, if we actually wanted to compute a sum, we would use the "is" predicate. We would write

```
?- X is 2+3.
```

or, just for fun, we could define a predicate add that relates two integers with their sum:

```
add(X,Y,Z) :- Z is X+Y.
```

In this definition, X and Y must be instantiated.

Chapter 3
Using Data Structures

The *Oxford English Dictionary* defines the word "recursion" in the following way:

RECURSION. [Now rare or *obs.* 1626]. A backward movement, return.

This definition is cryptic and perhaps outdated. Recursion is now a very popular and powerful technique in the world of non-numerical programming. It is used in two ways. It can be used to describe structures that have other structures as components. It can also be used to describe programs that need to satisfy a copy of themselves before they themselves can succeed. Sometimes, beginners view recursion with some suspicion, because, how is it possible for some relationship to be defined in terms of itself? In Prolog, recursion is the normal and natural way of viewing data structures and programs. We hope that the theme of this chapter, recursion, will be made explicit in a comfortable and unobtrusive way.

3.1 Structures and Trees

It is usually easier to understand the form of a complicated structure if we write it as a *tree*, in which each functor is a node, and the components are branches. Each branch may point to another structure, so we can have structures within structures. It is customary to write a tree diagram with the root at the top, and the branches at the bottom. For instance, the structure parents(charles,elizabeth,philip) is written as:

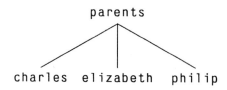

The structure a+b*c (or +(a,*(b,c)) is written as:

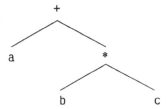

The structure book(moby_dick,author(herman,melville)) is written as:

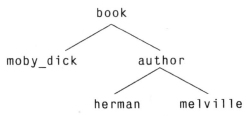

Notice that the last two structures have trees of the same shape, although the roots and leaves are different. Before going further, you should make sure that you can write tree diagrams for each of the structures you have seen in the previous chapters.

Suppose we are given the sentence "John likes Mary", and we need to represent the syntax of the sentence. A very simple syntax for English is that a sentence consists of a noun followed by a verb phrase. Additionally, a verb phrase consists of a verb and another noun. We can represent the structure of any such sentence by a structure of the form:

sentence(noun(X),verb_phrase(verb(Y),noun(Z))),

which has a tree like this:

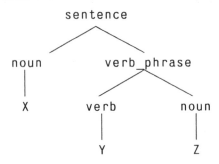

If we take our sentence ("John likes Mary"), and instantiate the variables in the structure with the words of the sentence, we obtain:

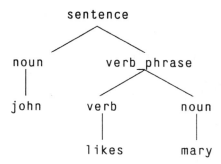

This shows how we can use Prolog structures and variables to represent the syntax of a class of very simple English sentences. In general, if we know the parts of speech of words in a sentence, it is possible to write a Prolog structure that makes explicit the relationships between different words in a sentence. This is an interesting topic in its own right, and later on we shall return to the question of how we can use Prolog to make the computer "understand" some simple English sentences.

Trees can also give a graphic description of variables inside structures, particularly showing how like-named variables share. For example, we can depict the structure of the term $f(X, g(X, a))$ by the following tree:

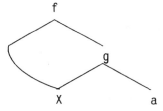

3.2 Lists

The *list* is a very common data structure in non-numeric programming. The list is an ordered sequence of elements that can have any length. "Ordered" means that the order of the elements in the sequence matters. The "elements" of a list may be any terms — constants, variables, structures — which of course includes other lists. These properties are helpful when we cannot predict in advance how big a list should be, and what information it should contain. Furthermore, lists can represent practically any kind of structure that one may wish to use in symbolic computation. Lists are widely used to represent parse trees, grammars, city maps, computer programs, and mathematical entities such as graphs, formulae, and functions. There is a programming language called LISP, in which the only data structures available are the constant and the list. However, in Prolog, the list is simply one particular kind of structure.

Lists can be represented as a special kind of tree. A list is either an *empty list,* having no elements, or it is a structure that has two components: the head and tail. The end of a list is customarily represented as a tail that is set to the empty list. The empty list is written as [ ], which is an opening square bracket followed by a closing square bracket. The head and tail of a list are components of the functor named ".", which is the dot. Thus, the list consisting of one element "a" is ". (a , [ ])", and its tree looks like this:

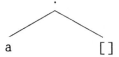

Also, the list consisting of the atoms a, b, and c is written . (a , . (b , . (c , [ ]))), and its tree looks like this:

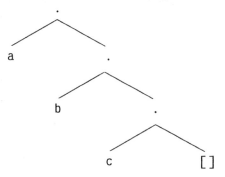

Some people like to write the tree diagram of a list with the tree "growing" from left to right, and with the "branches" hanging down. The above list looks like this in such a "vine" diagram:

In this vine diagram, the head component of the dot functor hangs down, and the tail component grows to the right. The end of the list is clearly marked by the last tail component being the empty list. The main advantage of the vine diagram for lists is that it can be written right-to-left on a piece of paper.

The vine diagram may be suitable for writing lists on paper when we need to see the structure of a list, but such diagrams are not used for writing lists into a Prolog program. As the dot notation is often awkward for writing complicated lists, there is another syntax that can be used for writing lists in a Prolog program. This *list notation* consists of the elements of the list separated by commas, and the whole list is enclosed in square brackets. For example, the above lists can be written in the list notation as [a] and [a,b,c].

It is useful for lists to contain other lists and variables. For example, the following lists are legal in Prolog:

```
[]
[the,men,[like,to,fish]]
[a,V1,b,[X,Y]]
```

Variables within lists are treated the same as variables in any other structure. They can become instantiated at any time, so judicious use of variables can provide a way to put "holes" in lists that can be filled with data at a later time.

To show the structure of lists within lists, the vine diagram for the previous list is:

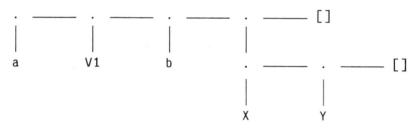

It is easy to see from this diagram that each horizontal "level" of the vine is a list having a certain number of elements. The top level is a list having four elements, one of which is a list. The second level, having two elements, is the fourth element of the top level list.

Lists are manipulated by splitting them up into a head and a tail. The head of a list is the first component of the "." functor that is used to construct lists. Notice that we speak of the "head" of a rule as well as the "head" of a list . These two things are different, and although they are both called "heads" by historical accident, it is easy enough to understand which "head" one is talking about at a particular time. The tail of a list is the second component of the "." functor. When a list appears in the square bracket notation, the head of the list is the first element of the list. The tail of the list is a *list* that consists of every element except the first. The examples in Table 3.1 show some heads and tails. Notice that the empty list has neither a head nor a tail. In the last example, the "+" operator is used as a functor for the structures +(X,Y) and +(x,y).

Because a common operation with lists is to split a list into its head and tail, there is a special notation in Prolog to represent "the list with head X and tail Y". This is written [X|Y], where the symbol separating the X and Y is the vertical bar. A pattern of this form will instantiate X to the head of a list, and Y to the tail of the list, as in the following example:

```
p([1,2,3]).
p([the,cat,sat,[on,the,mat]]).

?- p([X|Y]).
X=1    Y=[2,3] ;
X=the Y=[cat,sat,[on,the,mat]]

?- p([_,_,_,[_|X]]).
X=[the,mat]
```

More examples of the list syntax, showing how various lists match, are as follows, in which we attempt to match the two lists shown, obtaining the instantiations (if possible), shown in Table 3.2.

As the last example shows, it is possible to use the list notation to create structures that resemble lists, but which do not terminate with the empty list. One such structure, [white|horse], denotes a structure having head white and tail horse. The constant horse is neither a list nor the empty list, and we shall later see that such structures should be treated carefully when used at the tail of a list.

There is one final use for list syntax — representing strings. Occasionally one needs strings of characters for printing or reading text such as English sentences. If a string of characters is enclosed in double quotes, the string is

Table 3.1 Some lists with their head and tail.

List	Head	Tail
[a,b,c]	a	[b,c]
[]	(none)	(none)
[[the,cat],sat]	[the,cat]	[sat]
[the,[cat,sat]]	the	[[cat,sat]]
[the,[cat,sat],down]	the	[[cat,sat],down]
[X+Y,x+y]	X+Y	[x+y]

represented as a list of integer codes that represent the characters. The codes are taken from what is known as the "ASCII code", which is discussed in Section 2.2. For example, the string "system" is changed by Prolog into the list [115,121,115,116,101,109].

3.3 Recursive Search

We frequently need to search inside a Prolog structure to find some desired piece of information. When the structure may have other structures as its components, this results in a *recursive search* task.

Suppose, for example, we have a list of the names of those horses sired by Coriander who all won horseraces in Great Britain in the year 1927:

```
[curragh_tip, music_star, park_mill, portland]
```

Now suppose we want to find out if a given horse is in the list. The way we do this in Prolog is to find out whether the horse is the same as the head of the list: if it is, we succeed. If it is not, then we check to see if the horse is in the tail of the list. This means checking the head of the *tail* next time. And the head of *that* tail after that. If we come to the end of the list, which will be the empty list, we must fail: the horse is not in the list.

To write this in Prolog, we must first recognise that there is a relationship between an object, and a list it might appear in. This relationship, called

Table 3.2 Pairs of lists and how they match. If they match, variable instantiations are shown. One example does not match.

List 1	List 2	Instantiations
[X,Y,Z]	[john,likes,fish]	X = john Y = likes Z = fish
[cat]	[X|Y]	X = cat Y = []
[X,Y|Z]	[mary,likes,wine]	X = mary Y = likes Z = [wine]
[[the,Y]|Z]	[[X,hare],[is,here]]	X = the Y = hare Z = [[is,here]]
[golden|T]	[golden,norfolk]	T = [norfolk]
[vale,horse]	[horse,X]	(none)
[white|Q]	[P|horse]	P = white Q = horse

membership, is a common enough concept in our everyday lives. We talk about people being members of clubs, and so forth. We shall write a predicate member such that the goal member(X,Y) is true if the term that X stands for is a member of the list that Y stands for. There are two conditions to check. First, it is a fact that X will be a member of Y, if X is the same as the head of Y. In Prolog, this fact is:

```
member(X,[X|_]).
```

which represents, "X is a member of the list that has X as its head". Notice that we use the anonymous variable "_" to stand for the tail of the list. This is because we do not use the tail for anything in this particular fact. Notice that this rule also could have been written as:

```
member(X,[Y|_]) :- X = Y.
```

By this time you should understand why we can take a shortcut by using X in two places in the shorter version of the rule.

The second, and last, rule says that X is a member of a list providing it is in the tail, say Y, of that list. And, what better way to find out if Y is in the tail of the list, than to use member itself! This is the essence of recursion. In Prolog:

```
member(X,[_|Y]) :- member(X,Y).
```

which represents, "X is a member of the list if X is a member of the tail of the list". Notice that we have used the anonymous variable "_", because we do not care to have any named variable standing for the head of the list. The two rules together define the membership predicate, and they tell Prolog how to search a list from beginning to end, looking for an item in the list.

The most important point to remember, when encountering a recursively defined predicate, is to look for the *boundary conditions* and the *recursive case*. There are actually two boundary conditions for the member predicate. Either the object we are looking for is in the list, or it isn't in the list. The first boundary condition of member is recognised by the first clause, which will cause the search through the list to be stopped if the first argument of member matches the head of the second argument. The second boundary condition occurs when the the second argument of member is the empty list.

How are we assured that the boundary conditions will ever be satisfied? We must look at the recursive case, the second rule of member. Notice that each time member attempts to satisfy itself, the goal is given a *shorter* list. The tail of a list is always a shorter list than the original one. Eventually, one of two things will happen: either the first member rule will match, or member will be given a list of length 0, the empty list, as its second argument. When either of these things happens, the "recurrence" of member goals will come to an end. The first boundary condition is recognised by a fact, which does not cause any further subgoals to be considered. The second boundary condition is not recognised by any member clause, so member will fail. In Prolog:

```
member(X,[X|_]).
member(X,[_|Y]) :- member(X,Y).

?- member(d,[a,b,c,d,e,f,g]).
yes

?- member(2,[3,a,4,f]).
no
```

Suppose we asked the question

```
?- member(clygate,[curragh_tip,music_star,park_mill,portland]).
```

The second member rule would match, as clygate does not match curragh_tip. Variable Y becomes instantiated to [music_star, park_mill, portland], and the next goal is to see if clygate is a member of that. The second rule matches again, and the tail is taken again. The goal becomes member(clygate,[park_mill,portland]). This process recurs until we reach the goal where X is clygate, and Y is [portland]. The second rule matches once more, and now Y becomes the tail of [portland], which is the empty list, and the next goal becomes member(clygate,[]). No rule in the database matches this, so the goal fails, and the question is false.

It is most important to remember that each time that member uses its second clause to attempt to satisfy member, Prolog treats each recurrence of the member goal as a different "copy". This prevents the variables in one use of a clause from being confused with variables in another use of a clause.

As the membership predicate is so useful, we shall use it in many places in the remainder of this book. The member predicate is also important because it is one of the smallest useful examples of a predicate that is recursive — that is, the definition of member contains goals that can only be satisfied by member itself. Recursive definitions are frequently found in Prolog programs, and they are no different than any other type of definition. However, you must be careful that you do not write "circular" definitions, for example:

```
parent(X,Y) :- child(Y,X).
child(A,B) :- parent(B,A).
```

In this example, to satisfy parent, we set up child as a goal. However, the definition for child uses only parent as a goal. You should be able to see that asking a question about parent or child would lead to a loop in which Prolog would never infer anything new, and that the loop would never terminate.

One important problem to look out for in recursive definitions is that of *left recursion*. This arises when a rule causes the invocation of a goal that is essentially equivalent to the original goal that caused the rule to be used. Thus if we defined:

```
person(X) :- person(Y), mother(X,Y).
person(adam).
```

and asked

```
?- person(X).
```

Prolog would first use the rule, and generate the subgoal person(Y). In trying to satisfy this, it would again pick the rule first, and generate yet another equivalent goal. And so it would go on and on, until it ran out of space. Of course, if it had a chance to backtrack, it would find the fact about Adam and start producing solutions. The trouble is, that in order to backtrack, Prolog has to have failed after trying the first possibility. In this case, the task that it finds is infinitely long, and so it never gets a chance to succeed or fail. So the moral is:

> Don't assume that, just because you have provided all the relevant facts and rules, Prolog will always find them. You must bear in mind when you write Prolog programs how Prolog searches through the database and what variables will be instantiated when one of your rules is used.

In this example, the simple solution is just to put the fact before the rule, instead of after it. In fact, as a general heuristic, it is a good idea to put facts before rules whenever possible. Sometimes putting the rules in a particular order will work if they are used to solve goals of one form but will not if goals of another form are generated. Consider the following definition of islist, in which the goal islist(X) succeeds if X is a list in which the tail of its last element is the empty list:

```
islist([A|B]) :- islist(B).
islist([]).
```

If we use these rules to answer questions like:

```
?- islist([a,b,c,d]).
or
?- islist([]).
or
?- islist(f(1,2,3)).
```

then the definition will work fine. But when we ask:

```
?- islist(X).
```

the program will loop. A predicate similar to islist that is not susceptible to loops is provided by the following two facts:

```
weak_islist([]).
weak_islist([_|_]).
```

This version just tests the first part of the list, rather than checking whether the last tail is [ ]. This is not as strong a test as islist, but it will not loop if the argument is a variable.

3.4 Mapping

Given a Prolog structure, we frequently wish to construct a new structure that is similar to the old one but changed in some way. We traverse the old structure component-by-component, and construct the components of the new structure. We call this *mapping*.

For example, let us consider a Prolog program in which we type an English sentence and Prolog replies with another sentence that is an altered version of the one we typed in. This program for "talking back" to the programmer might produce a dialogue like this:

```
you are a computer
i am not a computer
do you speak french
no i speak german
```

Although this dialogue may seem like a forced but sensible conversation, it is very easy to write a computer program to carry out its "part" of the dialogue simply by following these steps:

1. Accept a sentence that is typed in by the user.

2. Change each you in the sentence to an "i".

3. Likewise, change any are to am not.

4. Change french to german.

5. Change do to no.

When applied to carefully chosen sentences, such as those in the above dialogue, this scheme will produce a sensible altered sentence. However, it does not work on every sentence, for example:

```
i do like you
i no like i
```

Once a simple program is written, it can be modified later to cope with sentences like this that produce awkward output.

A Prolog program to change one sentence into another can be written as follows. First, we need to recognise that there is a relationship between the original sentence and the altered sentence. So, we need to define a Prolog predicate, called alter, such that alter(X,Y) means that sentence X can be altered to give sentence Y. It is convenient for X and Y to be lists, with atoms standing for the words, so sentences can be written like this:

```
[this, is, a, sentence]
```

and once alter is defined, we could ask Prolog a question of the form

```
?- alter([do,you,know,french],X).
```

and Prolog would reply

```
X=[no,i,know,german].
```

Don't be concerned yet that the input and output sentences are not tidy, and do not look like normal sentences. In later chapters we will discuss ways of typing in and printing out structures in a way that is easy to read. For the moment we will only worry about changing one list into another.

Since alter deals with lists, the first fact about alter needs to deal with what happens if the list is empty. In this case, we will say that an empty list is altered into an empty list:

```
alter([],[]).
```

Or, in words, "it is a fact that altering the empty list gives the empty list". If the reason for treating the empty list is not apparent now, it should be clearer later. Next, we need to recognise that the main job of alter is to:

1. Change the head of the input list into another word, and let the head of the output list stand for that word.

2. alter the tail of the input list, and let the tail of the output list stand for the altered tail.

3. If we have reached the end of the input list, then there is nothing more to go onto the output list, so we can terminate the output list with an empty list [ ].

Translated into words that are closer to Prolog:

Altering a list with head H and tail T gives a list with head X and tail Y if:

changing word H gives word X, and
altering the list T gives the list Y.

Now we need to say what is meant by "changing" one word into another. This can be done by having a database of facts in which change(X,Y) means word X can be changed into word Y. At the end of the database we need a "catchall" fact, because if a word is not changed into another word it needs to be changed into itself. If the reason for a "catchall" is not apparent now, it should be clearer after we explain how the program works. The relevant catchall fact is change(X,X), which means word X is changed into itself. A database to handle the changes listed above is:

```
change(you,i).
change(are,[am,not]).
change(french,german).
change(do,no).
change(X,X).    /* this is the "catchall" */
```

Notice that we have treated the phrase "am not" as a list, so that it occupies only one argument of the fact.

Now we can translate the pseudo-Prolog text above into pure Prolog, remembering the notation [A|B] for the list with head A and tail B. We get something like this:

```
alter([],[]).
alter([H|T],[X|Y]) :- change(H,X), alter(T,Y).
```

The first clause in this procedure checks for an empty list. The same clause also checks for the end of the list as well. Why? Consider this worked example:

```
?- alter([you,are,a,computer],Z).
```

This question would match with the main alter rule, making variable H stand for you, and the variable T stand for [are, a, computer]. Next, the goal change(you,X) would succeed, setting X to stand for the word "i". As X is the head of the output list (in the goal of alter), the first word in the output list is "i". Next, the goal alter([are, a, computer],Y) would use the same rule. The word are is changed into the list [am, not] by the database, and another alter goal is generated:

    alter([a, computer], Y).

The fact change(a, X) is searched for, but as there is no change fact with "a" as its first argument, the catchall fact at the bottom of the database succeeds, changing "a" into "a" The alter rule is called for once again, with computer as the head of the input list, and the *empty list* [ ] as the tail of the input list. As previously, change(computer, X) matches against the catchall. Finally, alter is called with the empty list, which matches against the very first alter clause. The result is the empty list, which ends the sentence (remember that a list ends with an empty tail). Finally, Prolog answers the question by responding

Z = [i, [am, not], a, computer]

Notice that the phrase [am, not] appears in the list exactly as it was inserted.

The reasons for adding the fact alter([], []) and the catchall fact change(X, X) should now be clear. Facts like these are often included in a program when it is desirable to check for boundary conditions. It should be clear from the explanation above that boundary conditions occur when the input list becomes the empty list, and when all of the change facts have been searched through. In both of these boundary conditions, we wish certain actions to be performed. When the input list becomes the empty list, we wish to terminate the output list (by putting an empty list at its end). When all the change facts have been searched through without the given word being changed into another word, we wish to keep the word unchanged (by changing it into itself).

3.5 Recursive Comparison

As we saw in Chapter 2, Prolog provides predicates to compare integers. Comparing structures is generally more complicated, because it is necessary to consider all the individual components. When the components may themselves be structures, the comparison may have to be recursive. In applications dealing with words, such as using dictionaries, it is helpful to have a predicate to compare words for alphabetic order. This involves comparing lists recursively.

Consider a predicate we shall name aless. When aless(X, Y) is used as a goal, it will succeed if X and Y stand for atoms, and X is alphabetically less than Y. So,

    ?- aless(avocado, clergyman) would succeed, and

?- aless(windmill,motorcar) would fail. Also,

?- aless(picture,picture) should fail.

When comparing two words, we compare them letter-by-letter and, for each comparison, determine which of the following conditions is at hand:

1. We could reach the end of the first word without reaching the end of the second word. This happens when we try aless(book, bookbinder). In this case, aless must succeed.

2. We could find that the character in the first word was alphabetically less than the corresponding character in the second word. For example, with aless(elephant,elevator), The "p" of elephant is alphabetically less than the "v" of elevator. In this case, aless succeeds.

3. We could find that the character in the first word was alphabetically equal to the corresponding character in the second word. In this case, we need to try aless on the remaining characters in both words. F or example, given aless(lazy,leather), the "l" is the same at the beginning of both arguments, so we would need to try aless(azy,eather) as the next goal.

4. We could find that we reach the end of the first and second words at the same time. This would happen if we tried aless(apple,apple). In this case, aless must fail, because the two words are the same.

5. We could run out of characters in the second word before running out of characters in the first word, such as in aless(alphabetic,alp). In this case, aless must fail.

Once we have discovered the above conditions, it is a fairly simple task to translate them into Prolog. We shall represent words as lists of characters (small integers), so there must be a way to convert a Prolog atom into a list of characters. This is the purpose of the built-in predicate name. The goal name(X,Y) succeeds when the atom instantiated for X consists of the list of character codes (the ASCII codes) instantiated for Y. Refer to Chapter 2 for an explanation of ASCII codes. If one of the arguments is uninstantiated, then Prolog will attempt to instantiate it by creating the appropriate structure. So, we can use name to convert from words into the list of characters. For example, knowing that the ASCII code for "a" is 97, "l" is 108 and "p" is 112, the following questions could be asked of name:

```
?- name(X,[97,108,112]).
X = alp
```

```
?- name(alp,X).
X = [97,108,112]
```

A first attempt at a less is

```
aless(X,Y) :- name(X,L), name(Y,M), alessx(L,M).
```

We have simply converted the words into lists using name, and used a predicate alessx (not defined yet) for checking the lists for alphabetic order. Now we need to define alessx, using the set of conditions above. The first condition is true when the first argument is the empty list, and the second argument is any non-empty list:

```
alessx([],[_|_]).
```

The second condition is translated as:

```
alessx([X|_],[Y|_]) :- X < Y.
```

Remember that the arguments of alessx are lists of numbers, so it is permitted to compare them using the "<" predicate. The third condition is translated as:

```
alessx([A|X],[B|Y]) :- A = B, alessx(X,Y).
```

Finally, the last two conditions are what make the predicate fail, so if we do not supply any matching facts or rules, then the searching mechanism will fail any goal for which those conditions hold. Gathering the rules together,

```
aless(X,Y) :- name(X,L), name(Y,M), alessx(L,M).

alessx([],[_|_]).
alessx([X|_],[Y|_]) :- X < Y.
alessx([P|Q],[R|S]) :- P = R, alessx(Q,S).
```

Notice that the third rule could be written more conveniently as:

```
alessx([H|Q],[H|S]) :- alessx(Q,S).
```

We shall always use the more convenient form whenever possible.

Exercise 3.1: Work out what clause you need to add to this definition so that it succeeds when the two words are equal. This would create a predicate that checks if the first argument is alphabetically less than or equal to the second argument. Hint: look at condition (4) above, and insert a clause to handle it.

Exercise 3.2: Why does the first rule of alessx have [_|_]? Why is [_] insufficient for the purpose?

3.6 Joining Structures Together

The list processing predicate `append` is used to join two lists together to form another, new, list. For example, it is true that

```
append([a,b,c],[3,2,1],[a,b,c,3,2,1]).
```

Predicate `append` is most often used to create a new list from concatenating two others, like this:

```
?- append([alpha,beta],[gamma,delta],X).
X = [alpha,beta,gamma,delta]
```

But it can also be used in other ways:

```
?- append(X,[b,c,d],[a,b,c,d]).
X=[a]
```

Predicate `append` is defined as follows:

```
append([],L,L).
append([X|L1],L2,[X|L3]) :- append(L1,L2,L3).
```

The boundary condition is when the first list is the empty list. In this case, any list appended to the empty list is the same list. Otherwise, the following points show the principles of the second rule:

1. The first element of the first list (`X`) will always be the first element of the third list.

2. The tail of the first list (`L1`) will always have the second argument (`L2`) appended to it to form the tail (`L3`) of the third argument.

3. You actually have to use `append` to do the appending mentioned in point (2).

4. As we are continually taking the head from the remainder of the first argument, it will gradually be reduced to the empty list, so the boundary condition will occur.

We will refer to `append` in later examples, with further explanation. In later chapters we will discuss various properties and applications of the `append` predicate. But first, let us put it to work in another simple example of recursion.

Suppose we work in a bicycle factory, where it is necessary to keep an inventory of bicycle parts. If we want to build a bicycle, we need to know which parts to draw from the supplies. Each part of the bicycle may have sub-parts, for example each wheel has some spokes, a rim, and a hub.

Furthermore, the hub can consist of an axle and gears. Let us consider a tree-structured database that will enable us to ask questions about which parts are required to build a part of a bicycle. In a subsequent section we shall improve this basic program to calculate how many of each part are required.

There are two kinds of parts that we use to build our bicycle. These are assemblies and basic parts. Each assembly consists of a quantity of basic parts, such as the wheel, which consists of several spokes, a rim, and a hub. Basic parts are not made up of any smaller parts — they simply combine with other basic parts to form assemblies.

We can represent basic parts simply as facts, as follows:

```
basicpart(rim).
basicpart(spoke).
basicpart(rearframe).
basicpart(handles).
basicpart(gears).
basicpart(bolt).
basicpart(nut).
basicpart(fork).
```

Naturally, this is not a complete list of the basic parts required for a bicycle but it shows the general idea. Next, an assembly can be represented as the name of the assembly followed by a list of the basic parts, and the quantity of parts required. For example, the following fact represents that a bike is an assembly made up of two wheels and a frame:

```
assembly(bike,[wheel,wheel,frame]).
```

The database of assemblies required for our simplified bicycle is:

```
assembly(bike,[wheel,wheel,frame]).
assembly(wheel,[spoke,rim,hub]).
assembly(frame,[rearframe,frontframe]).
assembly(frontframe,[fork,handles]).
assembly(hub,[gears,axle]).
assembly(axle,[bolt,nut]).
```

Notice that this particular set of clauses does not perfectly describe a bicycle. We have not distinguished between the front hub and the rear hub — both have gears! The chain and pedals are missing, and there is no place for the rider to sit. Also, there is no indication of how to fit the parts together. This simply lists a few of the parts required.

Now we are ready to write the program that, given a part, will list all the basic parts required to construct it. If the part we want to construct is a basic part, then nothing more is required. However, if we want to construct an assembly, then we need to apply the same process to each part making up the assembly. Let us define a predicate partsof, to be used in goals of the form partsof(X,Y), where X is the name of a part, and Y is the list of basic parts that are required to construct X. In our first version of this program, we shall ignore how many of each kind of part are required to form assemblies. A better program will be presented in Chapter 7.

The boundary condition occurs when X is a basic part. In this case, we simply return X in a list:

```
partsof(X,[X]) :- basicpart(X).
```

The next condition is if X is an assembly. In this case, we need to find out if there is a matching assembly fact in the database, and if so, to use partsof on each member of the list of sub-parts. We shall use a predicate called partsoflist to handle this second task.

```
partsof(X,P) :-
            assembly(X,Subparts),
            partsoflist(Subparts,P).
```

Now partsoflist takes a list of parts (from the second argument of the assembly database above), and finds the partsof of each part. After calling itself to get the partsof for the tail of the list, partsoflist must glue the lists together with append:

```
partsoflist([],[]).
partsoflist([P|Tail],Total) :-
            partsof(P,Headparts),
            partsoflist(Tail,Tailparts),
            append(Headparts,Tailparts,Total).
```

The list which is constructed by partsof will not contain information about how many parts are required, and duplicate parts may appear in the list. In Chapter 7, we shall present an improved version of this program that handles these deficiencies.

There are two insights that indicate how partsof can be used to generate English sentences. First, sentences can be decomposed into hierarchical structures: a sentence has parts noun_phrase and verb_phrase; a noun_phrase has parts determiner and noun, and so forth. So, any simple grammar can be expressed in terms of "parts". Second, partsoflist always looks at the elements of its first argument from left to

right, and its result is appended together in left-to-right order. These two
properties of partsof show that we can use the same framework to generate
sentences from a grammar. Part of a typical "assembly" for a grammar
might look like this:

```
assembly(sentence,[noun_phrase, verb_phrase]).
assembly(noun_phrase, [determiner, noun]).
assembly(determiner, [the]).
assembly(noun, [clergyman]).
assembly(noun, [motorcar]).
```

and the words in the lexicon would be defined as basic parts:

```
basicpart(clergyman).
basicpart(motorcar).
```

At this point you may wish to experiment with generating sentences. You
should provide a reasonable grammar and a vocabulary. Satisfy yourself
that this modified program will produce all possible grammatical sentences
from the grammar and vocabulary you provide. As always, Prolog will stop
at each solution, and wait for you to type a semicolon to tell it to backtrack to
the next solution.

This is certainly not the last word on processing English language in this
book. The whole of Chapter 9 is devoted to a more sophisticated treatment of
analysing English language in Prolog.

3.7 Accumulators

Frequently we need to traverse a Prolog structure and calculate a result
which depends on what was found in the structure. At intermediate stages of
the traversal, we will have an interim value for the result. A common
technique is to use an argument of the predicate to represent the "answer so
far". This argument is called an *accumulator*.

In the following example, we show a definition of the predicate listlen
without using an accumulator, and then a definition using an accumulator.
The goal listlen(L,N) succeeds if the length of list L is N. Some Prolog
systems may have the built-in predicate length for this purpose. First, a
listlen without using an accumulator. There are two clauses, the
boundary condition and the recursive case. The boundary condition is a fact
stating that the empty list has length 0. The recursive case is a rule saying
that the length of a non-empty list can be calculated by adding one to the
length of the tail of the list:

```
listlen([],0).
listlen([H|T],N) :- listlen(T,N1), N is N1 + 1.
```

The alternative way to write this uses the same recursive principle, but the answer is accumulated at each recurrence in an extra argument used for this purpose. We use an auxiliary predicate lenacc, which is a generalisation of listlen. lenacc(L,A,N) means that the length of list L, when added to the number A, is the number N. Thus to use lenacc to find the length of a list, we need to give it the second argument 0 (zero). This is done in an introductory clause which gives the relation between listlen and lenacc.

```
listlen(L,N) :- lenacc(L,0,N).
```

```
lenacc([],A,A).
lenacc([H|T],A,N) :- A1 is A + 1, lenacc(T,A1,N).
```

Predicate lenacc also has two clauses. First, for the empty list, the length of the list will be whatever has been accumulated so far (A). In the second clause, we add 1 to the accumulated amount given by A, and recur on the tail of the list with a new accumulator value A1.

Note that the final argument of the recursive subgoal (N) is the same as the final argument in the head of the clause. This means that the length returned for the whole list will be the number that the recursive subgoal calculates. That is, the production of the final result is being delegated entirely to the recursive subgoal. All the extra information that is needed to construct this overall result is provided by the accumulator. If the second clause is used again for the recursive subgoal, once again the production of the final result is delegated to a recursive subgoal (with a modified accumulator). Thus we get a sequence of lenacc goals, all sharing the same last argument, each having the tail of the input list of the previous one and an accumulator that is 1 greater than the previous one. Here is what the sequence of subgoals would look like for finding the length of the list [a,b,c,d,e]:

```
lenacc([a,b,c,d,e],0,N)
lenacc([b,c,d,e],1,N)
lenacc([c,d,e],2,N)
lenacc([d,e],3,N)
lenacc([e],4,N)
lenacc([],5,N)
```

where all the N's share. The last goal has now met the boundary condition (the end of the input list has been reached), and so the first lenacc clause is now applicable. This instantiates the final argument to whatever the accumulator is at that point. Since the initial accumulator was 0 and each time we found an element in the list we passed on an accumulator 1 greater than the previous one, this value is the length of the list (5). Also since all the lenacc goals — including the very first one introduced by listlen — share their final argument, all these goals immediately get their final arguments instantiated to the length of the list. In particular, this means here that N in the listlen clause is instantiated to 5.

Accumulators needn't be integers. If we are producing a list as a result, an accumulator will hold the list built so far. This may be useful if we need to inspect our interim results (for example, to avoid adding duplicate elements to the list). Using an accumulator in this situation can also avoid much wasteful joining of structures. In general, for efficiency we may wish to avoid joining structures together too, often because these operations are expensive. For instance, if we use append to join two lists together, we make our way down the first list until it is empty. At each stage, we construct a new piece of list structure in the third argument. When we finally reach the end of the list, we fill in the final part of the output list with the second input list. In order to produce an output list that ends with the second input list, we essentially have to make a copy of the first input list. If the first input list is long, this can be a lot of work. Consider what happens in our parts inventory if we wish to find the parts that make up a bicycle. A bicycle assembly is given by the following:

```
assembly(bike,[wheel,wheel,frame]).
```

To find the parts of a bicycle, we use partsoflist to find the parts coming from the list [wheel,wheel,frame]. Because of the way partsoflist is defined, this involves:

- finding the parts of a frame,
- appending these to the empty list to give the parts of [frame],
- finding the parts of a wheel,
- appending these to the parts of [frame] to get the parts of [wheel,frame],
- finding the parts of a wheel,
- appending these to the parts of [wheel,frame] to get the parts of [wheel,wheel,frame].

This sequence of operations is wasteful because each list of parts for a subpart of a bicycle has to be built twice. It is built once when it is first worked out, and once when it is appended to the list of parts obtained so far. Because some of the subparts of a bicycle are themselves assemblies, this wastefulness will be repeated in deriving their parts as well. We can avoid this unnecessary extra work by using accumulators. As with the listlen example, we introduce auxiliary predicates with extra accumulator arguments and have a starting clause that calls one of these with an appropriately initialised accumulator. Here is a program for the parts inventory which uses accumulators. The clauses for basicpart and assembly are unchanged, so are not listed here. Notice that append is no longer used.

```
partsof(X,P) :- partsacc(X,[],P).

partsacc(X,A,[X|A]) :- basicpart(X).
partsacc(X,A,P) :-
    assembly(X,Subparts),
    partsacclist(Subparts,A,P).

partsacclist([],A,A).
partsacclist([P|Tail],A,Total) :-
    partsacc(P,A,Headparts),
    partsacclist(Tail,Headparts,Total).
```

The predicates partsacc and partsacclist are defined very similarly to the previous versions of partsof and partsoflist, except that they have an accumulator as their second argument. This argument represents the list of (basic) parts that have been found so far. So partsacc(X,A,P) means that the parts of object X, when added to the list A, give the list P. Notice the similarity with the meaning of lenacc. If we wish to use partsacc to find the parts of an object, we must provide it with the empty list as its second argument; hence the partsof clause.

The first clause of partsacc simply constructs a new list whose head is the object given in the first argument, and whose tail is the accumulated list of parts, and this will succeed if the object is a basic part. The second clause, which applies when the object is an assembly, first finds the list of subparts, and then uses partsacclist to find the subparts of each art in the list. Note that the accumulator (A) has been passed to partsacclist.

The first clause of partsacclist is the boundary case, in which the result is the accumulated list of subparts (A). The recursive case calls partsacc to find the subparts of the next part on the given list, and the recursive goal deals with the remainer of the list. Note that the second argument of the second clause (A) is used as the accumulator for the partsacc goal, and that the result of the partsacc goal (Headparts) is used as the accumulator for the recursive goal.

We make further use of accumulators throughout the book. In particular, we draw your attention to Sections 7.2, 7.5, and 7.8, as well as the next section.

3.8 Difference Structures

In the previous section, we used an accumulator to avoid unnecessary joining of structures. One unmentioned effect of this was to produce a resulting list in which the elements were in the *reverse* order to that in which they were produced from the original list. Sometimes, however, we may wish to generate elements in the *same* order as the original list. *Difference structures* (here difference *lists*) allow us to do this.

If we use the parts inventory program to find the parts of a bicycle, the version using accumulators works just as well as the original version, and indeed runs faster. However, if we use it for generating English sentences as suggested before, we encounter a problem: the words come out in reverse order! This did not matter for the bicycles, because the order of the parts is not important, but obviously with English sentences it matters what order the words come in. If we think about the way in which the list of "parts" is built, it is not surprising that it ends up in the reverse order to that in which the parts are originally discovered. For every time we come to a basic part, we create a new accumulator which has this part *before* all the parts found so far.

With accumulators, we use two arguments to organise the building of some output structure. One is for the "result so far" and one is for the "final result". With difference lists, we also use two arguments, but with a different interpretation. The first argument is for the "final result", and the second argument is for "a hole in the final result where further information can be put". The way we represent a "hole" in a structure is by a Prolog variable which shares with a component somewhere in the structure. Thus the following two terms represent a list together with a named "hole variable" where further information could be put:

```
[a,b,c|X]   X
```

If we have a list with a "hole" in it, we can further instantiate the list by passing the "hole variable" as an argument to a Prolog goal which instantiates this argument. In general, we will be interested in where further information can be inserted after this goal has succeeded. Thus we will require the goal to pass back a *new* hole through another argument. So here is a conjunction of goals that would create a list with a hole, add some elements to the list using predicate p and then fill in the hole that remains with the list [z]:

```
?- Res = [a,b,c|X], p(X,NewHole), NewHole = [z].
```

We can allow for the p goal not instantiating the list further by providing a clause which causes the original hole to be returned as the new hole:

```
p(Hole,Hole).
```

If this clause is chosen, the variable Res will have the value [a,b,c,z] when the question succeeds. Alternatively, we can provide a clause that causes the original hole to be instantiated to a structure containing a new variable and this variable to be passed back as the new hole:

```
p([d|NewHole],NewHole).
```

(in general, a clause like this will, of course, obtain these results partly through the effects of subgoals that it invokes). If this clause is chosen, the variable Res will have the value [a,b,c,d,z] when the question succeeds.

Here is a version of the parts inventory program that uses the difference lists technique:

```
partsof(X,P) :- partsacc(X,P,Hole), Hole = [].

partsacc(X,[X|Hole],Hole) :- basicpart(X).
partsacc(X,P,Hole) :-
    assembly(X,Subparts),
    partsacclist(Subparts,P,Hole).

partsacclist([],Hole,Hole).
partsacclist([P|Tail],Total,Hole) :-
    partsacc(P,Total,Hole1),
    partsacclist(Tail,Hole1,Hole).
```

First consider the partsof clause. When partsacc is initially called from the partsof clause, it will build its result in the second argument P and will return in Hole a variable. Because partsof calls partsacc only once, it is necessary to terminate the difference list by instantiating Hole with []. Note that a perfectly valid alternative definition of partsof is:

```
partsof(X,P) :- partsacc(X,P,[]).
```

This more succint version ensures that the very last hole is filled with [] even before the list is constructed.

The first clause of partsacc returns a difference list containing the object in the first argument, and this applies if the object is a basic part. The second clause, for assemblies, finds the list of subparts and delegates the traversal of the list to partsacclist, passing the two arguments making up the difference list (P and Hole). The second clause uses partsacc to list the subparts using the difference list with Total and Hole1. The recursive goal then returns the portion of the difference list starting at Hole1 and ending at Hole. The entire result, the list between Total and Hole, is the result of the second partsacclist clause. The way that the list is constructed by "weaving" together partial results can be conveyed with the aid of this illustration.

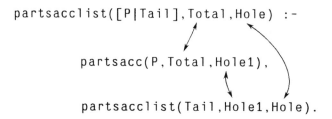

```
partsacclist([P|Tail],Total,Hole) :-

        partsacc(P,Total,Hole1),

    partsacclist(Tail,Hole1,Hole).
```

We make use of difference lists again in the definition of quisortx in section 7.7.

Chapter 4

Backtracking and the "Cut"

Let us summarise what we learned in Chapters 1 and 2 about what can happen to a goal:

1. An attempt can be made to satisfy a goal. When we satisfy a goal, we search the database from the top. Two things can happen:

   (a) A matching fact (or rule head) can be found. In this case, we say the goal has been matched. We mark the place in the database, and instantiate any previously uninstantiated variables that have matched. If we matched against a rule, we shall first have to attempt to satisfy the subgoals introduced by the rule. If the goal succeeds, we then attempt to satisfy the next goal. In our diagrams, this is the goal in the next box below the arrow. If the original goal appears in a conjunction, this will be the goal to its right in the program.

   (b) No matching fact (or rule head) can be found. In this case, we say the goal has failed. We then attempt to re-satisfy the goal in the box above the arrowhead. If the original goal appears in a conjunction, then this will be the goal on its left in the program.

2. We can attempt to re-satisfy a goal. First of all, we attempt to re-satisfy each of the subgoals in turn, the arrow retreating up the page. If no subgoal can be re-satisfied in a suitable way, we attempt to find an alternative clause for the goal itself. In this case, we must make uninstantiated any variables that became instantiated when the previous clause was chosen. This is what we mean by "undoing" all the work previously done by this goal. Next, we resume searching the database, but we begin the search from where the goal's place-marker was previously put. As before, this new "backtracked" goal may either succeed or fail, and either step (a) or (b) above would occur.

This chapter will look at backtracking in more detail. It will also look at a special mechanism that can be used in Prolog programs — the "cut". The cut allows you to tell Prolog which previous choices it need not consider again.

4.1 Generating Multiple Solutions

The simplest way a set of facts can allow multiple solutions to a question is when there are several facts that will match against the question. For instance, if we have the following facts in which father(X,Y) means that the father of X is Y:

```
father(mary,george).
father(john,george).
father(sue,harry).
father(george,edward).
```

The question

```
?- father(X,Y).
```

will have several possible answers. If we prompt with a semicolon, Prolog will give us the following:

```
X=mary, Y=george ;
X=john, Y=george ;
X=sue, Y=harry ;
X=george, Y=edward
```

It finds these answers by searching through the database to find the facts and rule about father in the order in which they were given. Prolog is not particularly clever about this — it does not remember anything about what it has shown before. So if we ask

```
?- father(_,X).
```

(for which X is X a father?) we will get:

```
X=george ;
X=george ;
X=harry ;
X=edward
```

with george repeated twice because George is the father of both Mary and John. If Prolog has two ways of showing the same thing, it treats them as two different solutions.

Backtracking happens in exactly the same way if the alternatives are embedded more deeply in the processing. For example, one rule in a definition of "one of the children of X is Y" might be

```
child(X,Y) :- father(Y,X).
```

Then, the question

```
?- child(X,Y).
```

would give

```
X=george, Y=mary ;
X=george, Y=john ;
X=harry, Y=sue ;
X=edward, Y=george
```

Because father(Y,X) has four solutions, so does child(X,Y). Moreover, the solutions are generated in the same order. All that is different is that the order of the arguments is different, as is specified in the definition of child. Similarly, if we defined

```
father(X) :- father(_,X).
```

(father(X) meaning that X is a father), then the question

```
?- father(X). would evoke:
```

```
X=george ;
X=george ;
X=harry ;
X=edward
```

If we mix facts and rules, the alternatives follow again in the order in which things are presented. Thus we might represent that adam is a person, anything is a person if it has a mother, and eve is a person. Also, various people have various mothers:

```
person(adam).
person(X) :- mother(X,Y).
person(eve).

mother(cain,eve).
mother(abel,eve).
mother(jabal,adah).
mother(tubalcain,zillah).
```

In this case, if we asked the question

```
?- person(X).
```

the answers would be:

```
X=adam ;
X=cain ;
X=abel ;
X=jabal ;
```

```
X=tubalcain ;
X=eve
```

Let us look now at a more interesting case — where there are two goals each of which has several solutions. Let us imagine we are planning a party and want to speculate about who might dance with whom. We can start writing a program as follows:

```
possible_pair(X,Y) :- boy(X), girl(Y).

boy(john).
boy(marmaduke).
boy(bertram).
boy(charles).

girl(griselda).
girl(ermintrude).
girl(brunhilde).
```

This program says that X and Y form a possible pair if X is a boy and Y is a girl. Now let's see what possible pairs there are:

```
?- possible_pair(X,Y).

X = john, Y = griselda ;
X = john, Y = ermintrude ;
X = john, Y = brunhilde ;
X = marmaduke, Y = griselda ;
X = marmaduke, Y = ermintrude ;
X = marmaduke, Y = brunhilde ;
X = bertram, Y = griselda ;
X = bertram, Y = ermintrude ;
X = bertram, Y = brunhilde ;
X = charles, Y = griselda ;
X = charles, Y = ermintrude ;
X = charles, Y = brunhilde
```

You should make sure that you understand why Prolog produces the solutions in this order. First of all, it satisfies the goal boy(X), finding john, the first boy. Then it satisfies girl(Y), finding griselda, the first girl. At this point, we ask for another solution by causing a failure. Prolog attempts to re-satisfy what it did last, which is the girl goal within the satisfaction of the possible_pair goal. It finds the alternative girl ermintrude, and so the second solution is john and ermintrude. Similarly, it generates john and brunhilde as the third solution. The next time it tries to re-satisfy girl(Y), Prolog finds that its place-marker is at the end of the database, and so the goal fails. Now it tries to re-satisfy boy(X). The place-marker for this was placed at the first fact for boy, and so the next solution found is the second boy (marmaduke). Now that it has re-satisfied this goal, Prolog looks to see what is next — it must now satisfy girl(Y) from the start again. So it finds griselda, the first girl. The next three solutions now involve marmaduke and the three girls. Next time we ask for an alternative, the girl goal cannot be re-satisfied again. So another boy is found, and the search through girls starts again from scratch. And so on. Eventually, the girl goal fails and there are also no more solutions to the boy goal either. So the program can find no more pairs.

These examples are all very simple. They just involve the specification of many facts or the use of rules to access those facts. Because of this, they can only generate a finite number of possible solutions. Sometimes we might want to generate an infinite number of possibilities — not because we want to consider them all, but because we may not know in advance how many we need. In this case we need a recursive definition (discussed in the previous chapter).

Consider the following definition of what it is to be an integer (where by integer we mean a whole number not less than 0). The goal is_integer(N) will succeed providing N is instantiated to an integer. If N is not instantiated at the time the goal is considered, then an is_integer(N) will cause an integer to be chosen, and N will be instantiated to it:

```
/* 1 */   is_integer(0).
/* 2 */   is_integer(X) :- is_integer(Y), X is Y+1.
```

If we ask the question

```
?- is_integer(X).
```

we will get as the possible answers all the integers in ascending order (0, 1, 2, 3, ...), one at a time. Each time we force backtracking to occur (perhaps by typing semicolon), is_integer will succeed with its argument instantiated to a new integer. So in principle this short definition generates an infinite number of answers. Why? Here is the sequence of events that leads to the first three solutions:

First solution:

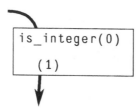

Second solution:

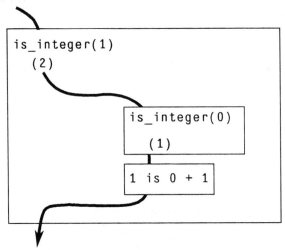

Third solution:

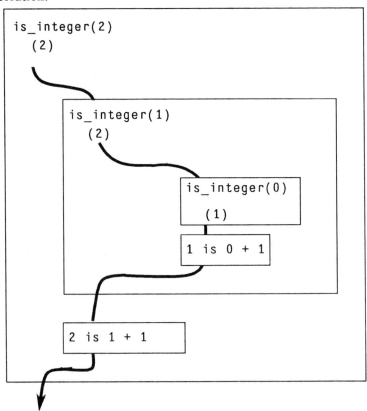

and so on. At each stage, the lowest (1) is where another choice will be made next. Initially, we have a choice between fact 1 and rule 2 to answer the question. If we choose fact 1, no more choices have to be made, and we get X = 0. Otherwise we choose rule 2 and have a choice how to satisfy the goal it introduces. If we choose fact 1, we end up with the answer X = 1; otherwise we use rule 2 and must again choose how to satisfy the subgoal produced. And so on. At each stage, the first thing Prolog does is to pick fact 1. Only on backtracking does it undo the last choice. Each time it does this, it goes back to where it last chose fact 1, and instead chooses rule 2. Once it has decided to use rule 2, a new subgoal is introduced. Fact 1 is the first possibility for satisfying it.

Most Prolog rules will give rise to alternative solutions if they are used for goals that contain a lot of uninstantiated variables. For instance, the relation of membership of a list (from Chapter 3):

```
member(X,[X|_]).
member(X,[_|Y]) :- member(X,Y).
```

will generate alternatives. If we ask

```
?- member(a,X).
```

(notice X in the question is uninstantiated) then the successive values of X will be partially-defined lists where a is the first, second, third, (and so on) member. See if you can see why this is.

A further result of allowing this definition of member to backtrack is that the question

```
?- member(a,[a,b,r,a,c,a,d,a,b,r,a]).
```

actually can succeed five times. Clearly, there are some applications of member where we only need it to succeed once, if at all, and then discard the other four choices. We can tell Prolog to discard choices in this way by using the "cut".

4.2 The "Cut"

This section looks at a special mechanism that can be used in Prolog programs — the "cut". The "cut" allows you to tell Prolog which previous choices it need not consider again when it backtracks though the chain of satisfied goals. There are two reasons why it may be important to do this:

- Your program will operate faster because it will not waste time attempting to satisfy goals that you can tell beforehand will never contribute to a solution;

- Your program may occupy less of the computer's memory space because more economical use of memory can be made if backtracking points do not have to be recorded for later examination.

In some cases, including a "cut" may mean the difference between a program that will run and a program that will not.

Syntactically, a use of "cut" in a rule looks just like the appearance of a goal which has the predicate "!" and no arguments. As a goal, this succeeds immediately and cannot be re-satisfied. However, it also has side-effects which alter the way backtracking works afterwards. The effect is to make inaccessible the place markers for certain goals so that they cannot be re-satisfied.

Let us see how this works in an example. Imagine that you are running a library and have a Prolog database containing information about what books there are, who has borrowed what and when books are due back. One thing you might be concerned about is which of the library facilities should be open to which people. Some facilities, which we might call basic facilities, should be open to everyone. These include the use of the reference library and the enquiries desk. On the other hand, the library might want to be selective about which people are allowed to use additional facilities, such as actually borrowing books or using inter-library loans. One rule that might be made is that, if a person has a book overdue, then the additional facilities will not be available to the person until the book is returned. Here is part of a program that uses this rule:

```
facility(Pers,Fac) :-
    book_overdue(Pers,Book),
    !,
    basic_facility(Fac).

facility(Pers,Fac) :- general_facility(Fac).

basic_facility(reference).
basic_facility(enquiries).

additional_facility(borrowing).
additional_facility(inter_library_loan).

general_facility(X) :- basic_facility(X).
general_facility(X) :- additional_facility(X).

book_overdue('C. Watzer',book10089).
book_overdue('A. Jones',book29907).
...
```

```
client('A. Jones').
client('W. Metesk').
  .
  .
  .
```

Why is there a cut in this program and what effect does it have? Let us assume that we wish to run through all our clients and find out what facilities are open to them. Thus we give Prolog the question:

```
?- client(X), facility(X,Y).
```

Prolog will start by finding the first client, 'A. Jones'. Let us assume that this client has several overdue books. In order to find what facilities are open to him, Prolog will start by using the first clause for facility. This introduces a new goal — to see whether he has any overdue books. After a short search among the book_overdue facts, the fact about the first overdue book for A. Jones is found (the second fact for this predicate). The next goal encountered is the "cut". This goal succeeds, and the effect is to commit the system to all the decisions made since the first facility clause was chosen. We can show the situation just before the "cut" is encountered in a diagram as follows:

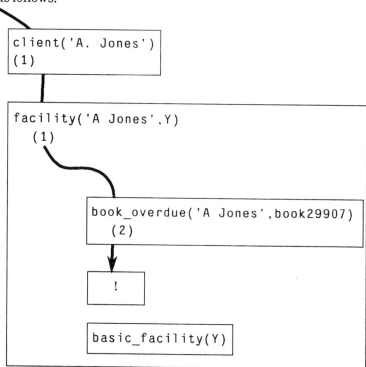

When the cut is encountered, it "cuts" the flow of satisfaction line so that if it is forced to retreat beyond this point it will have to take a short cut:

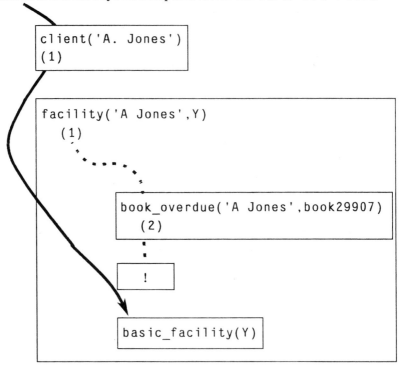

The effect of the "cut" in the facility rule (clause 1) is to commit the system to every choice it has made since it chose that rule. The flow of satisfaction path has been changed so as to avoid all the place markers between the facility goal and the "cut" goal inclusive. Thus if backtracking later causes a retreat back past this point, the facility goal will immediately fail. The system will not consider alternative solutions for the goal book_overdue('A. Jones',Book), and this is quite reasonable as we are only interested in whether the client has *any* overdue book, not what *all* the books are. Neither will the system consider clause 2 for facility, because the choice of the rule that the cut appears in is also bypassed on backtracking. This is again reasonable here, because we don't want to generate solutions that say that all facilities are open to A. Jones.

In summary, the effect of the "cut" in this example is to say:

> *If a client is found to have an overdue book, then only allow the client the basic facilities of the library. Don't bother going through all the client's overdue books, and don't consider any other rule about facilities.*

In this example, the cut committed the system to all the decisions made from it back to the `facility` goal. This is called the *parent goal* of the cut goal, because it is the goal that caused the use of the rule containing the cut. In our diagrams, the parent goal is always the goal whose box is the smallest one enclosing the "`!`" box. The formal definition of the effect of the cut symbol is as follows:

> When a cut is encountered as a goal, the system thereupon becomes committed to all choices made since the parent goal was invoked. All other alternatives are discarded. Hence an attempt to re-satisfy any goal between the parent goal and the cut goal will fail.

There are several ways of describing what has happened to the choices that are affected by a cut. One can say that the choices are cut or frozen, that the system commits itself to the choices made or that the alternatives are discarded. One can also look at the cut symbol as being rather like a fence that separates goals. In this conjunction of goals,

```
foo :- a, b, c, !, d, e, f.
```

Prolog will quite happily backtrack among goals a, b, and c, *until* the success of c causes the "fence" to be crossed to the right to reach goal d. Then, backtracking can occur among d, e, and f, perhaps satisfying the entire conjunction several times. However, if d fails, causing the "fence" to be crossed to the left, then no attempt will be made to re-satisfy goal c: the entire conjunction of goals will fail, and the goal f o o will also fail.

One further note before we go on to see more examples of the cut in use. We have said that if the cut appears in some rule and the cut goal is satisfied then Prolog becomes committed to all choices made since the parent goal was invoked. This means that the choice of that rule, and all other choices made since then, become fixed. We will see later that it is possible to provide alternatives within a single rule using the built-in predicate "`;`" (meaning "or"). The choices introduced by this facility are affected in exactly the same way. That is, when a cut goal is satisfied, all "or" choices that have been made since the rule was chosen are fixed.

4.3 Common Uses of the Cut

We can divide the common uses of "cut" into three main areas:

- The first concerns places where we want to tell the Prolog system that it has found the right rule for a particular goal. Here, the cut says "if you get this far, you have picked the correct rule for this goal."

- The second concerns places where we want to tell the Prolog system to fail a particular goal immediately without trying for alternative solutions. Here, we use the cut in conjunction with the fail predicate to say "if you get to here, you should stop trying to satisfy this goal."

- The third concerns places where we want to terminate the generation of alternative solutions through backtracking. Here, the cut says "if you get to here, you have found the only solution to this problem, and there is no point in ever looking for alternatives."

We will now look at some examples of these three uses. You should bear in mind, however, that the cut has a single meaning in all these applications. The division into three main areas of use is purely for tutorial reasons, and to show what kinds of reasons you might have for putting cuts into your programs.

4.3.1 Confirming the Choice of a Rule

Very often in a Prolog program, we wish to associate several clauses with the same predicate. One clause will be appropriate if the arguments are of one form, another will be appropriate if the arguments are of another form, and so on. Often we can specify which rule should be used for a given goal by providing patterns in the rule heads that will only match goals of the right types. However, this may not always be possible. If we cannot tell in advance what forms the arguments may take, or if we cannot specify an exhaustive set of patterns, we may have to compromise. This means giving rules for some specific argument types and then giving a "catchall" rule at the end for everything else.

As an example of this, consider the following program. The rules define the predicate sum_to such that giving Prolog the goal sum_to(N,X) with N having an integer value, causes X to be instantiated to the sum of the numbers from 1 to N. Thus, for instance, it produces the following:

```
?- sum_to(5,X).

X = 15 ;
no
```

because $1+2+3+4+5$ is 15. Here is the program.

```
sum_to(1,1) :- !.
sum_to(N,Res) :-
        N1 is N - 1,
        sum_to(N1,Res1),
        Res is Res1 + N.
```

This is a recursive definition. The idea is that the boundary condition occurs when the first number is 1. In that case, the answer is also 1. The second clause introduces a recursive sum_to goal. However, the first number of the new goal is one less than the original one. The new goal that this goal will invoke will have its first argument one less again. And so on until the boundary condition is reached. Since the first arguments are always getting less, the boundary condition must be reached eventually (assuming that the original goal has a first argument not less than 1), and the program will terminate.

The interesting thing about this program is how we have handled the two cases — when the number is 1, and when it is something else. When we defined predicates that talked about lists, it was easy to specify the two cases that would normally arise — when the list was [ ] and when it was of the form [A|B]. With numbers, things are not so easy, because we cannot specify a pattern that will only match an integer not equal to 1. The solution adopted in this example is to provide a pattern for the "1" case and just to leave a variable to match against anything else. We know from the way Prolog searches through the database that it will try to match the number against 1 first and will only try the second rule if this fails. So the second rule should only be used for numbers not equal to 1. However, this is not the whole story. If Prolog ever backtracks and comes to reconsider the choice of rule when applied to the number 1, it will find that the second rule is applicable. As far as it can see, both rules provide alternatives for the goal sum_to(1,X). We must tell it that on no account is the second rule ever to be tried if the number is 1. One way of doing this is to put a cut in the first rule (as shown). This tells Prolog that, once it has got this far in the first rule, it must never remake the decision about which rule to use for the sum_to goal. It will only get this far if the number is in fact 1. Let us see what this looks like in terms of the flow of satisfaction. If we call sum_to(1,X) in the context:

```
go :- sum_to(1,X), foo(apples).

?- go.
```

and the goal foo(apples) fails, then at the point of failure we will have:

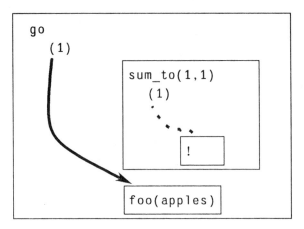

When Prolog tries to re-satisfy the goals in reverse order, it will find that two of the goals cannot be re-satisfied because the flow of satisfaction path has been re-routed. Hence it will correctly avoid trying alternative ways of satisfying sum_to(1,X).

Exercise 4.1: What happens if the "cut" is left out here and backtracking gets round to reconsidering the sum_to goal? What alternative results, if any, are produced, and why?

The last example showed how "cut" can be used to make Prolog behave sensibly when we cannot distinguish between all the possible cases by specifying patterns in the heads of the rules. A more usual situation in which we cannot specify patterns to decide which rule to use arises when we want to provide extra conditions, in the form of Prolog goals, which will decide on the appropriate rule. Consider the following alternative form of the above example:

```
sum_to(N,1) :- N =<· 1, !.
sum_to(N,R) :-
        N1 is N - 1,
        sum_to(N1,R1),
        R is R1 + N.
```

In this case, we say that the first rule is the one to choose if the number provided is less than or equal to one. This is slightly better than the previous formulation, because it means that the program produces an answer (rather than running on indefinitely) if the first argument is given as 0 or a negative number. If the condition is true, the result 1 can be produced immediately, and no more recursive goals are necessary. Only if the condition is not true do we want ever to try the second rule. We must tell Prolog that once it has proved N =< 1, it must never reconsider the choice about what rule to choose. This is what the cut does.

It is a general principle that uses of cut to tell Prolog when it has picked the only correct rule can be replaced by uses of not. This is a Prolog built-in predicate, which means that its definition is already provided when you start your Prolog session. So you can use it in your own programs without having to write down a definition each time (built-in predicates are described more fully in Chapter 6). Predicate not is defined in such a way that the goal not(X) succeeds only if X, when seen as a Prolog goal, fails. So not(X) means that "X is not satisfiable as a Prolog goal". As an example of replacing cuts with uses of not, the two possibilities given for the sum_to definition can be rewritten as:

```
sum_to(1,1).
sum_to(N,R) :-
      not(N=1),
      N1 is N-1, sum_to(N1,R1), R is N+R1.
```

or

```
sum_to(N,1) :- N =< 1.
sum_to(N,R) :-
      not(N =< 1),
      N1 is N - 1,
      sum_to(N1,R1),
      R is N + R1.
```

In fact, Prolog provides suitable built-in predicates to substitute for both of these uses. For example, we can replace not(N=1) by N\=1, and not(N=<1) by N>1. In general, we will not be able to do this with all the conditions we dream up.

It is good programming style to replace cuts by the use of not. This is because programs containing cuts are in general harder to read than programs not containing them. If one can localise all occurrences of cut to inside the definition of not, then the program will be easier to understand. However, the definition of not involves trying to show that the goal it is given can be satisfied. Therefore, if we have a program of the general form:

```
A :- B, C.
A :- not(B), D.
```

Prolog may well end up trying to satisfy B twice. It will have to try to satisfy B when it looks at the first rule. Also, if it ever backtracks and considers the second rule, it will have to try to satisfy B again to see if not(B) can be satisfied. This duplication could be very inefficient if the condition B was rather complicated. This would not be the case if instead we had:

```
A  :-  B,  !,  C.
A  :-  D.
```

So one must sometimes weigh up the advantages of a clear program against those of a program that will run quickly. The discussion of efficiency leads us to our last example of the cut being used to fix the choice of a rule. Consider the definition of append:

```
append([],X,X).
append([A|B],C,[A|D])  :-  append(B,C,D).
```

If we are always using append for the case where we have two known lists and want to know what list consists of the first appended onto the front of the second, we may feel that it is inefficient that when backtracking gets to reconsider how to deal with a goal like append([],[a,b,c,d],X) it must try to use the second rule, even though the attempt is bound to fail. We know in this context that if the first list is [] then the first rule is the only correct one, and this information can be given to Prolog by a use of the cut. In general, Prolog implementations will be able to make better use of the available storage if they are told things like this than if they have to keep a record of apparent choices that are not really there. So we could rewrite our definition as:

```
append([],X,X)  :-  !.
append([A|B],C,[A|D])  :-  append(B,C,D).
```

Assuming our restricted use of append, this does not affect at all which solutions the program finds. It only increases the space and time efficiency to some extent. In exchange for this, we are liable to find that other kinds of uses of append will no longer work as expected, as is shown in Section 4.4.

4.3.2 The "cut-fail" Combination

In the second major application area, the cut is used in conjunction with the built-in fail predicate. This is another built-in predicate, like not. It has no arguments, which means that the success of the goal fail does not depend on what any variables stand for. Indeed, fail is defined in such a way that as a goal it always fails and causes backtracking to take place. This is just like what happens if we try to satisfy a goal for a predicate with no facts or rules. When fail is encountered after a cut, the normal backtracking behaviour will be altered by the effect of the cut. In fact, the particular combination "cut-fail" turns out to be quite useful in practice.

Let us consider how we might use this combination in a program to calculate how much tax somebody should pay. One thing we might want to know is whether the person is an "average taxpayer" — in this case, the calculations might be quite simple and not have to involve considering lots of special cases. Let us define a predicate `average_taxpayer` where `average_taxpayer(X)` means that X is an average taxpayer. For instance, Fred Bloggs, who is married with 2 children and works in a bicycle factory, might be considered quite average. However, the managing director of an oil company may be earning too much, and a student may be earning too little for the same kinds of tax calculations to be appropriate. We should start by considering a possible special case. It may be that special tax laws apply to somebody who is a native of another country, because he may have obligations to that country as well. Therefore, however average he may be in other respects, a foreigner will not be classed as an average taxpayer. We can start writing rules about this as follows:

```
average_taxpayer(X) :- foreigner(X), fail.
average_taxpayer(X) :- ...
```

In this extract, *which is not correct yet*, the first rule attempts to say "if X is a foreigner then the goal `average_taxpayer(X)` should fail." The second rule is to apply the general criterion for being an average taxpayer for the cases when X is not a foreigner. The trouble is that if we asked the question:

```
?- average_taxpayer(widslewip).
```

about a foreigner called `widslewip` the first rule would match and the `foreigner` goal would succeed. Next, the `fail` goal would initiate backtracking. In attempting to re-satisfy the `average_taxpayer` goal, Prolog would find the second rule and start applying the general criterion to `widslewip`. Now it is quite likely that he would pass the further tests, being average in other ways, in which case the question would incorrectly be answered "yes". So our first rule has been completely ineffective in rejecting our friend as an average taxpayer.

Why is this? The answer is that during backtracking Prolog tries to re-satisfy *every* goal that has succeeded. So in particular it will investigate alternative ways of satisfying `average_taxpayer(widslewip)`. In order to stop Prolog finding alternatives for this, we need to "cut" the choice (freeze the decision) before failing. We can do this by inserting a cut before the `fail` goal. A slightly more comprehensive definition of `average_taxpayer` incorporating this change, is given below:

```
average_taxpayer(X) :- foreigner(X), !, fail.
average_taxpayer(X) :-
     spouse(X,Y),
     gross_income(Y,Inc),
```

```
      Inc > 3000,
      !, fail.
average_taxpayer(X) :-
      gross_income(X,Inc),
      2000 < Inc, 20000 > Inc.

gross_income(X,Y) :-
      receives_pension(X,P),
      P < 5000,
      !, fail.
gross_income(X,Y) :-
      gross_salary(X,Z),
      investment_income(X,W),
      Y is Z+W.

investment_income(X,Y) :-   ...
```

Note the use in this program of several other "cut-fail" combinations. In the second rule for average_taxpayer we say that the attempt to show that someone is an average taxpayer can be abandoned if we can show that that person's spouse earns more than a certain amount. Also, in the definition of the predicate gross_income we say (in the first rule) that if somebody receives a pension that is below a certain amount then, whatever their other circumstances, we will consider them not to have any gross income at all.

An interesting application of the "cut-fail" combination is in the definition of the predicate not. Most Prolog implementations provide this already defined, but it is interesting to consider how we can provide rules for it. We require that the goal not(P), where P stands for another goal, succeeds if and only if the goal P fails. This is not exactly in accord with our intuitive notion of "not true" — it is not always safe to assume that something is not true if we are unable to prove it. However, here is the definition:

```
not(P) :- call(P), !, fail.
not(P).
```

The definition of not involves invoking the argument P as a goal, using the built-in predicate call. Predicate call simply treats its argument as a goal and attempts to satisfy it. We want the first rule to be applicable if P can be shown, and the second to be applicable otherwise. So we say that if Prolog can satisfy call(P) it should thereupon abandon satisfying the not goal. The other possibility is that Prolog cannot show call(P). In this case, it never gets to the cut. Because the call(P) goal failed, backtracking takes place, and Prolog finds the second rule. Hence the goal not(P) will succeed when P is not provable.

As with the first use of "cut", we can replace uses of "cut-fail" with uses of not. This involves rather more reorganisation of the program than before, but does not introduce the same inefficiency. If we were to rewrite our average_taxpayer program, it would start off something like:

```
average_taxpayer(X) :-
   not(foreigner(X)),
   not((spouse(X,Y), gross_income(Y,Inc), Inc>3000)),
   gross_income(X,Inc1),
   :
   :
```

Note that in this example, we have to enclose a whole conjunction of goals inside the not. In order to show unambiguously that the commas join the goals into a conjunction (rather than separating multiple not arguments), we have enclosed the not argument in an extra set of brackets.

4.3.3 Terminating a "generate and test"

Now we come to look at the last major use of "cut" in Prolog programs — to terminate a "generate and test" sequence. Very often a program will have parts that conform to the following general model. There will be a sequence of goals that can succeed in many ways, and which generates many possible solutions on backtracking. After this, there are goals that check whether a solution generated is acceptable for some purpose. If these goals fail, backtracking will lead to another solution being proposed. This will be tested for appropriateness, and so on. This process will stop when either an acceptable solution is generated (success), or when no more solutions can be found (failure). We can call the goals that are yielding all the alternatives the "generator" and those that check whether a solution is acceptable the "tester". Let us consider an example of this: a program to play the game "Noughts and Crosses" ("Tic-Tac-Toe"). In case you haven't come across this game, it involves two players taking turns to occupy squares on a 3×3 board. We can number the nine squares on the board as shown here to identify them uniquely:

```
 1 | 2 | 3
---+---+---
 4 | 5 | 6
---+---+---
 7 | 8 | 9
```

One player occupies squares with pieces marked o, and the other one with pieces marked x. The object of the game is to get three of one's own pieces in a (vertical, horizontal or diagonal) line before the other player does. We shall next give part of a program. The program uses the built-in predicates var and arg, which are fully discussed in Chapter 6.

```
forced_move(Board,Sq)  :-
    aline(Squares),
    threatening(Squares,Board,Sq),
    !.

aline([1,2,3]).
aline([4,5,6]).
aline([7,8,9]).
aline([1,4,7]).
aline([2,5,8]).
aline([3,6,9]).
aline([1,5,9]).
aline([3,5,7]).

threatening([X,Y,Z],B,X)  :-
    empty(X,B), cross(Y,B), cross(Z,B).

threatening([X,Y,Z],B,Y)  :-
    empty(Y,B), cross(X,B), cross(Z,B).

threatening([X,Y,Z],B,Z)  :-
    empty(Z,B), cross(X,B), cross(Y,B).

empty(Sq,Board)  :- arg(Sq,Board,Val), var(Val).

cross(Sq,Board)  :-
    arg(Sq,Board,Val), nonvar(Val), Val = x.

nought(Sq,Board)  :-
    arg(Sq,Board,Val), nonvar(Val), Val = o.
```

The program is assumed to be looking at the game from the point of view of the player who puts o's on the board. The predicate forced_move is used to answer the question "Am I forced to put a piece in a particular position?" This will be the case if the o player cannot immediately win (we do not deal with this here), but the x is threatening to win on his next move.

For instance, in the position shown below, the o player is forced to play in square 4, because if he does not, his opponent will be able to fill the line 1-4-7 in his next turn. The program works by trying to find a line, two of whose

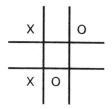

squares are occupied by crosses, and the other of which is empty. If it can, then the player is forced to move into the empty square.

In the clause for forced_move, the goal aline(Squares) serves as a "generator" of possible lines. This goal can succeed in many ways , with Squares instantiated as one of the possible lists of square numbers that represent lines. Once a possible line has been suggested, it is necessary to see whether the opponent is threatening to claim this line. This is the purpose of the "tester" goal: threatening(Squares,Board,Sq). In this goal, the variable Board is supposed to hold a representation of the current state of the board — what squares are occupied by what pieces — and the variable Sq becomes instantiated to the number of the square where the o player is forced to play (assuming the goal succeeds). The basic idea of the program is very simple. First, aline proposes a line, and then threatening looks to see whether that line is threatening. If so, the original forced_move goal succeeds. Otherwise, backtracking occurs and aline comes up with another possible line. Now this is tested also, and maybe backtracking occurs again. If we get to the point when aline can generate no more lines, then the forced_move goal will correctly fail (there is no forced move).

Now consider what happens if this program, as part of a larger system, successfully finds a forced move. Variable Sq will become instantiated to the number of the square where the move should be, and this information will be used somewhere else in the program. Suppose that somewhere later a failure occurs, and Prolog eventually tries to re-satisfy the forced_move goal. Then aline will start producing more possible lines to be checked. This makes no sense, because it cannot possibly be useful to find alternative forced moves. If we have found one of them, then we cannot do anything better than carry it out: failure to do so would guarantee losing the game. Most of the time, there will be no alternative anyway, and forced_move will search through all the untried lines in vain, before itself failing. However, in the case of forced moves, we know that even if there is an alternative solution, it cannot be of any use in a context where a failure occurred in spite of the first solution. We can prevent Prolog from wasting time searching for different forced moves by putting a "cut" at the end of the clause. This has the effect of freezing the last successful aline solution. Including the "cut" amounts to saying "when I look for forced moves, it is only the first solution that is important."

From the point of view of understanding this use of "cut", it is only necessary to consider the overall structure of this program. However, some of the details are also of interest. The program assumes the board to be represented by a structure with nine components. Each component represents what is occupying the square of the appropriate number. Thus at any time the value for square 4 can be obtained by looking at the fourth argument of the current board structure (we use the built-in predicate arg for this). The value is an uninstantiated variable if the square is unoccupied; otherwise it is one of the atoms o and x. We use var and nonvar to determine whether the square is occupied or not.

Let us look at another example of a program that works by a "generate and test" method. We came across the idea of "integer division" in Section 2.5. Most Prolog systems provide this facility automatically, but here is a program for integer division that only uses addition and multiplication.

```
divide(N1,N2,Result) :-
    is_integer(Result),
    Product1 is Result*N2,
    Product2 is (Result+1)*N2,
    Product1 =< N1, Product2 > N1,
    !.
```

This rule uses the predicate is_integer (as defined before) to generate the number Result which is the result of "dividing" N1 by N2. For instance, the result of dividing 27 by 6 is 4, because

4 * 6 is less than or equal to 27, and 5 * 6 is greater than 27.

The rule uses is_integer as a "generator", and the rest of the goals provide the appropriate "tester". Now we know in advance that, given specific values of N1 and N2, divide(N1,N2,Result) can only succeed for one possible value for Result. For although is_integer can generate infinitely many candidates, only one will ever get past the tests. We can indicate this knowledge by putting a cut at the end of the rule. This says that if we ever successfully generate a Result that passes the tests for being the result of the division, we need never try any more. In particular, we need never reconsider any of the choices that were involved in looking for rules for divide, is_integer, and so on. We have found the only solution, and there is no point in ever looking for another. If we did not put in the cut here, any backtracking would eventually start finding alternatives for is_integer again. So we would carry on generating possible values for

Result again. None of these other values would be the correct result of the division, and so we would continue generating indefinitely.

4.4 Problems with the Cut

We have already seen that we must sometimes take into account the way Prolog searches the database and what state of instantiation our goals will have in deciding the order in which to write the clauses of a Prolog program. The problem with introducing cuts is that we have to be even more certain of exactly how the rules of the program are to be used. For, whereas a cut when a rule is used one way can be harmless or even beneficial, the very same cut can cause strange behaviour if the rule is suddenly used in another way. Consider the modified append from the last section:

```
append([],X,X) :- !.
append([A|B],C,[A|D]) :- append(B,C,D).
```

When we are considering goals like:

```
append([a,b,c],[d,e],X)
```

and

```
append([a,b,c],X,Y)
```

the cut is quite appropriate. If the first argument of the goal already has a value, then all the cut does is to reaffirm that only the first rule will be relevant if the value is [ ]. However, consider what happens if we have the goal

```
?- append(X,Y,[a,b,c]).
```

This goal will match the head of the first rule, giving:

```
X=[], Y=[a,b,c]
```

but now the cut is encountered. This will freeze all the choices we have made, and so if we ask for another solution, the answer will be **no** even though there actually are other solutions to the question.

Here is another interesting example of what can happen if a rule containing a cut is used in an unexpected way. Let us define a predicate number_of_parents, which can express information about how many parents somebody has. We can define it as follows:

```
number_of_parents(adam,0) :- !.
number_of_parents(eve,0) :- !.
number_of_parents(X,2).
```

That is, the number of parents is 0 for adam and eve, but.2 for everybody else. Now if we are always using our definition of number_of_parents to find the number of parents of given people, this is fine. We will get

```
?- number_of_parents(eve,X).

X=0 ;
no
?- number_of_parents(john,X).

X=2 ;
no
```

and so on, as required. The cut is necessary to prevent backtracking ever reaching the third rule if the person is adam or eve. However, consider what will happen if we use the same rules to verify whether given people have given numbers of parents. All is well, except that we get:

```
?- number_of_parents(eve,2).

yes
```

You should work out for yourself why this happens. It is simply a consequence of the way Prolog searches through the database. Our implementation of "otherwise" with a cut simply does not work properly any more. There are two possible modifications we could make to recover from this:

```
number_of_parents(adam,N) :- !, N = 0.
number_of_parents(eve,N) :- !, N = 0.
number_of_parents(X,2).
```

or

```
number_of_parents(adam,0).
number_of_parents(eve,0).
number_of_parents(X,2) :- X \= adam, X \= eve.
```

Of course, these will still not work properly if we give goals such as

```
?- number_of_parents(X,Y).
```

expecting backtracking to enumerate all the possibilities. So the moral is: *If you introduce cuts to obtain correct behaviour when the goals are of one form, there is no guarantee that anything sensible will happen if goals of another form start appearing.* It follows that it is only possible to use the cut reliably if you have a clear policy about how your rules are going to be used. If you change this policy, all the uses of cut must be reviewed.

Chapter 5
Input and Output

Thus far, the only means we have seen of providing information to a Prolog program has been by asking questions of the Prolog system. Also, the only method of finding out what a variable stands for at some point in the satisfaction of a goal has been by asking a question in such a way that Prolog will print out the answer in the "X = *answer*" form. Much of the time, such direct interaction with questions is all that is required to ensure that a program is working properly. However, for many occasions it is useful to write a Prolog program that initiates a conversation with you by itself.

Suppose you have a database of world events in the 16th Century, arranged as facts containing dates and headlines. To start with, dates can be represented as integers, and headlines can be represented as lists of atoms. We shall have to enclose some of the atoms in single quotes because they begin with an upper-case letter, and we should not want them to be interpreted as variables:

```
event(1505,['Euclid',translated,into,'Latin']).
event(1510,['Reuchlin-Pfefferkorn',controversy]).
event(1523,['Christian','II',flees,from,'Denmark']).
```

Now if we wish to know about a particular date, we could ask a question as follows:

```
?- event(1505,X).
```

and Prolog would print the reply

```
X=[Euclid,translated,into,Latin].
```

Representing the history headlines as lists of atoms confers the advantage that "searches" can be made to find out the date when certain key events happened. For example, consider the predicate we shall define, called when. The goal when(X,Y) succeeds if X is mentioned in year Y according to our history headlines:

```
when(X,Y) :- event(Y,Z), member(X,Z).

?- when('Denmark',D).

D = 1523
```

One disadvantage of using lists of atoms is that they are awkward to type in, especially if atoms begin with an upper-case letter. Another possibility, which has advantages and disadvantages of its own, is to represent history headlines as lists of characters. From a previous chapter we know that lists of characters can be typed by putting them between double quotes:

```
event(1511, "Luther visits Rome").
event(1521, "Henry VIII made Defender of the Faith").
event(1524, "Vasco da Gama dies").
event(1529, "Berquin burnt at Paris").
event(1540, "Reopening of war with Turks").
```

This is easier to type in, but consider asking the question

```
?- event(1524,X).
```

If you try this, Prolog will print out an incomprehensible list of ASCII codes corresponding to the characters in the string to which X is instantiated! Although the list of characters is easy to type in, the question-and-answer sequence is not sufficient to print out a legible answer.

It would be more convenient, instead of asking Prolog questions of this form, to write a program that first asks what date you want to know about, and then prints out the appropriate headline on the computer terminal's display. Headlines could then be represented in any way desired. In order to do these kinds of tasks, Prolog makes available some built-in predicates that print out their arguments on your computer terminal's display. There are also predicates that wait for you to type in text from the computer terminal's keyboard, and instantiate a variable to whatever you typed in. In this way, your program can interact with you, accepting *input* from you, and printing *output* to you. When a program waits for you to type some input from you, we say that it is *reading* the input. Likewise, when a program is printing some output to you, we say it is *writing* the output.

In this chapter we describe various methods for reading and writing. One of our examples will be printing headlines from the history database, and we conclude with a program that accepts normal sentences and converts them into a list of constants that can be processed by other programs. This conversion program, called read_in, can be used as a building block with which to create programs that analyse English language. Such analysis programs are discussed in later chapters, especially Chapter 9.

5.1 Reading and Writing Terms

5.1.1 Writing Terms

Perhaps the most useful way to print some term on the computer terminal's display is to use the built-in predicate write. If X is instantiated to a term, then the goal write(X) will cause the term to be printed out on the display. If X is not instantiated, a uniquely numbered variable (such as '_253') will be printed. However, if two variables are "sharing" within the same argument of write then they will have the same number. The write predicate cannot be re-satisfied. It only succeeds once, and it fails if an attempt is made to re-satisfy it.

Why would it not be a good idea to use write to write out the historical headline in our example above? Remember that a string is actually represented as a list of character codes. If we were to write out such a list, it would be printed as a sequence of integers, separated by commas, and enclosed in square brackets!

There are two more predicates to introduce, and then we will see our first example using write. The built-in predicate nl is used to force all succeeding output to be printed on the next line of the display. The name "nl" means "new line". Like write, nl succeeds only once. Next, the built-in predicate tab is used to print a number of blank spaces across the display screen. The goal tab(X) succeeds only once, and it causes the cursor on the display to move to the right by X space characters. It is assumed that X is instantiated to an integer. The name tab is perhaps poorly chosen, because it does not actually have anything to do with the "tab stops" on a standard typewriter or on the display of a computer terminal.

When printing lists, it is helpful for the items of a list to be printed in a way that is easy to understand. Lists that contain other "nested" lists are especially difficult to read, especially when there are structures inside as well. We shall define a predicate pp such that the goal pp(X,Y) prints out the list (to which X is instantiated) in a helpful way. The name "pp" means "pretty print". The second argument of pp is explained later. Each author of a pretty-print program has his own style of making lists more legible. Just for simplicity, we shall adopt a method where the elements of a list are printed in a vertical column. If the element is itself a list, its elements are printed in a column which is shifted over to the right. This is essentially a "vine diagram" (Chapter 3) on its side. For example, the list [1,2,3] is pretty-printed as

```
1
2
3
```

and the list $[1,2,[3,4],5,6]$ is printed as

```
1
2
    3
    4
5
6
```

Notice that we have decided to remove the separating commas and the square brackets. If the element of a list is a structure, we will treat it as though it is an atom. This way we do not have to "get inside" structures to pretty-print their contents. The following program implements the pretty-print method we have specified:

```
pp([H|T],I) :- !, J is I+3, pp(H,J), ppx(T,J), nl.
pp(X,I) :- tab(I), write(X), nl.

ppx([],_).
ppx([H|T],I) :- pp(H,I), ppx(T,I).
```

Here we see the second argument of pp revealed as a column counter. The "top level" goal for printing a list might look like

```
..., pp(L,0), ...
```

which initialises the column counter to 0. The first clause of pp handles the special case: if the first argument is a list. If so, we have to set up a new column by increasing the column counter by some amount (3 here). Next, we need to "pretty print" the head of the list, because it might be a list itself. Next, we need to print each element of the tail of the list all in the same column. This is what ppx does. And, ppx needs to pp each element in case it is a list. The second clause of pp matches if we wish to pretty-print something that is not a list. We simply indent to the specified column, use write to print the term, and print a new line. The first clause of pp also needs to terminate each list with a new line, hence the nl there.

Let us consider the event facts from the beginning of this chapter. Given one of the history headlines represented as a list of atoms, we can use write to print out each atom, with a space in between each atom. Consider the predicate phh (for "print history headline"):

```
phh([]) :- nl.
phh([H|T]) :- write(H), tab(1), phh(T).
```

So, the following question would print out any history headline that
mentions "England":

```
?- event(_,L), member('England',L), phh(L).
```

Notice the use of backtracking to search the database. Everytime the
member goal fails, an attempt is made to re-satisfy event, which causes the
entire database to be searched top-to-bottom for events that mention the
atom England.

The predicate write is clever about how it prints a term, because it takes
into account what operator declarations have been made. For instance, if we
have declared an atom as an infix operator, then a term with this atom as
functor and two arguments will be printed out with the atom between the
two arguments. There is another predicate that behaves in exactly the same
way as write, except that it ignores any operator declarations that have
been made. This predicate is called display. The difference between
write and display is illustrated by the following:

```
?- write(a+b*c*c), nl, display(a+b*c*c), nl.
a+b*c*c
+(a,*(*(b,c),c))
yes
```

Notice how display has treated the atoms + and * just like any other atoms
for printing out this term. We do not usually want to see our structures
printed out in this way, because having operators usually helps us to read
program output as well as prepare program input. However, using display
can be quite helpful if we are not quite sure about the precedences of our
operators.

5.1.2 Reading Terms

The predicate read will read the next term that you type in from the
computer terminal's keyboard. The term must be followed by a dot "." and a
non-printing character such as a space or a RETURN. If X is uninstantiated,
the goal read(X) will cause the next term to be read, and X to be
instantiated to the term.

As with the other input/output predicates we have encountered thus far,
read only succeeds once. If its argument is instantiated at the time it is used
as a goal, then the next term will be read, and matched with the argument

given to read. The goal will succeed or fail, depending on the success of the match.

Using read and phh as defined above, we can write a Prolog program to print the historical headlines from the event database as follows:

```
hello :-
      phh(['What', date, do, you, 'desire? ']),
      read(D),
      event(D,S),
      phh(S).
```

We have defined a predicate hello, having no arguments. When we ask the question

```
?- hello.
```

Prolog will print:

What date do you desire?

and wait for a response. Suppose we type in:

```
1523.
```

Remember that we need to type in the dot and RETURN after 1523. Prolog will respond:

Christian II flees from Denmark

Notice also that the first clause of the body of hello uses phh, even though it is not intended to print a history headline. This simply shows that phh suffices also to print any list of atoms, no matter where that list came from.

5.2 Reading and Writing Characters

The smallest entity that can be written and read is the character. As we have seen thus far, characters are treated as small integers corresponding to the ASCII code for the character. Prolog has several built-in predicates for reading and writing characters.

5.2.1 Writing Characters

If X is instantiated to a character (an ASCII code represented as an integer), it will be printed when Prolog encounters the goal put(X). The predicate put always succeeds, and it cannot be re-satisfied (it fails when an attempt is made to re-satisfy it). As a "side effect", put prints its argument as a character on your terminal's display. For example, we can print the word hello in a rather awkward way by:

```
?- put(104), put(101), put(108), put(108), put(111).
```
hello

The result of this conjunction of goals is that Prolog prints the characters h, e, l, l, o, printing them out after the question as shown above.

We have already seen that it is possible to start printing at the beginning of the next line by using the n l predicate, which has no arguments. What n l actually does is to print some control characters that cause the cursor on your computer terminal's display to move to the beginning of the next line. The question

```
?- put(104), put(105), nl, put(116), put(104),
   put(101), put(114), put(101).
```

causes the following to be printed:

hi
there

Another goal we have seen is tab(X), which prints X spaces (ASCII code 32). Of course, X must be instantiated to an integer. Notice that tab(X) could have been defined as:

```
tab(0) :- !.
tab(N) :- put(32), M is N-1, tab(M).
```

We are now able to define a predicate that we shall call printstring. If we instantiate X to a list of character codes (a string), the goal printstring(X) will print it out using put for each element of the list. As in all such programs, the boundary condition is the empty list. This is what we will use to terminate the recursion. Otherwise, we simply use put to print the head of the list, and use printstring to print the tail of the list:

```
printstring([]).
printstring([H|T]) :- put(H), printstring(T).

?- printstring("Charles V abdicates at Brussels").
```

Charles V abdicates at Brussels

If we choose to represent a history headline as a string, rather than a list of atoms, such a definition will suffice to print the strings in the event database above.

5.2.2 Reading Characters

Characters may be read from the keyboard by using the goals get0(X) and get(X). These goals always succeed if their argument is uninstantiated, and they also cannot be re-satisfied. When they are used, they make the computer wait until some characters have been typed by you. They are slightly different because get0(X) will instantiate X to the very next character that is typed, no matter what it is. On the other hand, get(X) will skip all *non-printing* characters, and instantiate X to the first *printing* character. As we said in Chapter 2, a printing character is one that makes a mark on the computer terminal's display.

If X is already instantiated, then the goal get(X) will skip all non-printing characters and compare the next printing character with whatever X is instantiated to. The goal succeeds or fails depending on the outcome of the test. The goal get0(X) compares the next character for equality, and succeeds or fails depending on the outcome of the equality test.

The next section shows some examples of reading characters. An important consideration is what happens when we need to backtrack over a get goal.

5.3 Reading English Sentences

We shall now present the program that reads in a sentence typed at the terminal and converts it to a list of Prolog atoms. The program defines the predicate read_in with one argument. The program must know when one word of the input ends and the next begins. In order to know this, it assumes that a word consists of any number of letters, digits, and special characters. Letters and digits are the same as those discussed in Section 2.1, and we will consider the single quote "'" and the hyphen "-" to be special characters. Also, the characters ",", ";", ":", "?", and "!" are taken to form words on their own. Any other characters just mark space between words. The sentence is deemed to have finished when one of the words ".", "?", or "!" appears. Upper-case letters are automatically converted to lower-case, so that the same word always gives rise to the same atom. As a result of this definition, the program will produce question and answer sequences like:

```
?- read_in(S).
The man, who is old, saw Joe's hat.
S = [the,man,',',who,is,old,',',saw,'joe''s',hat,'.']
```

We have actually inserted extra single-quote characters in this to make it clear that the punctuation marks are atoms.

The program uses the predicate get0 to read in characters from the terminal. The trouble with get0 is that, once a character has been read from the terminal by it, that character has "gone for ever", and no other get0 goal or attempt to re-satisfy a get0 goal will ever get hold of that character again. So we must avoid ever backtracking over a use of get0 if we want to avoid "losing" the character it reads in. For instance, the following program to read in characters and print them out again, converting a's to b's (character codes 97 to code 98) <u>will not work</u>:

```
go :- do_a_character, go.

do_a_character :- get0(X), X=97, !, put(98).
do_a_character :- get0(X), put(X).
```

This is not a particularly good program anyway, because it will run for ever. However, consider the effect of attempting to satisfy the do_a_character goal. If the first do_a_character rule reads in an X which is not 97, backtracking then causes the second rule to be tried instead. However, the get0(X) goal in the second rule will cause X to be instantiated to the *next* character after the one already found. This is because the satisfaction of the original get0 goal was an irreversible process. So this program would actually fail to print out all the characters. It would even sometimes print out a's.

How does our read_in program cope with the problem of backtracking over input? The answer is that we must design it in such a way that it always reads one character ahead, and makes tests on a character inside a different rule to the one where it was read. When a character is found somewhere and cannot be used at that point, it is passed back to the rules that will be able to use it. Hence, our predicate to do with reading a single word, readword, actually has three arguments. The first is for the character that was found by whichever rule last satisfied a get0 goal but could not find a use for the character. The second is for the Prolog atom that will be constructed for the word. The last argument is for the first character that is read after the word. In order to see where a word ends, it is necessary to read up to the next character after it. This character must be passed back, because it might provide the valuable first character of another word.

Here then is the program:

```
/* Read in a sentence */

read_in([W|Ws]) :-
        get0(C), readword(C,W,C1), restsent(W,C1,Ws).
/*
   Given a word and the character after it, read in
   the rest of the sentence.
*/
```

```
restsent(W,_,[]) :- lastword(W), !.
restsent(W,C,[W1|Ws]) :-
        readword(C,W1,C1), restsent(W1,C1,Ws).

/*
   Read in a single word, given an initial character,
   and remembering what character came after the word.
*/

readword(C,W,C1) :-
        single_character(C), !, name(W,[C]), get0(C1).
readword(C,W,C2) :-
        in_word(C,NewC),
        !,
        get0(C1),
        restword(C1,Cs,C2),
        name(W,[NewC|Cs]).
readword(C,W,C2) :- get0(C1), readword(C1,W,C2).

restword(C,[NewC|Cs],C2) :-
        in_word(C,NewC),
        !,
        get0(C1), restword(C1,Cs,C2).
restword(C,[],C).

/* These characters form words on their own */

single_character(44).    /* , */
single_character(59).    /* ; */
single_character(58).    /* : */
single_character(63).    /* ? */
single_character(33).    /* ! */
single_character(46).    /* . */

/*
   These characters can appear within a word.    The
   second in_word clause converts characters to lower-
   case
*/

in_word(C,C) :- C>96, C<123.               /* a b...z */
in_word(C,L) :- C>64, C<91, L is C+32.     /* A B...Z */
in_word(C,C) :- C>47, C<58.                /* 1 2...9 */
in_word(39,39).                            /* ' */
in_word(45,45).                            /* - */
```

```
/* These words terminate a sentence */
lastword('.').
lastword('!').
lastword('?').
```

Exercise 5.1: Explain what each variable in the above program is used for.

Exercise 5.2: Write a program to read in characters indefinitely, printing them out again with a's changed to b's.

5.4 Reading and Writing Files

The predicates previously discussed in this chapter were used only for reading from or writing to your computer terminal, but they are actually more general than that. The Prolog system recognises a *current input stream*, from which all input is read. All output is written to the *current output stream*. The computer terminal's keyboard is normally the current input stream, and the terminal's display is normally the current output stream. Often it is useful to read or write *files*, which are sequences of characters on a secondary storage medium. The particular medium depends on your particular computer installation, but nowadays we usually read and write files that are stored on magnetic discs. It is assumed that each file has a *filename* that we use to identify it. In order for this section to be understandable, you should be familiar with the conventions for organising and naming files at your computer installation. In Prolog, filenames are represented as atoms, but we cannot rule out the possibility of further installation-dependent restrictions on the syntax of filenames.

Files have a certain length. That is, they contain a certain number of characters. At the end of a file, there is a special marker, called the *end of file marker*. We did not discuss the end of file marker previously, because it is more usual to encounter the end of file marker on a file than on a computer terminal. If a program is reading from a file, the end of file marker can be detected whether the program is reading terms or characters. If a get0(X) encounters the end of a file, X will be instantiated to a control character, normally the one with ASCII code 26. If read(X) encounters the end of a file, X will be instantiated to some special term that depends on your particular Prolog system. The special term is usually the atom end_of_file. If an attempt is made to read beyond the end of a file, an error is generated.

There is a built-in file called user. Reading this file causes input to come from your computer terminal's keyboard, and writing to this file will cause characters to be written on the display. This is the normal mode of operation. When input is from the computer terminal's keyboard, an end of file can be generated by typing the end-of-file control character (ASCII code 26, or control-Z). This will make get0 and read behave as though the end of a file has been encountered.

5.4.1 Writing Files

Terms and characters can be written to files by using exactly the same predicates as discussed earlier. The only difference is that when we wish to write to a file, we must change the *current output stream* to be the file instead of the computer terminal's display. The current output stream is changed by using the tell predicate. If X is instantiated to a filename, which must be an atom, the goal tell(X) switches the current output stream so that any writing (done by write, put, and so forth) will be done to the file, instead of to the computer terminal's display. The tell(X) goal succeeds only once (it cannot be re-satisfied). Also, when Prolog backtracks over a tell goal, it does not reset the current output to what it was previously. As well as changing what Prolog considers to be the current output stream, tell also performs other operations in certain situations. The first time that we satisfy tell(X) for a particular X, Prolog assumes that we want to start a new file with that name. Therefore if X is instantiated to an atom that names a file that already exists, then any characters already in the file will be removed. On the other hand, if X is instantiated to an atom that does not name any existing file, then a file with that name will be created. In either case, the file is now considered open (for output). This means that subsequent writing to the file will add characters at the end of the file until we say explicitly that the file is complete (until we close the file). At that point, if we try to write to it again, Prolog will assume that we want to write a new version as before. If we try to satisfy tell(X) when X is not instantiated, or is instantiated to an object other than a filename, then an error occurs. The specific behaviour taken by the Prolog system when an error occurs depends on the particular implementation of Prolog you are using.

The predicate telling is used to find out the name of the file that is the current output stream. The goal telling(X) succeeds when X is instantiated to the name of the current output file. As you might expect, if X is uninstantiated, then telling will instantiate it to the atom that makes the goal succeed.

When all writing to a file has been completed, the predicate told will end the file and close it (for output). Also, it will cause the current output to revert to the computer terminal's display. So, a typical sequence of goals to write some characters on a file would be:

```
...tell(fred), write(X), told, ...
```

If the current output stream is switched without using told on the previous file, the previous file will not be closed, but it is still available for writing. This allows you to write to a file at several different times, as in this example:

```
...tell(X), write(A), tell(user),
       write(B), tell(X), write(C), told.
```

5.4.2 Reading Files

The predicates that Prolog makes available for switching the current input stream are analogues of those discussed above. The goal see(X) switches the current input stream to the filename specified. As with tell, the goal cannot be re-satisfied, and the operation is not undone on backtracking. The first time we satisfy see(X) for some file X, that file becomes open (for input), and we start at the beginning of the file. Subsequent input continues from where it last left off, until we explicitly close the file. After that point, a new attempt to read from the file will open it and start from the beginning as before. The current input stream can be discovered by satisfying seeing(X), and the current input stream may be switched back to the computer terminal's keyboard by seen, which also closes the file.

5.4.3 Consulting

Reading and writing files is most helpful when our programs deal with more terms than we care to type in by hand each time we want to put them in the database. In Prolog, files are used mainly to store programs. If we have the text of a Prolog program in a file, we can read all of the clauses in the file, and put them into the database by using the predicate consult. When X is instantiated to the name of a file, the goal consult(X) will read Prolog clauses and goals from the file. Most implementations of Prolog have a special notation for consult, which allows a list of files to be consulted, one after another. If a list of atoms is given as a Prolog question, then Prolog will consult each file in the list. An example of this notation is:

```
?- [file1, mapper, expert].
```

This behaves as though Prolog were executing a goal consultall(X), where X is the list that we give the question, and where consultall might be defined as follows:

```
consultall([]).
consultall([H|T]) :- consult(H), consultall(T).
```

However, the shorthand list notation reduces effort, and this is especially
important when one considers that the very first act that the practising
Prolog programmer does is to `consult` a list of files to make available his
favourite predicates. The `consult` predicate automatically stops reading
clauses when the end of the file is encountered. Section 6.1 describes
`consult` in more detail.

5.5 Declaring Operators

Operators are considered in this "input and output" chapter because
operators provide syntactic convenience when reading or writing terms.
There is no other reason for having operators. Let us first briefly review
Section 2.3, and then tell how operators are declared.

The Prolog syntax provides for operators, each having three properties: a
position, precedence class, and associativity. The position can be infix,
postfix, or prefix (an operator with two arguments can go between them; an
operator with one argument can go after or before it). The precedence class is
an integer whose range depends on the actual Prolog implementation, but we
shall assume the range used by most Prolog systems: from 1 to 1200. The
precedence class is used to disambiguate expressions where the syntax of the
terms is not made explicit through the use of brackets. The associativity is to
disambiguate expressions in which there are two operators in the expression
that have the same precedence. In Prolog, we associate a special atom with
an operator, which specifies its position and associativity. The possible
specifiers for infix operators are:

   xfx   xfy   yfx   yfy.

To understand these specifiers, it helps to see them as "pictures" of possible
uses of the operators. In the pictures, the letter f represents the operator,
and x and y represent arguments. So in all of the above, the operator must
appear *between* two arguments — that is, it is an infix operator.   In
accordance with this convention,

   fx   fy

are two specifiers for prefix operators (the operator comes *before* its one
argument). Also,

   xf   yf

are possible specifiers for postfix operators. You may be wondering why
there are two letters available for indicating arguments. The choice of x's
and y's in these positions enables associativity information to be conveyed.
Assuming that there are no brackets, a y means that the argument can

contain operators of the same or lower precedence class than this operator. On the other hand, an x means that any operators in the argument must have a strictly lower precedence class than this operator. Consider what this means for the operator +, declared as y f x. If we look at

```
a + b + c
```

there are two possible interpretations:

```
(a + b) + c   or   a + (b + c)
```

the second of these is ruled out, because it requires the argument after the first + to contain an operator of the same precedence (another +, for example). This contradicts the presence of an x after the f of the specifier.

Thus, in particular, an operator declared y f x is left associative. Similarly, an operator declared x f y is right associative. If we know the desired associativity of an infix operator we are declaring, this means that the specifier is uniquely determined.

Note that the meanings of x and y (in terms of what other operators can appear unbracketed in the relevant position) are the same in all the other cases as well. This means that, for instance, the sequence

```
not not a
```

is legal syntactically if not is declared as f y, but is illegal if it is declared f x.

In Prolog, if we wish to declare that an operator with a given position, precedence class, and associativity is to be recognised when terms are read and written, we use the built-in predicate op. If Name is the desired operator (the atom that we want to be an operator), Prec the precedence class (an integer within the appropriate range), and Spec the position/associativity specifier (one of the above atoms), then the operator is declared by providing the following goal:

```
?- op(Prec,Spec,Name).
```

If the operator declaration is legal, then the goal will succeed.

As an example of declaring operators, the following is a complete list of declarations for the "core" operators discussed in this book. Particular implementations of Prolog may have slightly different operators as "standard" ones, and the precedence classes may be scaled to fit within another range. However, the order of operators within the precedence hierarchy is normally conventional.

```
?- op(  1200,   xfx,    :-   ).
?- op(  1200,   fx,     ?-   ).
?- op(  1100,   xfy,    ;    ).
```

```
?- op(   1000,    xfy,    ',' ).
?- op(   900,     fy,     not ).
?- op(   700,     xfx,    =   ).
?- op(   700,     xfx,    is  ).
?- op(   700,     xfx,    =.. ).
?- op(   700,     xfx,    \=  ).
?- op(   700,     xfx,    ==  ).
?- op(   700,     xfx,    \== ).
?- op(   700,     xfx,    <   ).
?- op(   700,     xfx,    >   ).
?- op(   700,     xfx,    =<  ).
?- op(   700,     xfx,    >=  ).
?- op(   500,     fx,     +   ).
?- op(   500,     fx,     -   ).
?- op(   400,     yfx,    *   ).
?- op(   400,     yfx,    /   ).
?- op(   300,     xfx,    mod ).
```

Chapter 6
Built-in Predicates

In this chapter we introduce some of the *built-in* predicates that a Prolog system might provide. What do we mean when we say that a predicate is built-in? We mean that the predicate's definition is provided in advance by the Prolog system, instead of by your own clauses. Built-in predicates may provide facilities that cannot be obtained by definitions in pure Prolog. Or they may provide convenient facilities just to save each programmer from having to define them himself. We have already encountered some built-in predicates: the predicates for reading and writing discussed in Chapter 5. Also, the "cut" could be regarded as a built-in predicate.

The input/output predicates illustrate the fact that a built-in predicate may have "side effects". That is, satisfying a goal involving the predicate may cause changes apart from the instantiation of the arguments. Another important fact about built-in predicates is that they may expect particular sorts of arguments. For instance, consider the predicate "<", defined so that X < Y succeeds if the number X is less than the number Y. Such a relation cannot be defined in Prolog without some outside help that knows something about numbers. So "<" is provided as a built-in predicate, and its definition involves the use of some underlying machine operation for testing the comparative size of numbers (represented as binary patterns, or whatever).

What should happen if we introduce a X < Y goal where X is an atom, or even if both X and Y are uninstantiated? The definition in terms of the machine will simply not apply. So we must stipulate that X < Y is only a sensible goal if both X and Y are instantiated to numbers when an attempt is made to satisfy it. What happens if this condition is not met will depend on the individual Prolog implementation. One possibility is that the goal will simply fail. The other possibility is that an error message will be printed out, and the system will take some appropriate action (like abandoning trying to answer the current question).

6.1 Entering New Clauses

When you write a Prolog program, you will want to tell the system what clauses to use, as well as ask questions about them. You may want to type in new clauses at the terminal, or to tell Prolog to take clauses from a file that you have prepared in advance. In fact, these two operations look the same from Prolog's point of view, because the terminal is seen as just another file, having the name user. There are two basic built-in predicates for reading in new clauses: consult and reconsult. In addition, there is a convenient notation for when you want to read in clauses from more then one file: the list notation. If you are interested, simple definitions in Prolog of consult and reconsult are given in Section 7.13.

consult(X)

The built-in predicate consult is meant for those situations when you want the clauses in some file (or to be typed at the terminal) to *augment* those already in the database. The argument must be an atom giving the name of the file the clauses are to be taken from. Which atoms constitute a legal file name will, of course, depend on your particular computer. Examples of possible consult goals for various computers are:

```
?- consult(myfile).
?- consult('/usr/john/pl/chat').
?- consult('lib:iorout.pl').
```

When it has to satisfy a consult goal, Prolog reads through the file, adding the clauses it finds at the end of the database. As a result, the new clauses will appear after any already existing clauses for the same predicates. If a question is found in the file, this will be treated just like an ordinary question, except that the answer will not be printed out. It does not usually make sense to interleave questions with new clauses in a file, except to do things like declare new operators and print out helpful messages.

reconsult(X)

The predicate reconsult is just like consult, except that the clauses read in are taken to *supersede* all existing clauses for the same predicate. Because of this, reconsult is appropriate for correcting programming mistakes. If you read in several files of clauses and then discover that there is a mistake in one clause, you may be able to correct it without having to read in all the files again. To do this, you just have to reconsult a file containing a correct set of clauses for the predicate in question. You can give the corrected clauses by either typing them at the terminal (reconsult(user)) or by editing a file without exiting from Prolog (only possible in some implementations) and then reconsult-ing that file. Of course, typing in revised clauses at the terminal will alter what Prolog sees in the *database* but it will not change the *file* that the original, faulty, clauses came from! Section 8.5 shows consult and reconsult being used in the development of a program.

The List Notation

Prolog provides a special notation that makes it more convenient to specify `consult` and `reconsult` goals, especially when you want Prolog to look at more than one file. The notation involves simply putting the file names (as Prolog atoms) into a list, and giving that list as a goal to be satisfied. If you want a file to be `consulted`, you put the name into the list as it is, and if you want a file to be `reconsulted`, you precede the name with a "-" sign. Thus the question:

```
?- [file1,-file2,'fred.1',-'bill.2'].
```

is exactly equivalent to the longer version:

```
?- consult(file1), reconsult(file2),
   consult('fred.1'), reconsult('bill.2').
```

The list notation is purely a notational convenience, and does not offer any extra facilities over and above those provided by `consult` and `reconsult`. Some Prolog implementations may use a different sign than "-" in the list notation, but the effect is the same.

6.2 Success and Failure

In the normal course of executing a Prolog program, a goal succeeds when it can be satisfied, and it fails when there is no way to satisfy it. There are two predicates that make it more convenient to specify when a goal succeeds or fails. These are the `true` and the `fail` predicates.

true

This goal always succeeds. It is not actually necessary, as clauses and goals can be reordered or recombined to obviate any use of `true`. However, it exists for convenience.

fail

This goal always fails. There are two places where it is helpful. One place is the "cut fail" combination, which was described in Section 4.3. A conjunction of goals of the form

```
..., !, fail.
```

is used to say, "if execution proceeds to this point, then one can abandon attempting to satisfy this goal". The conjunction fails due to the `fail`, and the parent goal fails because of the cut.

Another place to use fail is where you explicitly want another goal to backtrack through all solutions. You may want to print out all the solutions. For instance,

```
?- event(X,Y), phh(Y), fail.
```

would print out all the events in the database of Section 5.1, using event and phh (and would then fail). See the definition of retractall in Section 7.13 for another use of fail.

6.3 Classifying Terms

If we wish to define predicates which will be used with a wide variety of argument types, it is useful to be able to distinguish in the definition what should be done for each possible type. At the crudest level, we might wish a different clause to apply if an argument is an integer than if the argument is an atom. Or we might want one clause to apply if the argument is instantiated and another if it is not. The following predicates allow the programmer to put these extra conditions in his clauses.

var(X)

The goal var(X) succeeds if X is currently an *uninstantiated* variable. Thus we would expect the following behaviour:

```
?- var(X).
yes
?- var(23).
no
?- X = Y, Y = 23, var(X).
no
```

An uninstantiated variable can represent part of a structure that has not yet been filled in. Examples are the unmarked squares in the noughts-and-crosses board of Section 4.3.3, and the unfilled parts of the sorted tree dictionary in Section 7.1. When such structures are being examined, the predicate var can be essential to determine whether some part has already been filled in. This can prevent the variable from being "accidentally" instantiated to something when the intent was to examine it. For example, in the sorted tree dictionary, one might wish to know whether there is already an entry for some key without creating one. In the noughts-and-crosses game, one might want to know whether a square is occupied or not. Attempting to match the variable with an o or an x would simply put the value into the square if the variable was uninstantiated at the time.

nonvar(X)

The goal nonvar(X) succeeds if X is *not* currently an uninstantiated variable. The predicate nonvar is therefore the opposite of var. Indeed, it could be defined in Prolog by:

```
nonvar(X) :- var(X), !, fail.
nonvar(_).
```

atom(X)

The goal atom(X) succeeds if X currently stands for a Prolog atom. As a result, the following behaviour takes place:

```
?- atom(23).
no
?- atom(apples).
yes
?- atom('/us/chris/pl.123').
yes
?- atom("this is a string").
no
?- atom(X).
no
?- atom(book(bronte,w_h,X)).
no
```

integer(X)

The goal integer(X) succeeds if X currently stands for an integer (a whole number). For example, Section 7.12 shows how we can use this predicate in the definition of a simplifier for arithmetic expressions, where we need to know whether the expression is just an integer .

atomic(X)

The goal atomic(X) succeeds if X currently stands for either an integer or an atom. Predicate atomic can be defined in terms of atom and integer by

```
atomic(X) :- atom(X).
atomic(X) :- integer(X).
```

6.4 Treating Clauses as Terms

Prolog allows the programmer to examine and alter the program (the clauses that are used to satisfy his goals). This is particularly straightforward, because a clause can be seen as just an ordinary Prolog structure. Therefore Prolog provides built-in predicates to allow the programmer to:

- Construct a structure representing a clause in the database,

- Add a clause, represented by a given structure, to the database,

- Remove a clause, represented by a given structure, from the database.

Most operations on the database can be performed by the use of these predicates, together with the normal Prolog operations of constructing and decomposing structures. In addition to the examples given here, Section 7.8 shows some of the uses one can make of predicates to add and remove clauses.

Before we look at the relevant built-in predicates, it is important to see just how a Prolog clause can be seen as a structure. For a simple fact, the structure is just the predicate with the arguments. That is, something like

```
likes(john,X)
```

can be seen as an ordinary structure, with functor likes, and two arguments john and X. A rule, on the other hand, can be seen as a structure whose main functor is ":-", with two arguments. This functor is declared as an infix operator. The first argument is the head of the clause, and the second is the body. Thus

```
likes(john,X) :- likes(X,wine)
```

is really just

```
':-'(likes(john,X),likes(X,wine))
```

which is a perfectly normal structure. Finally, when there is more than one goal in a rule, the goals are considered bound together by the functor "," (with two arguments). This is also declared as an infix operator. Thus

```
grandparent(X,Z) :- parent(X,Y), parent(Y,Z)
```

is really just

```
':-'(grandparent(X,Z), ','(parent(X,Y),parent(Y,Z))
```

Here now are the predicates that enable the programmer to examine and alter clauses.

<u>listing(A)</u>

Satisfying a goal of the form listing(A), where A is instantiated to an atom, causes all the clauses with the atom as predicate to be written out, as Prolog terms, on the current output file. This is how you check up on what clauses you currently have for some predicate. The exact format of the output will depend on your Prolog implementation. Notice that you will see all the clauses with that atom as predicate, regardless of how many arguments it has. Using listing can help you discover a mistake in your

program. For instance, in the following example session, the programmer
discovers that he has not defined reverse properly.

```
?- [test].
test consulted
yes

?- reverse([a,b,c,d],X).
no
```

```
?- listing(reverse).

reverse([],[]).
reverse([_44|_45],_38) :-
        reverse(_45,_47),
        appenD(_47,[_44],_38).

yes
```

The listing of the reverse clauses reveals that the atom append was mis-
spelled in the program (as appenD).

clause(X,Y)

Satisfying a goal of the form clause(X,Y) causes X and Y to be matched
with the head and body of an existing clause in the database. When an
attempt is made to satisfy the goal, X must be instantiated enough so that
the main predicate of the clause is known. If there are no clauses for the
predicate, the goal just fails. If there is more than one clause that matches,
Prolog will choose the first one. In this case, if an attempt is made to re-
satisfy the goal, the other matching clauses will be chosen, one at a time.

Notice that, although clause always has an argument for the body of a
clause, not every clause actually has a body. If a clause does not have a body,
it is considered to have the dummy body true. We have been calling such
clauses "facts". By providing X's and Y's that are more or less instantiated,
you can look for either all the clauses for a given predicate and number of
arguments, or all the ones that match some pattern. Thus, for instance:

```
append([],X,X).
append([A|B],C,[A|D]) :- append(B,C,D).

?- clause(append(A,B,C),Y).
A = [], B = _3, C = _3, Y = true ;
A = [_3|_4], B = _5, C = [_3|_6], Y = append(_4,_5,_6) ;

no
```

The predicate clause is very important if we wish to construct programs that examine or execute other programs (see Section 7.13).

asserta(X), assertz(X)

The two built-in predicates asserta and assertz allow one to add new clauses to the database. The two predicates act in exactly the same way, except that asserta adds a clause at the *beginning* of the database, whereas assertz adds a clause at the *end*. This convention can be remembered because a is the first letter of the alphabet, and z is the last. In a goal asserta(X), X must be already instantiated to something representing a clause; indeed, as for clause, it must be sufficiently instantiated that the main predicate is known.

It is important to stress that the action of adding a clause to the database is *not* undone when backtracking takes place. Therefore, once we have used asserta or assertz to add a new clause, that clause will only be removed if we explicitly say so (using retract). See Section 7.8 for examples of asserta in use.

retract(X)

The built-in predicate retract enables a program to remove clauses from the database. The predicate takes a single argument, representing a term that the clause is to match. The term must be sufficiently instantiated that the predicate of the clause can be determined (as for asserta, clause, *etc.*). When an attempt is made to satisfy a goal retract(X), X is matched with the first clause in the database that it can be matched with, and that clause is removed. When an attempt is made to re-satisfy the goal, Prolog searches on from that clause, looking for another one that will match. If it finds one, the same thing happens as before. If an attempt is made to re-satisfy it again, the search continues for another appropriate clause. And so on. Note that, once a clause has been removed it is never reinstated, even when backtracking tries to re-satisfy the retract goal. If at any time the search cannot find any more matching clauses, the goal fails.

Because the argument X is matched with a clause as it is removed, it is possible to see exactly which clause has been removed, even if X originally stood for something with lots of uninstantiated variables in it. So one can use retract to duplicate the function of clause, in the case that one wants to remove the clause after finding it. This is how it is used in the definition of gensym (Section 7.8).

6.5 Constructing and Accessing Components of Structures

Normally when we want to access a structure of a certain kind in a Prolog program, we do so by just "mentioning" such a structure. That is, if a predicate needs to handle a variety of different kinds of structures appearing in an argument position, we normally just provide a separate clause for each kind of structure. A good example of this is the definition of symbolic differentiation in Section 7.11. There are separate clauses for the functors +, -, *, and so on. We have anticipated all the structures that might appear, and have provided clauses for each one.

In some programs we cannot anticipate all the structures that may appear. For instance, we might want to write a "pretty print" program that can print out any Prolog structure, using multiple lines and indentation (see Section 5.1 for a version of such a program that only handles lists). So, for instance, we might want the term

```
book(b29,author(bronte,emily),wh)
```

to "pretty print" as

```
book
    b29
    author
        bronte
        emily
    wh
```

The important point is that we want this program to work *whatever* kind of structure we give it. One possibility, of course, is to provide a clause for every functor we can possibly think of. But this is a task that we will never finish, because in some programs there might be infinitely many of them! The way to write this kind of program is to use built-in predicates that perform operations on arbitrary structures. We will now describe some of these — the predicates functor, arg, and "=..". We will also describe a predicate that works on atoms, the predicate name.

functor(T,F,N)

The predicate functor is defined in such a way that functor(T,F,N) means, "T is a structure with functor F and arity (number of arguments) N". It can be used in basically two ways. In the first way, T is already instantiated. The goal fails if T is not an atom or a structure. If T is an atom or structure, F is matched with the functor and N is matched with the integer giving the arity (number of arguments) of the functor. Note that in this context, an atom is considered to be like a structure with arity 0. Here are some examples of goals involving `functor`:

```
?- functor(f(a,b,g(Z)),F,N).
Z = _23, F = f, N = 3
?- functor(a+b,F,N).
F = +, N = 2
?- functor([a,b,c],F,N).
F = ., N = 2
?- functor(apple,F,N).
F = apple, N = 0
?- functor([a,b,c],'.',3).
no
?- functor([a,b,c],a,Z).
no
```

Before we go on to look at `arg`, we should consider the second possible use for `functor`. This occurs when the first argument of the goal (T) is uninstantiated. In this case, both of the others must be instantiated — specifying a functor and a number of arguments respectively. A goal of this form will always succeed, and as a result T will become instantiated to a structure with the functor and number of arguments provided. So this is a way of *constructing* arbitrary structures, given a specification in terms of a functor and its number of arguments. The arguments of such a structure constructed by `functor` are uninstantiated variables. Hence the structure will match any other structure with the same functor and number of arguments.

A common use of `functor` to create a structure is when we wish to make a "copy" of an existing structure with new variables as the arguments of the principal functor. We can encapsulate this use in the definition of a predicate `copy`, as follows:

```
copy(Old,New) :- functor(Old,F,N), functor(New,F,N).
```

Here, two `functor` goals occur adjacently. If the `copy` goal has the first argument instantiated and the second uninstantiated, then the following will happen. The first `functor` goal will involve the first possible use of the predicate (because the first argument will be instantiated). Hence F and N will become instantiated to the functor and number of arguments of this existing structure. The second `functor` goal uses the predicate in the second way. This time the first argument is uninstantiated, and the information in F and N is used to *construct* the structure New. This is a structure involving the same functor and number of arguments as `Old`, but with variables as its components. Thus we would get interactions like:

```
?- copy(sentence(np(n(john)),v(eats)),X).
X = sentence(_23,_24)
```

We shall use a combination of `functor` goals in this way in the definition of `reconsult` in Section 7.13.

arg(N,T,A)

The predicate `arg` must always be used with its first two arguments instantiated. It is used to access a particular argument of a structure. The first argument of `arg` specifies which argument is required. The second specifies the structure that the argument is to be found inside. Prolog finds the appropriate argument and then tries to match it with the third argument. Thus `arg(N,T,A)` succeeds if the Nth argument of T is A. Let us look at some goals involving `arg`.

```
?- arg(2,related(john,mother(jane)),X).
X = mother(jane)

?- arg(1,a+(b+c),X).
X = a

?- arg(2,[a,b,c],X).
X = [b,c]

?- arg(1,a+(b+c),b).
no
```

We use `arg` in our definition of substitution in Section 7.12.

Sometimes we will want to use `functor` and `arg` when the possible structures *are* known. This is because there may be so many arguments that it is inconvenient to specify them every time. Consider an example where we use structures to represent books. We might have a component for the title, the author, the publisher, the date of publication, and so on. Let us say that the resulting structures have fourteen components. We might write the following useful definitions:

```
is_a_book(book(_,_,_,_,_,_,_,_,_,_,_,_,_,_)).
title(book(T,_,_,_,_,_,_,_,_,_,_,_,_,_),T).
author(book(_,A,_,_,_,_,_,_,_,_,_,_,_,_),A).
```

In fact, we can write these much more compactly as:

```
is_a_book(X) :- functor(X,book,14).
title(X,T) :- is_a_book(X), arg(1,X,T).
```

```
author(X,A) :- is_a_book(X), arg(2,X,T).
```

X =.. L

The predicates functor and arg provide one way of creating and accessing arguments of arbitrary structures. The predicate "=.." (pronounced "univ" for historical reasons) provides an alternative way, which is useful if you want to obtain the arguments of a structure all together, or if you want to construct a structure, given a list of arguments. The goal X =.. L means, "L is the list consisting of the functor of X followed by the arguments of X." Such a goal can be used in two ways, in the same way that a functor goal can. If X is instantiated, Prolog constructs the appropriate list and tries to match it with L. Alternatively, if X is uninstantiated, the list will be used to construct an appropriate structure for X to stand for. In this case, the head of L must be an atom (it will become the functor of X). Here are some examples of =.. goals:

```
?- foo(a,b,c) =.. X.
X = [foo,a,b,c]

?- append([A|B],C,[A|D]) =.. L.
A = _2, B = _3, C = _4, D = _5, L = [append,[_2|_3],_4,[_2|_5]]

?- [a,b,c,d] =.. L.
L = ['.',a,[b,c,d]].

?- (a+b) =.. L.
L = [+,a,b].

?- (a+b) =.. [+,X,Y].
X = a, Y = b.

?- [a,b,c,d] =.. [X|Y].
X = '.', Y = [a,[b,c,d]]

?- X =.. [a,b,c,d].
X = a(b,c,d).

?- X =.. [append,[a,b],[c],[a,b,c]].
X = append([a,b],[c],[a,b,c])
```

Examples of the use of =.. are given in Section 7.12.

name(A,L)

Whereas functor, arg, and =.. are used for constructing and accessing arbitrary structures, the predicate name is for dealing with arbitrary atoms. Predicate name relates an atom to the list of characters (ASCII codes) that make it up. This can be used either to find the characters for a given atom, or to find the atom that has some given characters. The goal name(A,L) means that "the characters for the atom A are the members of the list L". If the argument A is instantiated, Prolog creates the list of characters and tries to match them with L. Otherwise Prolog uses the list L to make an atom for A to stand for. Example uses of name are as follows:

```
?- name(apple,X).
X = [97,112,112,108,101]
?- name(X,[97,112,112,108,101]).
X = apple
?- name(apple,"apple").
yes
?- name(apple,"pear").
no
```

In Section 9.5, we use name to access the internal structure of English words represented as Prolog atoms.

6.6 Affecting Backtracking

There are two built-in predicates that affect the normal sequence of events that happens during backtracking. Basically, "!" removes possibilities for the re-satisfaction of goals, and repeat makes new alternatives where there were none before.

!

The "cut" symbol can be viewed as a built-in predicate that commits the Prolog system to certain choices it has made. For more details about the "cut" see Chapter 4.

repeat

The built-in predicate repeat is provided as an extra way to generate multiple solutions through backtracking. Although it is built-in, it can be thought of as behaving as though defined as follows:

```
repeat.
repeat :- repeat.
```

What is the effect of this if we put repeat as a goal in one of our rules? First of all, the goal will succeed, because of the fact which is the first clause of repeat. Secondly, if backtracking reaches this point again, Prolog will be able to try an alternative — the rule that is provided as the second clause of repeat. When it uses this rule, another goal repeat is generated. Since this matches the first fact, we have succeeded again. If backtracking reaches here again, Prolog will again use the rule where it used the fact before. To satisfy the extra goal generated, it will again pick the fact as the first option. And so on. In fact, the goal repeat will be able to succeed infinitely many times on backtracking. Note the importance of the order of the clauses here. (What would happen if the fact appeared after the rule?).

Why is it useful to generate goals that will always succeed again on backtracking? The reason is that they allow one to build — from rules that have no choices in them — rules that *do* have choices. And we can make them generate different values each time.

Consider the built-in predicate get0, which is described in Chapter 5. If Prolog attempts to satisfy a goal get0(X), it takes this as an instruction to look at the next character (letter, digit, space or whatever) that has been input to the system and to try to match the integer representation of this character with whatever value X has. If it will match, the goal succeeds; otherwise it fails. There is no choice involved. Predicate get0 always only considers the character which comes next at the time it is invoked. The next time a goal involving get0 is invoked, it will find the character after this, but again there will be no choice. We can define a new predicate new_get as follows:

```
new_get(X) :- repeat, get0(X).
```

The predicate new_get has the property that it generates the values of all the next characters (in the right order) one by one as its alternative solutions. Why is this? When we first call new_get(X), the subgoal repeat succeeds and the subgoal get0(X) succeeds with the value of the next character associated with X. When we backtrack, the last place where there was a choice is in the satisfaction of repeat. So Prolog forgets everything it has done since then and succeeds in establishing repeat in another way. It now has to look at the subgoal get0(X) again. By now, the "next character" is the one after what we last saw, and so X ends up with the second character as its value.

We can use our definition of new_get to define another useful predicate. The predicate get is normally provided as a built-in predicate in Prolog systems. When Prolog finds a goal get(X), it treats this as an instruction to read characters until it finds the next proper printing character (not a space, newline or whatever). It then tries to match the integer representation of this character with X. We can write an approximate definition of get as follows:

```
get(X) :- new_get(X), X > 32.
```

To understand this definition, one must realise that (in the ASCII code) the printing characters all have integer values above 32, whereas the others all have values 32 or less. What happens when we try to satisfy get(X)? First of all, new_get(X) matches X against the next character coming in. If the value is less than or equal to 32, the next goal will fail, and new_get will have to generate the next character as the next possible solution. This will then be compared to 32, and so on. Eventually, new_get will find a printing character, the comparison will succeed, and the value of this character will be returned as the result of get.

Exercise 6.1   The above definition of get will not necessarily work if we invoke the goal get(X) when X is already instantiated. Why is this?

One trouble with repeat is that it always has a choice to redo when backtracking reconsiders it. So backtracking will never be able to reconsider choices made earlier than the last call of repeat unless we manage to cut out the choice in some way. Because of this, the above definitions should be rewritten as:

```
new_get(X) :- repeat, get0(X).

get(X) :- new_get(X), X > 32, !.
```

Note that this definition will still only work if we attempt to satisfy get(X) with X uninstantiated. Because of the problem of backtracking over repeat choices, everything using new_get should be responsible for cutting out the choice as soon as the character generated is satisfactory for its purposes.

6.7 Constructing Compound Goals

In rules and questions of the form X :- Y or ?- Y, the term appearing as Y may consist of a single goal, or a conjunction of goals, or a disjunction of goals. Furthermore, it is possible to have variables as goals, and to satisfy a goal when the goal actually fails by using not. The predicates described in this section provide ways to specify these complicated ways of expressing goals.

X , Y

The "," operator specifies a conjunction of goals. This operator was introduced in Chapter 1. Where X and Y are goals, the goal X , Y succeeds if X succeeds and if Y succeeds. If X succeeds and then Y fails, then an attempt is made to re-satisfy X. If X fails, then the entire conjunction fails. This is the essence of backtracking. The "," has a built-in declaration as a right associative infix operator, so that X , Y , Z is equivalent to X , (Y , Z).

X ; Y

The ";" operator specifies a disjunction (meaning *or*) of goals. When X and Y are goals, the goal X ; Y succeeds if X succeeds or if Y succeeds. If X fails, then an attempt is made to satisfy Y. If Y then fails, the entire disjunction fails. We can use the ";" operator to express alternatives *within the same clause*. For instance, let us say that something is a person if it is either Adam or Eve, or if it has a mother. We can express this in a single rule as follows:

```
person(X) :- (X=adam; X=eve; mother(X,Y)).
```

In this rule, we have actually specified three alternatives. However, as far as Prolog is concerned, this breaks down into two alternatives, one of which itself introduces two alternatives. Because ";" has a built-in declaration as a right associative infix operator, the clause is actually the same as:

```
person(X) :- ';'( X=adam, ';'(X=eve,mother(X,Y)) )
```

So the first possibility is that X is adam. The second possibility involves the two alternatives that X is eve or X has a mother.

We can put disjunctions anywhere where we can put any other kind of goal in Prolog. However, it is advisable to add extra brackets to avoid confusion about how the operators ";" and "," interact. We can usually replace a use of disjunction with a use of several facts and rules, possibly involving the definition of an extra predicate. For instance, the above example is exactly equivalent to:

```
person(adam).
person(eve).
person(X) :- mother(X,Y).
```

This version is more conventional and perhaps easier to read. On many Prolog systems, it may actually be more efficient than using ";".

The effect of a "cut" includes committing the system to any choices made because of disjunctions since the rule was matched (Chapter 4). Because of this, there are some cases where a program with cuts cannot be translated into one without disjunctions. However, in general you are not recommended to use ";" excessively. Refer to Chapter 8 for warnings on how injudicious use of ";" may lead to programs that are difficult to understand.

call(X)

It is assumed that X is instantiated to a term that can be interpreted as a goal. The call(X) goal succeeds if an attempt to satisfy X succeeds. The call(X) goal fails if an attempt to satisfy X fails. At first sight, this

predicate may seem redundant, because one might ask why the argument of
`call` shouldn't simply appear by itself as a goal? For instance, the goal

     ..., call(member(a,X)), ...

can always be replaced by

     ..., member(a,X), ...

However, if we are *constructing* goals by using the "`=..`" predicate or its
friends, then it is possible to call goals that have a functor that is *unknown* at
the time you type in your program. In the definition of `consult` in Section
7.13, for instance, we want to be able to treat any term read after a "`?-`" as a
goal. Assuming that P, X, and Y are instantiated to a functor and arguments
appropriately, `call` can be used as follows:

     ..., Z =.. [P,X,Y], call(Z), ...

The above line can be thought of as a way of expressing the following sort of
call, which is *not correct syntax* in the standard version of Prolog we are using
in this book:

     ..., P(X,Y), ...

However, some versions of Prolog do permit the use of variable functors in
goals.

not(X)

It is assumed that X is instantiated to a term that can be interpreted as a
goal. The not(X) goal succeeds if an attempt to satisfy X fails. The not(X)
goal fails if an attempt to satisfy X succeeds. In this way, `not` is rather like
`call`, except that the success or failure of the argument, interpreted as a
goal, is reversed.

What is the difference between the following two questions?

     ?- member(X,[a,b,c]), write(X).

     ?- not(not(member(X,[a,b,c]))), write(X).

One might be tempted to say that there is no difference, because in the
second question,

              member(X,[a,b,c])   succeeds, so
          not(member(X,[a,b,c]))   fails, and so
      not(not(member(X,[a,b,c]))) succeeds.

This is partly right. However, the first question would cause the atom "a" to
be written, and the second goal would cause an *uninstantiated variable* to be
written. This is what happens when an attempt is made to satisfy the first
goal of the second question above:

1. The member goal succeeds, instantiating X to a.

2. An attempt is made to satisfy the first not goal, and it fails because the member goal, its argument, succeeded. Now remember that when a goal fails, any variables that became instantiated, such as X in the example, must now "forget" what they stood for. Hence X becomes uninstantiated.

3. An attempt is made to satisfy the second not goal, and it succeeds, because its argument, not(member(...)), failed. X is still uninstantiated.

4. An attempt is made to satisfy the write goal, with X uninstantiated. The uninstantiated variable, as described in Section 6.9, is printed in a special way.

6.8 Equality

This section deals briefly with the various built-in predicates for testing and making things equal in Prolog.

X = Y

When Prolog encounters a goal X = Y, it attempts to make X and Y equal by matching them together. If it can match them, the goal succeeds (and X and Y may have become more instantiated). Otherwise the goal fails. A fuller discussion of this predicate is given in Section 2.4. The equality predicate is defined as though by

```
X = X.
```

See if you can understand how this definition works.

X \= Y

The "\=" predicate is the opposite of the "=" predicate in terms of success and failure. That is, X \= Y succeeds if X = Y fails, and vice versa. If the goal X \= Y succeeds (X and Y could not be matched), the instantiation of X and Y will not have been changed at all. If "\=" happened not to be a built-in predicate, we could define it in Prolog, thus:

```
X \= Y :- X=Y, !, fail.
X \= Y.
```

X == Y

The predicate "==" represents a much stricter equality test than "=". That is, if X == Y ever succeeds then X = Y does as well. On the other hand, this is not so the other way round. The way that "==" is more strict is by the way it considers variables. The "=" predicate will consider an uninstantiated variable to be equal to anything, because it will match anything. On the other hand, "==" will only consider an uninstantiated variable to be equal to another uninstantiated variable that is already sharing with it. Otherwise the test will fail. So we get the following behaviour:

```
?- X == Y.
no
?- X == X.
X = _23
?- X=Y, X==Y.
X = _23, Y = _23
?- append([A|B],C) == append(X,Y).
no
?- append([A|B],C) == append([A|B],C).
A = _23, B = _24, C = _25
```

X \== Y

This predicate is to "==" as "\=" is to "=". That is, a goal involving it succeeds exactly when the same goal for "==" would fail, and vice versa. Again, we could imagine it defined in Prolog, thus:

```
X \== Y :- X == Y, !, fail.
X \== Y.
```

6.9 Input and Output

The predicates made available for reading and writing characters and terms were descibed in Chapter 5. Here we summarise each one.

get0(X)

This goal succeeds if X can be matched with the next character encountered on the current input stream. get0 succeeds only once (it cannot be re-satisfied). The operation of moving to the next character is not undone on backtracking, because there is no way to put a character back onto the current input stream.

get(X)

This goal succeeds if X can be matched with the next printing character encountered on the current input stream. Printing characters have an ASCII code that is greater than 32. Any non-printing characters are skipped. get succeeds only once (it cannot be re-satisfied). The operation of

get is not undone on backtracking, because there is no way to put a
character back onto the current input stream.

skip(X)

This goal reads and skips over characters from the current input stream
until a character is found that matches with X. A skip succeeds only once.

read(X)

This goal reads the next term from the current input stream and matches it
with X. A read succeeds only once. The term must be followed by a dot ".",
which does not become a part of the term, and at least one non-printing
character. The dot is removed from the current input stream.

put(X)

This goal writes the integer X as a character on the current output stream.
put succeeds only once. An error occurs if X is not instantiated.

nl

Writes a control sequence to the current output stream that causes a "new
line". On a computer display, all characters after the use of nl appear on the
next line of the page. nl succeeds only once.

tab(X)

Writes a quantity of X "space" characters to the current output stream. An
error occurs if X is not instantiated. tab succeeds only once.

write(X)

This goal writes the term X to the current output stream. write succeeds
only once. Any uninstantiated variables in X are written as uniquely
numbered variables beginning with an underscore, such as "_239". Sharing
variables within the same argument to write have the same number when
they are printed out. The predicate write takes account of current operator
declarations when it prints a term. Thus an infix operator will be printed out
between its arguments, for instance.

display(X)

The predicate display works in exactly the same way as write, except that
it ignores any operator declarations. When display is used, any structure
is printed out with the functor first and the arguments in brackets
afterwards.

op(X,Y,Z)

This goal declares an operator having precedence class X, position and associativity Y, and name Z. The position and associativity specification is taken from the following set of atoms:

fx   fy   xf   yf   xfx   xfy   yfx   yfy

If the operator declaration is legal, then op will succeed. See Section 5.5 for more details.

6.10 Handling Files

The predicates that Prolog makes available for altering the current input and current output streams were introduced in Chapter 5. Here we summarise each one.

see(X)

This goal opens file X, if it is not already open, and defines the current input stream to originate from file X. An error occurs if X is not instantiated, or if X names a file that does not exist.

seeing(X)

This goal succeeds if the name of the current input stream matches with X, and fails otherwise.

seen

This goal closes the current input stream, and defines the current input stream to be the user's computer terminal's keyboard.

tell(X)

This goal opens file X, if it is not already open, and defines the current output stream to write into the file. An error occurs if X is not instantiated. The first time tell is used on a file not already open, if X names a file that does not exist, then a file of that name is created. Otherwise, if X names a file that exists, then the previous contents of the file are destroyed.

telling(X)

This goal succeeds if X matches with the name of the current output stream, and fails otherwise.

told

This goal closes the current output stream, causing an end-of-file marker to be written on the file. The current output stream reverts to the user's computer terminal's display.

6.11 Evaluating Arithmetic Expressions

Arithmetic was first discussed in Section 2.5. Here we summarise the use of the "is" predicate, and what functors are available for constructing arithmetic expressions.

X is Y

Y must be instantiated to a structure that can be interpreted as an arithmetic expression as described in Section 2.4. First, the structure instantiated for Y is evaluated to give an integer, called the *result*. The result is matched with X, and the is succeeds or fails based on the match. The functors that can be used to make up the structure on the right-hand side of an is are as follows:

X + Y

The addition operator. When evaluated by is its result is the numerical sum of its two arguments. The arguments must be instantiated to integers or to structures that evaluate to integers.

X - Y

The subtraction operator. When evaluated by is, its result is the numerical difference of its two arguments. The arguments must be instantiated to integers or to structures that evaluate to integers.

X * Y

The multiplication operator. When evaluated by is, its result is the numerical product of its two arguments. The arguments must be instantiated to integers or to structures that evaluate to integers.

X / Y

The integer division operator. When evaluated by is, its result is the integer quotient of its two arguments. The arguments must be instantiated to integers or to structures that evaluate to integers.

X mod Y

The integer remainder operator. When evaluated by is, its result is the integer remainder that is generated when X is divided by Y. The arguments must be instantiated to structures that evaluate to integers.

Particular Prolog implementations may include more arithmetic operations such as exponentiation. The examples shown in this book only require the ones listed here.

6.12 Comparing Numbers

Six predicates are provided for comparing numbers (integers). These predicates were first presented in Section 2.5 when we discussed arithmetic. Each predicate is written as an infix operator having two arguments.

X = Y

The equality predicate, described in Section 6.8, also succeeds when two integer arguments are the same.

X \= Y

The inequality predicate of Section 6.8 also holds for integers, succeeding when the two arguments are not the same integer.

X < Y

The less than predicate succeeds when the left-hand integer argument is less than the right-hand integer argument. Both arguments must be instantiated.

X > Y

The greater than predicate succeeds when the left-hand integer argument is greater than the right-hand integer argument. Both arguments must be instantiated, or an error occurs.

X >= Y

The greater than or equal to predicate succeeds when the left-hand integer argument is greater than or equal to the right-hand integer argument. Both arguments must be instantiated.

X =< Y

The less than or equal to predicate succeeds when the left-hand argument is less than or equal to the right-hand argument. Both arguments must be instantiated. Notice that the predicate is spelled as "=<" rather than "<=", so that "<=" is free to be used as an operator that looks like an arrow.

6.13 Watching Prolog at Work

This section describes the built-in predicates that enable you to watch your program as it runs. We will only describe the built-in predicates here, and refer you to Chapter 8 for a more detailed discussion of debugging and tracing.

trace

The effect of satisfying the goal trace is to turn on exhaustive tracing. This means that afterwards you will get to see every goal that your program generates at each of the four main ports.

notrace

The effect of the goal notrace is to stop exhaustive tracing from now on. However, any tracing due to the presence of spy points will continue.

spy P

The predicate spy is used when you want to pay special attention to goals involving some specific predicates. You do this by setting *spy points* on them. The predicate is defined as a prefix operator, and so you do not need to put brackets round the argument. The argument can be any of the following:

- An atom. In this case, a spy point is put on all predicates with this atom, however many arguments are used. Thus if we had clauses for sort with both two and three arguments, the goal spy sort would cause spy points to be set on both sets of clauses.

- A structure of the form Name/Arity, where Name is an atom and Arity is an integer. This specifies a predicate with functor Name and arity Arity. Thus spy sort/2 would cause spy points to be set on goals for the predicate sort with two arguments.

- A list. In this case, the list must be terminated with "[ ]", and each element of the list must itself be an allowable argument to spy. Prolog will put spy points in all the places specified in the list. Thus spy [sort/2, append/3] would cause spy points to be set on sort with two arguments and append with three.

debugging

The built-in predicate debugging allows you to see which spy points you currently have set. The list of spy points is printed out as a side-effect of the goal debugging being satisfied.

nodebug

The goal nodebug causes all your current spy points to be removed.

nospy

Like spy, nospy is a prefix operator. nospy is more selective than nodebug, because you can specify exactly which spy points you wish to have removed. You do this by providing an argument in exactly the same form as for spy. Thus the goal nospy [reverse/2, append/3] will remove any spy points on reverse with two arguments and append with three arguments.

Chapter 7

More Example Programs

Each section of this chapter deals with a particular application of Prolog programming. We suggest that you read all of the sections in this chapter. Do not be concerned if you do not understand the purpose of a program because you are not acquainted with the particular application. For example, only those readers who have been introduced to Calculus will appreciate the value of symbolic differentiation. Read it anyway, because the program for finding symbolic derivatives demonstrates how to use pattern matching to transform one kind of structure (an arithmetic expression) into another one. What is important is to gain an understanding of programming techniques available to the Prolog programmer, regardless of the particular application.

We hope that we have included enough applications to satisfy most tastes. Naturally, all of the applications deal with areas that suit Prolog's way of representing the world. You will not find how to calculate the flow of heat through a square metal pipe, for example. It is possible to solve such problems using Prolog, but the expressiveness and power of Prolog is not shown to advantage on problems which are essentially repetitious calculations over arrays of numbers. We would like to be able to discuss large Prolog programs, such as those that are used by Artificial Intelligence researchers for understanding natural language. Unfortunately, the aims of a book like this one preclude discussion of programs that are longer than a page of text and which would appeal only to a specialised audience.

7.1 A Sorted Tree Dictionary

Suppose we wish to make associations between items of information, and retrieve them when required. For example, an ordinary dictionary associates a word with its definition, and a foreign language dictionary associates a word in one language with a word in another language. We have already seen one way to make a dictionary: with facts.

If we wanted to make an index of the performance of horses in the British Isles during the year 1938, we could simply define facts `winnings(X,Y)` where X is the name of the horse, and Y is the number of guineas (a unit of currency) won by the horse. The following database of facts could serve as part of such an index:

```
winnings(abaris,582).
winnings(careful,17).
winnings(jingling_silver,300).
winnings(maloja,356).
```

If we wanted to find out how much was won by maloja, we would simply ask the right question, and Prolog would give us the answer:

```
?- winnings(maloja,X).
X=356
```

Remember that when Prolog searches through a database to find a matching fact, it starts at the top of the database and works its way down. This means that if our dictionary database is arranged in alphabetical order, as is the one above, then Prolog will take a short amount of time to find the winnings for ablaze, and it will take longer to find the winnings for zoltan. Although Prolog can look through its database much faster than you could look through a printed index, it is silly to search the index from beginning to end if we know that the horse we are looking for is at the end. Also, although Prolog has been designed to search its database quickly, it is not always as fast as we would wish. Depending on how large your index is, and depending on how much information you have stored about each horse, Prolog might take an uncomfortably long amount of time to search the index.

For these reasons and others, computer scientists have devoted much effort to finding good ways to store information such as indices and dictionaries. Prolog itself uses some of these methods to store its own facts and rules, but it is sometimes helpful to use these methods in our programs. We shall describe one such method for representing a dictionary, called the *sorted tree*. The sorted tree is both an efficient way of using a dictionary, and a demonstration of how lists of structures are helpful.

A sorted tree consists of some structures called *nodes*, where there is one node for each entry in the dictionary. Each node has four components. It contains the two associated items of information, rather like winnings, above. One of these items, called the *key*, is the one whose name determines its place in the dictionary (the name of the horse in our example). The other is used to store any other information about the object involved (the winnings in our example). In addition, each node contains a tail (like the tail of a list) to a node containing a key whose name is alphabetically *less than* the name of the key in the node itself. Furthermore, the node contains another tail, to a node whose name is alphabetically *greater than* the key in the node. Let us use a structure called w(H,W,L,G) (w is an abbreviation of "winnings") where H is the name of a horse (an atom) used as the key, W is the amount of guineas won (an integer), L is a structure with a horse whose name is less than H 's, and G is a structure with a horse whose name is greater than H's. If there are no structures for L and G, we will leave them uninstantiated. Given a small set of horses, the structure might look like this when written as a tree:

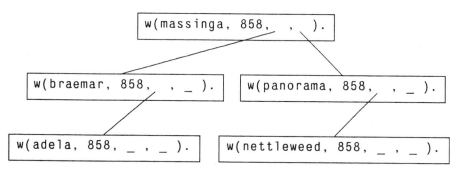

Represented as a structure in Prolog, and indented so as not to be too wide to fit on the page, this would look like:

```
w(massinga,858,
   w(braemar,385,
      w(adela,588,_,_),
   _),
   w(panorama,158,
      w(nettleweed,579,_,_),
   _)
).
```

Now given a structure like this, we wish to "look up" names of horses in the structure to find out how many guineas they won during 1938. The structure would have the format w(H,W,L,G) as above. The boundary condition is when the name of the horse we are looking for is H. In this case, we have succeeded and need not try any alternatives. Otherwise, we must use aless, defined in Chapter 3, to decide which "branch" of the tree, L or G, to look up recursively. We use these principles to define the predicate lookup for which the goal lookup(H,S,G) means that horse H, when looked up in index S (a w structure), won G guineas:

```
lookup(H, w(H,G,_,_), G) :- !.
lookup(H, w(H1,_,Before,_), G) :-
```

```
          aless(H,H1),
          lookup(H,Before,G).
 lookup(H, w(H1,_,_,After), G) :-
          not(aless(H,H1)),
          lookup(H,After,G).
```

If we use this predicate to search a sorted tree, in general we examine fewer horses than if we arranged them in a single list, and searched that from start to finish.

There is a suprising and interesting property of this lookup procedure: if we look for the name of a horse which is not in the structure, then whatever information we supply about the horse when we use lookup as a goal will be instantiated in the structure when lookup returns from its recursion. For example, the interpretation of lookup in this question

```
 ?- lookup(ruby_vintage,S,X).
```

is: "Construct a structure, instantiated to S, such that ruby_vintage is paired with X." So, lookup is inserting new components in a partially specified structure. We can therefore use lookup repeatedly to create a dictionary. For instance,

```
 ?- lookup(abaris,X,582), lookup(maloja,X,356).
```

would instantiate X to be a sorted tree with two entries. The actual means by which lookup functions for both storing and retrieving components takes advantage of what you should know already about Prolog, so we urge you to work this out by yourself. Hint: when lookup(H,S,G) is used in a conjunction of goals, the "changes" made to S only hold over the scope of S.

Exercise 7.1. Experiment with the lookup predicate to determine what difference it makes to insert items in the dictionary in a different order each time. For example, what does the dictionary tree look like when entries have been inserted in the order: massinga, braemar, nettleweed, panorama? In the order: adela, braemar, nettleweed, massinga?

7.2 Searching a Maze

It is a dark and stormy night. As you drive down a lonely country road, your car breaks down, and you stop in front of a splendid palace. You go to the door, find it open, and begin looking for a telephone. How do you search the palace without getting lost, and know that you have searched every room? Also, what is the shortest path to the telephone? It is just for such emergencies that maze-searching methods have been devised.

In many computer programs, such as those for searching mazes, it is useful to keep lists of information, and search the list if some information is needed at a later time. For example, if we decide to search the palace for a telephone, we might need to keep a list of the room numbers visited so far, so we don't go round in circles visiting the same rooms over and over again. What we do is to write down the room numbers visited on a piece of paper. Before entering a room, we check to see if its number is on our piece of paper. If it is, we ignore the room, since we must have been to it previously. If the room number is not on the paper, we write down the number, and enter the room. And so on until we find the telephone. There are some refinements to be made to this method, and we will do so later when we discuss graph searching. But first, let's write down the steps in order, so we know what problems there are to solve:

1. Go to the door of any room.

2. If the room number is on our list, ignore the room and go to Step 1. If there are no rooms in sight, then "backtrack" through the room we went through previously, to see if there are any other rooms near it.

3. Otherwise, add the room number to our list.

4. Look in the room for a telephone.

5. If there is no telephone, go to Step 1. Otherwise we stop, and our list has the path that we took to come to the correct room.

We shall assume that room numbers are constants, but it does not matter whether they are integers or atoms. First, we can solve the problem of how to look up room numbers on the piece of paper by using the member predicate defined in Section 3.3, representing the piece of paper as a list. Now we can get on with the problem of searching the maze. Let us consider a small example, where we are given the floor plan of a house, with letters labelling the different rooms, like this:

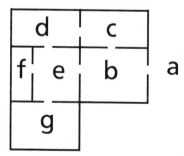

Notice that gaps in the walls are meant to represent doors, and that room a is simply a representation of the space outside the house. There are doors from rooms a to b, from c to d, from f to e, and so forth. The facts about where there are doors can be represented as Prolog facts:

```
d(a,b).
d(b,e).
d(b,c).
d(d,e).
d(c,d).
d(e,f).
d(g,e).
```

Notice that the information about doors is not redundant. For example, although we have said that there is a door between room g and room e, we have not said that there is a door between room e and room g: we have not asserted d(e,g). To get around this problem of representing two-way doors, we could write a duplicate d fact for each door, reversing the arguments. Or, we could make the program recognise that each door fact can be interpreted in two ways. This is the alternative we choose in the program that follows.

To go from one room to another, we must recognise one of two cases:

- we are in the room we want to go to, or

- we have to pass through a door, and recognise these cases again (recursively).

Consider the goal go(X,Y,T), which succeeds if it is possible to go from room X to room Y. The third argument T is our piece of paper that we carry, that has a "trail" of the room numbers that we have visited so far.

The boundary condition for going from room X to room Y is if we are already at room Y (this is, if X = Y). This is represented as the clause:

```
go(X,X,T).
```

Otherwise we choose some adjoining room, call it Z, and see if we have been to it before. If we haven't, then we "go" from Z to Y, adding Z to our list. All of this is represented as the following clause:

```
go(X,Y,T) :- d(X,Z), not(member(Z,T)), go(Z,Y,[Z|T]).
```

In words, this could be interpreted as:

> To "go" from X to Y, not passing though the rooms on T, find a door from X to anywhere (Z), ensure that Z is not already on the list, and "go" from Z to Y, using the list T with Z added to it.

There are three ways that failures can occur in the use of this rule. First, if there is no door from X to anywhere. Second, if the door we choose is on the list. Third, if we cannot "go" to Y from the Z we chose because it fails deeper in the recursion. If the first goal d(X,Z) fails, then it will cause this use of go to fail. At the "top level" (not a recursive call), this means that there is no path from X to Y. At lower levels, it simply means we must backtrack to find a different door.

The program as stated treats each door as a "one-way" door. If we assume that having a door from room a to room b is just the same as having a door from room b to room a, then we must make this explicit, as indicated above. Instead of supplying a duplicate fact for each d fact but with the arguments reversed, there are two ways to put this information in the program. The most obvious way is to add another rule, giving:

```
go(X,X,T).
go(X,Y,T) :- d(X,Z), not(member(Z,T)), go(Z,Y,[Z|T]).
go(X,Y,T) :- d(Z,X), not(member(Z,T)), go(Z,Y,[Z|T]).
```

Or, the semicolon predicate (for disjunction) can be used:

```
go(X,X,T).
go(X,Y,T) :-
        (d(X,Z) ; d(Z,X)),
        not(member(Z,T)),
        go(Z,Y,[Z|T]).
```

Now for finding the telephone. Consider the goal hasphone(X) which succeeds if room X has a telephone. If we want to say that room g has a telephone, we simply write our database with

```
hasphone(g).
```

in it. Supposing we start at room a, one possible question we ask to find the path to the telephone is:

```
?- go(a,X,[]), hasphone(X).
```

This question is a "generate and test", which finds possible rooms, then checks them for a telephone. Another way is to satisfy hasphone(X) first, then see whether we can go from a to X:

```
?- hasphone(X), go(a,X,[]).
```

This method is more efficient, but it implies that we "know" where the telephone is before we have begun the search, however.

Initialising the third argument to the empty list means that we start with a clean piece of paper. This can be changed to provide variety: the question,

"Find the telephone without entering rooms d and f" would be expressed in Prolog a

```
?- hasphone(X), go(a,X,[d,f]).
```

In Section 7.9 we will describe some general graph searching procedures, including a program that finds the shortest path through a graph.

Exercise 7.2: Annotate the above program so that it will print messages such as "entering room Y" and "found telephone in room Y" with the appropriate room numbers filled in.

Exercise 7.3: Can alternate paths be found by this program? If so, where do you put the "cut" goal to prevent more than one path from being found?

Exercise 7.4: What determines the order in which rooms are searched?

7.3 The Towers of Hanoi

The Towers of Hanoi is a game played with three poles and a set of discs. The discs are graded in diameter, and fit onto the poles by means of a hole cut through the centre of each disc. Initially all the discs are on the left-hand pole. The object of the game is to move all of the discs onto the centre pole. The right-hand pole can be used as a "spare" pole, a temporary resting place for discs. Each time a disc is moved from one pole to another, two constraints must be observed: only the top disc on a pole can be moved, and no disc may be placed on top of a smaller one.

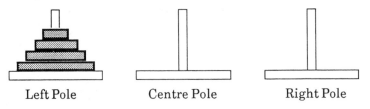

Left Pole   Centre Pole   Right Pole

Many people who play this game never actually discover the quite simple strategy which will correctly play the Towers of Hanoi game with three poles and N discs. To save you the effort of finding it, we reveal it here:

- The boundary condition occurs when there are no discs on the source (the left-hand) pole.

- Move $N-1$ discs from the source pole to the spare pole (the right-hand one), using the destination as a spare. Notice that this is a recursive move.

- Move a single disc from the source pole to the destination pole.

- Finally, move N-1 discs from the spare to the destination, using the source as the spare.

The Prolog program that implements this strategy is defined as follows. We define a predicate hanoi having one argument, such that hanoi(N) means to print out the sequence of moves when N discs are on the source pole. Of the two move clauses, the first one is the boundary condition as described above, and the second clause implements the recursive cases. The predicate move has four arguments. The first argument is the number of discs to be moved. The other three represent the poles which are the source, destination and spare for moving the discs. The predicate inform uses write to print out the names of the poles that are involved in moving a disc.

```
hanoi(N) :- move(N,left,centre,right).

move(0,_,_,_) :- !.
move(N,A,B,C) :-
    M is N-1,
    move(M,A,C,B),inform(A,B),move(M,C,B,A).

 inform(X,Y) :-
    write([move,a,disc,from,
                        the,X,pole,to,the,Y,pole]),
    nl.
```

7.4 Parts Inventory

In Chapter 3 we discussed a program for printing a list of parts required in constructing an assembly when given an inventory of parts. In the improved program described in this section, we shall take into account how many of each part is required, by accumulating the quantities of parts required as we descend from assemblies to their constituents. The improved program also handles duplicates properly: the collect procedure removes duplicates, while summing up the quantities of each part required, before the answer is printed out.

The structure of the inventory database is similar to that described in Chapter 3. An assembly is represented as a list of structures of the form quant(X,Y), where X is the name of some part (a basic part or an assembly), and Y is the quantity of such parts needed. For example, the list of structures for a bicycle having two wheels and a frame would look like this:

```
[quant(wheel,2), quant(frame,1)] .
```

This can just as well be used for any list of items, such as a grocery list:

```
[quant(apple,12), quant(banana,2), quant(loaf,2)] .
```

We now list each predicate of the modified program, together with a description of its purpose:

partlist(A): prints out a list of all of the basic parts required, and the quantities of each, for the construction of assembly A.

partsof(N,X,P): P is a list of structures quant(Part,Num) giving the part name Part and the quantity Num of each required for the construction of N X's. N is an integer and X is an atom which is the name of some part.

partsoflist(N,S,P): P is a list of quant structures as above, required for the construction of the sum of all the members of the list S, given that N such lists are required. N is an integer, S is a list of quant structures.

collect(P,A): P and A are lists of quant structures. A is a list with the same members as P except that there are no duplicate parts, and for any duplicates in P, the quantity of that part in A is the sum of all the corresponding quantities in P. We use collect to collect several descriptions of collections of like parts. For instance, "3 screws, 4 cushions, and 4 screws" is collected to form "7 screws and 4 cushions".

collectrest(X,M,L,O,N): L and O are lists of quant structures. O is the list of all the members of L except for those which have X as their part. X is an atom which is the name of some part. N is the sum of all the quantities of X in list L, added to M. M is an integer that is used to accumulate the quantity of X's in L, and is passed down to each call of collectrest. At the end of the recursion, which is caught by the boundary condition, M is returned as N.

printpartlist(P): P is a list of quant structures, printed one structure per line of output. The put(9) goal prints the ASCII code 9, which is a horizontal tab motion.

append(A,B,C) is the predicate we have seen many times before.

The complete Prolog program is as follows:

```
partlist(T) :-
            partsof(1,T,P),
            collect(P,Q),
            printpartlist(Q).

partsof(N,X,P) :- assembly(X,S), partsoflist(N,S,P).
partsof(N,X,[quant(X,N)]) :- basicpart(X).

partsoflist(_,[],[]).
partsoflist(N,[quant(X,Num)|L],T) :-
            M is N * Num,
```

```
                partsof(M,X,Xparts),
                partsoflist(N,L,Restparts),
                append(Xparts,Restparts,T).
collect([],[]).
collect([quant(X,N)|R],[quant(X,Ntotal)|R2]) :-
                collectrest(X,N,R,0,Ntotal),
                collect(0,R2).
collectrest(_,N,[],[],N).
collectrest(X,N,[quant(X,Num)|Rest],Others,Ntotal) :-
                !,
                M is N + Num,
                collectrest(X,M,Rest,Others,Ntotal).
collectrest(X,N,[Other|Rest],[Other|Others],Ntotal) :-
                collectrest(X,N,Rest,Others,Ntotal).
printpartlist([]).
printpartlist([quant(X,N)|R]) :-
                tab(4), write(N), put(9), write(X), nl,
                printpartlist(R).
```

7.5 List Processing

In this section we shall describe some basic predicates that are useful for manipulating lists. Because Prolog makes arbitrary data structures available to you, lists may not take on the omnipresent rôle that they do in other programming languages such as LISP and POP-2. Whether or not your programs will make use of lists, it is always important to understand how the predicates defined in this section work, because they employ principles that can be applied to manipulating any kind of data structure .

Finding the last element of a list: The goal last(X,L) succeeds if element X is the last element of list L. The boundary condition is when there is only one element in L. The first rule checks for this. The usual kind of recursive case forms the second rule.

```
last(X,[X]).
last(X,[_|Y]) :- last(X,Y).

?- last(X,[talk,of,the,town]).
X=town
```

Checking for consecutive elements: the goal nextto(X,Y,L) succeeds if elements X and Y are consecutive elements of list L. Due to the way variables work, either X, or Y, or both could be uninstantiated when an attempt is made to satisfy the goal. The first clause, which checks for the boundary condition, must also assume that there may be more elements in the list after X and Y. This is why the anonymous variable appears, holding down the tail of the list.

```
nextto(X,Y,[X,Y|_]).
nextto(X,Y,[_|Z]) :- nextto(X,Y,Z).
```

Appending lists: We have seen this example before in Section 3.6. The goal append(X,Y,Z) succeeds when Z is a list constructed by appending Y to the end of X. For example,

```
?- append([a,b,c],[d,e,f],Q).
Q=[a,b,c,d,e,f]
```

It is defined as follows:

```
append([],L,L).
append([X|L1],L2,[X|L3]) :- append(L1,L2,L3).
```

The boundary condition occurs when the first argument is the empty list. This is because appending the empty list to a list does not change the list. Furthermore, we will gradually approach the boundary condition because each recursion of append removes an element from the head of the first argument.

Notice that any two of the arguments of append can be instantiated, and append will instantiate the third argument to the appropriate result. This property is true of many of the predicates defined in this chapter. Because of the flexibility of append, we can actually define several other predicates in terms of it:

```
last(El,List) :- append(_,[El],List).

next_to(El1,El2,List) :- append(_,[El1,El2|_],List).

member(El,List) :- append(_,[El|_],List).
```

Reversing a list: the goal rev(L,M) succeeds if the result of reversing the order of elements in list L is list M. The program uses a standard technique, where we reverse a list by appending its head to the reverse of its tail. And, what better way to reverse the tail than to use rev itself! The boundary condition is when the first argument is reduced to the empty list, in which case the result is also the empty list.

```
rev([],[]).
rev([H|T],L) :- rev(T,Z), append(Z,[H],L).
```

Notice that we have enclosed H in square brackets in the second argument of append. This is because H was selected as the head of the first argument, and the head of a list is not necessarily a list. By convention, the tail of a list is always a list.

For a more efficient implementation of rev, we can incorporate the appending into the clauses for rev:

```
rev2(L1,L2) :- revzap(L1,[],L2).
revzap([X|L],L2,L3) :-
                    revzap(L,[X|L2],L3). revzap([],L,L).
```

The second argument of revzap is used to hold the "answer so far", in other words, an accumulator, as introduced in Section 3.7. Whenever a new piece (X) of the answer is discovered, the accumulator passed to the rest of the program is the old accumulator combined with the new piece X. At the end, the last accumulator is passed back to be the answer in the original goal. A similar technique is used in the definition of integer_name in Section 7.8.

Deleting one element: the goal efface(X,Y,Z) removes the first occurrence of element X from list Y, giving a new effaced list Z. If there is no such element X in the list Y, the predicate fails. The boundary condition is when we have found the element. Otherwise, we recur on the tail of Y.

```
efface(A,[A|L],L) :- !.
efface(A,[B|L],[B|M]) :- efface(A,L,M).
```

It is easy to add a clause so that the predicate does not fail when the second argument becomes reduced to the empty list. The new clause, which recognises a new boundary condition, is

```
efface(_,[],[]).
```

Deleting all occurrences of an element: the goal delete(X,L1,L2) constructs a list L2 by deleting all the elements X from list L1. The boundary condition is when L1 is the empty list, meaning that we have recurred down the entire length of the list. Otherwise, if X is in the list, then the result is the tail of the list, except that we delete from that as well. The final case is if we have seen something other than X in the second argument: we simply recur.

```
delete(_,[],[]).
delete(X,[X|L],M) :- !, delete(X,L,M).
delete(X,[Y|L1],[Y|L2]) :- delete(X,L1,L2).
```

Substitution: this is quite similar to delete, except instead of deleting a desired element, we substitute some other element in its place. The goal subst(X,L,A,M) will construct a new list M made up from elements of list L, except that any occurrences of X will be replaced by A. There are three cases. The first one is the boundary condition, exactly as for delete. The second one is in case an X is found in the second argument, and the third is in case something *other than* X is found.

```
subst(_,[],_,[]).
subst(X,[X|L],A,[A|M]) :- !, subst(X,L,A,M).
subst(X,[Y|L],A,[Y|M]) :- subst(X,L,A,M).
```

Sublists: list X is a sublist of list Y if every item in also appears in Y, consecutively, and in the same order. The following goal would succeed:

    sublist([of,the,club],[meetings,of,the,club,will,be,held]).

The sublist program requires two predicates: one to find a matching first element, and one to ensure that the remainder of the first argument matches element-for-element with the remainder of the second argument:

```
sublist([X|L],[X|M]) :- prefix(L,M), !.
sublist(L,[_|M]) :- sublist(L,M).

prefix([],_).
prefix([X|L],[X|M]) :- prefix(L,M).
```

Removing duplicates: The predicate remdup runs through a list of any elements, and makes a new list. Although duplicate elements may exist in the input, we want the output list to contain at most one of each element. The goal remdup(L,M) succeeds if L is the input list, and M is a list of the elements appearing in L without duplication. The definition uses an auxiliary predicate dupacc in which the accumulator (see Section 3.7) is the second argument, initialised to the empty list. We also use predicate member (from Section 3.3).

```
remdup(L,M) :- dupacc(L,[],M).

dupacc([],A,A).
dupacc([H|T],A,L) :- member(H,A), dupacc(T,A,L).
dupacc([H|T],A,L) :- dupacc(T,[H|A],L).
```

Predicate dupacc has three clauses. The boundary condition states that, when the input list is empty, the result will be whatever we have accumulated so far. The second clause checks whether the next element of the list is a member of the accumulated list. If it is, we simply recur on the tail, making no change to the accumulator. Otherwise, using the next clause, we recur on the tail of the input list, with an accumulator that has the new element (H) added.

Mapping: a powerful technique is the ability to convert one list into another list by applying some function to each element of the first list, using the successive results as the successive members of the second list. Our program in Chapter 3 for changing one sentence into another is an example of mapping. We say that we are "mapping one sentence into another."

Mapping is so useful that it justifies a section of its own. Furthermore, because lists in Prolog are simply special cases of structures, we will postpone discussion of mapping lists until Section 7.12. Mapping appears in other guises also. Section 7.11, on symbolic differentiation, describes a way to map arithmetic expression onto other ones.

7.6 Representing and Manipulating Sets

The set is one of the most important data structures used in Mathematics, and operations with sets find some applications in computer programming as well. A set is a collection of elements, rather like a list, but it does not make sense to ask where or how many times something is an element of a set. Thus, the set {1,2,3} is the same as the set {2,3,1}, because all that matters is whether a given item is an element of the set or not. Sets may also have other sets as members. The most fundamental operation on a set is to determine whether some element is a member of some given set.

It should come as no suprise that a convenient representation for sets is as lists. A list can contain arbitrary elements including other lists, and it is possible to define a membership predicate over lists. However, when we represent a set as a list, we will arrange that the list only has one element for each thing that belongs to the set. Dealing with lists without duplicated elements simplifies some operations such as removing elements. So we will deal only with lists without duplicates. The predicates described in this section expect and maintain this property.

It is usual to define the following operations over sets. We shall include the usual mathematical notation for those who are accustomed to it:

Set membership: $X \in Y$
X is a member of some set Y if X is one of the elements of Y.
Example: $a \in \{c,a,t\}$

Subset: $X \subset Y$
Set X is a subset of set Y if every element of X is also an element of Y. Y may contain some elements that X does not.
Example: $\{x,r,u\} \subset \{p,q,r,s,t,u,v,w,x,y,z\}$

Intersection: $X \cap Y$
The intersection of sets X and Y is the set containing those elements which

are members of X and which are members of Y.

Example: {r,a,p,i,d} ∩ {p,i,c,t,u,r,e} = {r,i,p}

Union: X ∪ Y

The union of sets X and Y is the set consisting of members from X, or Y, or both.

Example: {a,b,c} ∪ {c,d,e} = {a,b,c,d,e}

These are the basic operations that are normally used to manipulate sets. We can now write Prolog programs to implement each one. The first basic operation, membership, is the same member predicate that we have seen several times before. However, the definition of member that we use does not contain the "cut" symbol in the boundary case so that we can generate successive elements of the list by backtracking.

```
member(X,[X|_]).
member(X,[_|Y]) :- member(X,Y).
```

Next, a predicate subset for which subset(X,Y) will succeed if X is a subset of Y. The second clause in the definition embodies the mathematical notion that the empty set is a subset of every set. In Prolog, this notion turns into a way of checking the boundary condition on the first argument, since we recur on its tail.

```
subset([A|X],Y) :- member(A,Y), subset(X,Y).
subset([],Y).
```

Next, the most complicated example, intersection. The goal intersection(X,Y,Z) will succeed if the intersection of X and Y is Z. Here is where we have to assume that the lists contain no duplicated elements.

```
intersection([],X,[]).
intersection([X|R],Y,[X|Z]) :-
        member(X,Y),
        !,
        intersection(R,Y,Z).
intersection([X|R],Y,Z) :- intersection(R,Y,Z).
```

Finally, union. The goal union(X,Y,Z) will succeed if the union of X and Y is Z. Notice that union looks rather like an arranged marriage between intersection and append:

```
union([],X,X).
union([X|R],Y,Z) :- member(X,Y), !, union(R,Y,Z).
union([X|R],Y,[X|Z]) :- union(R,Y,Z).
```

This completes our repertoire of set-processing predicates. Although sets may not feature in the kind of programming you intend to do, it is worthwhile to study these examples to obtain a clear understanding of how you can make recursion and backtracking work for you.

7.7 Sorting

Sometimes it is helpful to sort a list of elements into order. If the elements of the list are integers, we can use the "<" predicate to decide whether two integers are in order. The list [1,2,3] is sorted into order because the predicate "<" succeeds for each consecutive pair of integers in the list. If the elements are atoms, we can use aless as discussed in Chapter 3. The list [alpha, beta, gamma] is sorted into order because the predicate aless succeeds for each consecutive pair of atoms in the list.

Computer scientists have developed many techniques for sorting a list into order when given some predicate that tells us whether consecutive elements are in order. We will show Prolog programs for four such sorting methods: naïve sort, insertion sort, bubble sort, and Quicksort. Each program will use a predicate order which can be defined by using "<" or aless or any other predicate you desire, depending on what kind of structure you are sorting. We assume that the goal order(X,Y) will succeed if objects X and Y are in the desired order, that is, if X is less than Y in some sense.

One way of sorting objects into ascending order is first to generate some permutation of the objects, and then test to see if the resulting list of objects is in ascending order. If they are not, then we generate some other permutation of the objects. This method is known as the *naïve* sort:

```
sort(L1,L2) :- permutation(L1,L2), sorted(L2), !.
permutation([],[]).
permutation(L,[H|T]) :-
        append(V,[H|U],L),
        append(V,U,W),
        permutation(W,T).
sorted([]).
sorted([X]).
sorted([X,Y|L]) :- order(X,Y), sorted([Y|L]).
```

The predicate append is defined numerous times previously in this book. In this program, the predicates have the following meanings: sort(L1,L2) means that L2 is the list which is the sorted version of L1; permutation(L1,L2) means that L2 is a list consisting of all the elements of list L1 in one of the many possible orders — this is a *generator* in the terminology of Section 4.3. Predicate sorted(L) means that the numbers in the list are sorted into increasing order — this is a *tester*.

The goal of finding the sorted version of a list consists of generating a permutation of the elements and testing to see if it is sorted. If it is, we have found the unique answer. Otherwise we must carry on generating permutations. This is not a very efficient way to sort a list.

In the *insertion sort* method, each item of the list is considered one at a time, and each item is inserted into a new list in the appropriate position. If you play card games, then you probably use this method when you sort your hand, picking up one card at a time. The goal insort(X,Y) succeeds when list Y is a sorted version of list X. Each element is removed from the head of the list and passed to insortx, which inserts the element in the list and returns the modified list:

```
insort([],[]).
insort([X|L],M) :- insort(L,N), insortx(X,N,M).

insortx(X,[A|L],[A|M]) :-
        order(A,X), !, insortx(X,L,M).
insortx(X,L,[X|L]).
```

A convenient way to obtain a more general-purpose insertion sorting predicate is to use the ordering predicate as an argument of insort. We use the "=.." predicate as discussed in Chapter 6:

```
insort([], [], _).
insort([X|L],M,O) :- insort(L,N,O), insortx(X,N,M,O).

insortx(X,[A|L],[A|M],O) :-
        P =.. [O,A,X],
        call(P), !,
        insortx(X,L,M,O).
insortx(X,L,[X|L],O).
```

Then we can use goals such as insort(A,B,'<') and insort(A,B,aless) without requiring a predicate named order. This technique can be applied to the other sorting algorithms in this section.

The *bubble sort* checks the list to see if two adjacent elements are out of order. If so, then they are exchanged. This process is repeated until no more exchanges are necessary. Whereas the insertion sort makes elements "sink" down to the appropriate level, the bubble sort is so named because it makes elements "float" up to the appropriate level.

```
busort(L,S) :-
        append(X,[A,B|Y],L),
```

```
      order(B,A), !,
      append(X,[B,A|Y],M),
      busort(M,S).
busort(L,L).

append([],L,L).
append([H|T],L,[H|V]) :- append(T,L,V).
```

Notice that the append predicate is the same as we have seen before, and that in this example it must be able to backtrack on each solution found. Hence, a "cut" does not appear in the first clause of append. This is another example of what some people call "non-deterministic" programming, because we are using append to select arbitrary members of list L. It is the responsibility of append to ensure that the set of selections from L is complete.

Quicksort is a more sophisticated sorting method due to C.A.R. Hoare. To implement Quicksort in Prolog we first need to split a list consisting of head H and tail T into two lists L and M such that:

- all the elements of L are less than H;

- all the elements of M are greater than or equal to H, and

- the order of elements within L and M is the same as in [H|T].

Once we have split the list, we Quicksort each list (this is the recursive part), and append M onto the back of L. The goal split(H,T,L,M) partitions the list [H|T] into L and M as described above:

```
split(H,[A|X],[A|Y],Z) :-
      order(A,H), split(H,X,Y,Z).
split(H,[A|X],Y,[A|Z]) :-
      not(order(A,H)), split(H,X,Y,Z).
split(_,[],[],[]).
```

The Quicksort program is now:

```
quisort([],[]).
quisort([H|T],S) :-
      split(H,T,A,B),
      quisort(A,A1),
      quisort(B,B1),
      append(A1,[H|B1],S).
```

It is also possible to build the append into the sorting program, giving the more efficient program:

```
quisortx([],X,X).
quisortx([H|T],S,X) :-
    split(H,T,A,B),
    quisortx(A,S,[H|Y]),
    quisortx(B,Y,X).
```

In this case the third argument is used as a temporary work area, and it is initialised to the empty list when quisortx is used as a goal.

More information on sorting can be found in Volume 3 (Sorting and Searching) of *The Art of Computer Programming* by Donald Knuth, published in 1973 by Addison-Wesley. Hoare's Quicksort method is described in his paper in *Computer Journal* 5 (1962), pages 10 to 15.

Exercise 7.5: Verify that, when given a known list as L1, permutation(L1,L2) will generate all the permutations of L1 (once each) as the alternative values of L2. In what order are the solutions generated?

Exercise 7.6 Quicksort works best on large lists because it converges to a solution more rapidly. However, the amount of work done at each recurrence of quisort is more than the other methods, because it must use split. So, perhaps when sorting small lists, then quisort's recursive calls could be replaced by calls to some other sorting method, say insertion sort. Develop a "hybrid" sorting program that uses Quicksort to sort the large partitions (the lists made by the split predicate), but switches to another sorting method when the size of the partition becomes sufficiently low that the insertion sort can be used. Hint: since split has to look at every element of the list anyway, it can be used to compute the length of a list.

7.8 Using the Database: random, gensym, findall

In all of the programs discussed so far, we have used the database only to store facts and rules that define predicates. It is possible to use the database to store ordinary structures, such as the structures that are constructed as a program executes. Until now, we have been passing such structures from one predicate to another by using arguments. However, one reason for storing information in the database, rather than passing it around through arguments, is that sometimes a piece of information may be needed by many parts of a program, and that the alternative would involve something like one or two extra arguments to most predicates. Another reason is to retain information over backtracking. In this section we describe three predicates that take advantage of the database for storing structures that have a lifetime that extends further than is possible by using variables. The three predicates are random, which generates a pseudorandomly chosen integer each time it is called; findall, which generates a list of all the structures that make a given predicate succeed, and gensym, which generates atoms with unique names.

7.8.1 Random

The goal random(R,N) instantiates N to a randomly chosen integer between 1 and R. The method of choosing a random integer is to use a congruential method, using a "seed" that is initialised to an arbitrary integer. Each time a random integer is desired, the answer is computed using the existing seed, and a new seed is determined, and stored until the next time that a random integer is desired. We use the database to store the seed between calls to random. After the seed is used, we retract the old information about its value. Then, the new seed is computed, and new information is asserted. The initial seed is simply a fact in the database, with functor seed having one component, the integer value of the seed.

```
seed(13).

random(R,N) :-
    seed(S),
    N is (S mod R) + 1,
    retract(seed(S)),
    NewSeed is (125 * S + 1) mod 4096,
    asserta(seed(NewSeed)), !.
```

We can take advantage of the semantics of retract to simplify the definition of random in the following way:

```
random(R,N) :-
    retract(seed(S)),
    N is (S mod R)+1,
    NewSeed is (125*S+1) mod 4096,
    asserta(seed(NewSeed)), !.
```

To print out a lot of random numbers between 1 and 10, but stopping when 5 has been generated, all that is required is:

```
?- repeat, random(10,X), write(X), nl, X = 5.
```

7.8.2 Gensym

The predicate gensym provides a way of generating new Prolog atoms. If we have a program that is assimilating information about the world (perhaps by understanding English sentences about it), we have the problem of dealing with the situation when a new object is discovered. A natural way to represent an object is with a Prolog atom. If the object has not been encounted before, we must ensure that the atom we assign to it does not accidentally coincide with the one representing some other object. That is, we require the ability to generate a new atom. We might as well require that the atom have some mnemonic significance as well, so that we can understand the program's output. If we were representing students, say, a reasonable solution would be to name the first student student1, the second student2, the third student3, and so on. Then if in addition we had to represent teachers, we could pick atoms teacher1, teacher2, teacher3 and so on to represent them.

The purpose of gensym is to generate new atoms from given roots (like student and teacher). For each root, it remembers what number was last used, so that next time it is asked to generate an atom from that root it can guarantee that it will be different from the ones generated before. Thus, the first time the question:

```
?- gensym(student,X).
```

is asked, the answer is

X = student1

The next time, the answer will be **X = student2** and so on. Note that these different solutions are not generated on backtracking (gensym(X,Y) can never be resatisfied), but are generated by subsequent goals involving the predicate.

The definition of gensym makes use of the subsidiary predicate current_num. It is by putting facts about current_num into the database (and also by removing facts that are no longer applicable) that gensym keeps track of which number to use next with a given root. The fact current_num(Root,Num) means that the last number used with root Root was Num. That is, the last atom generated for this root had the characters derived from Root followed by those derived from Num. The normal course of action when Prolog tries to satisfy a gensym goal is that the last current_num fact about the given root is removed from the database, 1 is added to the number involved and a new current_num fact is added to replace it. Meanwhile, the new number is used as the basis for generating an atom. It is very convenient to keep the current_num information in the database. The only alternative is to have every predicate directly or indirectly involved in a gensym carry the information about current numbers in extra arguments.

The last few clauses of this program define the predicate integer_name, which is used to derive a list of characters from a number. The atoms created by gensym are made up by using the built-in name predicate to make an atom whose characters consist of the characters of the root followed by the

characters of the number. Some Prolog implementations use a version of the
name predicate which will perform the functions of integer_name, but it is
quite instructive to see how it can be defined in Prolog. One fact that is used
implicitly in the definition is that the ASCII character codes for the digits 0,
1, 2, etc are 48, 49, 50, etc in that order. Therefore, in order to convert from a
number less than 10 to its character, one only has to add 48. To get the list of
characters for a number greater than 9 is more complex. We can easily get
hold of the last digit of a number, because this is simply the remainder on
division by 10 (the number mod 10). It is therefore easy to generate the
characters of a number in reverse order: we just keep on finding the last
digit, getting hold of the rest of the number (the result of integer division by
10), finding its last digit, and so on. The Prolog definition of this is:

```
reverse_chars(N,[C]) :- N < 10, !, C is N + 48.
reverse_chars(N,[C|Cs]) :-
    C is (N mod 10) + 48,
    N1 is N / 10,
    reverse_chars(N1,Cs).
```

To get the characters in the right order, we adopt a neat trick. We introduce
an extra argument to the predicate, expressing the list of characters
generated so far. Using this argument, we can find the characters in reverse
order, as above, but put together the list in the right order. This works as
follows. Assume we have the number 123. We start with the "list built so
far", [ ]. First, the number 3 is discovered and converted into the character
code 51. We then invoke a recursive integer_name goal, to find the
characters of 12. The "list so far" given to this goal is made up of the
character generated put on the front of the original "list so far": it is the list
[51]. The second integer_name goal generates the character code 50 (for
the 2) and tries to satisfy integer_name again, this time with the number 1
and the "list so far" [50,51]. This final goal succeeds and, because the
number was less than 10, gives the answer [49,50,51]. This answer is passed
up through the arguments of the various integer_name goals and forms
the answer of the original question (what are the characters corresponding to
123?). Here is the program:

```
gensym(Root,Atom) :-
    get_num(Root,Num),
    name(Root,Name1),
    integer_name(Num,Name2),
    append(Name1,Name2,Name),
    name(Atom,Name).
```

```
get_num(Root,Num)  :-
    retract(current_num(Root,Num1)),  !,
    Num is Num1+1,
    asserta(current_num(Root,Num)).
get_num(Root,1)  :- asserta(current_num(Root,1)).

/* Convert from an integer to a list of characters */

integer_name(Int,List)  :- integer_name(Int,[],List).
integer_name(I,Sofar,[C|Sofar])  :-
    I < 10,  !,  C is I + 48.
integer_name(I,Sofar,List)  :-
    Tophalf is I/10,
    Bothalf is I mod 10,
    C is Bothalf+48,
    integer_name(Tophalf,[C|Sofar],List).
```

7.8.3 *Findall*

In some applications it is helpful to determine all of the terms that satisfy
some predicate. For example, we might want to make a list of all of the
children of Adam and Eve using the parents predicate of Chapter 1 (and
assuming we had a database of parents facts). For this we could use a
predicate called findall, which we shall define below. The goal
findall(X,G,L) constructs a list L consisting of all of the objects X such
that the goal G is satisfied. It is assumed that G is instantiated to an ordinary
term, except that findall treats it as a Prolog goal. Also, X will appear
somewhere inside G. So, G can be instantiated to a Prolog goal of arbitrary
complexity. Here is how we could find out all the children of Adam and Eve:

```
?- findall(X, parents(X,eve,adam), L).
```

The variable L would be instantiated to a list of all of the X's that satisfy
parents(X,eve,adam). All that findall needs to do is to repeatedly
attempt to satisfy its second argument, and each time it succeeds it should
take whatever X is instantiated to, and put it in the database. When the
attempt to satisfy the second argument finally fails, then we go back and
collect all of the X's that we put into the database. The resulting list is
returned as the third argument. If the attempt to satisfy the second
argument *never* succeeds, then the third argument will be instantiated to the
empty list. To put items into the database, we use the built-in asserta
predicate, which inserts terms *before* those that have the same functor. To
record that an item X has been found, we add a fact to the database about the
predicate found. The Prolog clauses for findall are as follows:

```
findall(X,G,_) :-
    asserta(found(mark)),
    call(G),
    asserta(found(X)),
    fail.
findall(_,_,L) :- collect_found([],M), !, L = M.
collect_found(S,L) :-
    getnext(X),
    !,
    collect_found([X|S],L).
collect_found(L,L).

getnext(X) :- retract(found(X)), !, X \== mark.
```

The findall predicate first adds a special marker fact for found, in the form of a fact with argument mark. This special marker serves to mark the place in the database before which all of the X's satisfying G in this use of findall will be asserted. Next, an attempt is made to satisfy G, and each time it succeeds, then found(X) is inserted in the database. The fail forces backtracking to occur, attempting to re-satisfy G (asserta succeeds at most once). When G finally fails, backtracking will force the first findall clause to fail, and an attempt will be made to satisfy the second one. The second clause calls collect_found to retract each found structure back out of the database, inserting its component in a list. The collect_found predicate puts each element into a variable that holds the "list so far", the trick revealed when explaining gensym above. As soon as the component mark is encountered, getnext fails, so the second clause of collect_found is satisfied, which shares its second argument (the result) with its first (the collected list).

Notice that the presence of the found(mark) in the database indicates a particular use of findall. This means that findall can be used recursively. Any occurrence of findall used within the second argument of another findall will be treated correctly. Also, remember that because the term found(mark) serves a special purpose, the term mark should be unique within the application. More unlikely marker names can be used to ensure uniqueness.

In Section 7.9 we develop a program that uses findall to construct a list of all of the descendants of a node in a graph. This is used to implement a breadth-first graph searching program.

Exercise 7.7: Write a Prolog program that defines the predicate random_pick, for which the goal random_pick(L,E) instantiates E to a

randomly chosen element of list L. Hint: Use the random number generator
and define a predicate that returns the Nth element of a list.

Exercise 7.8: Given the goal findall(X,G,L), what happens when there
are uninstantiated variables not sharing with X in G?

7.9 Searching Graphs

Graphs are networks of nodes connected by arcs. For example, a map can be
seen as a graph, in which the nodes are villages and the arcs are roads
connecting the villages. If you want to find the shortest journey between two
villages, you have to solve the problem of finding the shortest path between
nodes of a graph.

The easiest way to represent a graph is by using a database of facts to
represent the arcs between nodes of a graph. For example, the graph
consisting of the following pattern of nodes and arcs can be represented as
facts as shown in Figure 7.1.

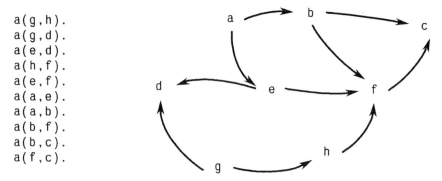

```
a(g,h).
a(g,d).
a(e,d).
a(h,f).
a(e,f).
a(a,e).
a(a,b).
a(b,f).
a(b,c).
a(f,c).
```

Figure 7.1. Representing a directed graph.

So to go from node a to node c, we could take the path a, e, f, c, or one of
several other possible paths indicated by the arrowheads on the arcs. Thus
the predicate a is interpreted such that a(X,Y) means that there is an arc
from X to Y, which *does not* imply an arc from Y to X.

The easiest program for searching a graph represented as above is the
following:

```
go(X,X).
go(X,Y) :- a(X,Z), go(Z,Y).
```

This program is more strict that the one presented in Section 7.2, because
paths are found only in the direction of the arcs. As before, it is possible for
this program to get into a loop. We could simply add the arc

```
a(d,a).
```

to the above, obtaining a cyclic graph. This is why, as before, we should use list T to keep a "trail" of the nodes we have visited at any particular recurrence of the predicate:

```
go(X,X,T).
go(X,Y,T) :- a(X,Z), legal(Z,T), go(Z,Y,[Z|T]).
legal(X,[]).
legal(X,[H|T]) :- X \== H, legal(X,T).
```

Note that the predicate legal is nothing more than a "non-membership" test.

This program does what is called a "depth first" search, because at first only one of the neighbours of a node in the graph is considered. The other neighbours are ignored until later failure causes backtracking to the node so another neighbour can be considered.

Now let's assume that the graph is *undirected* — that is, all arcs are two-way. Then it is necessary to use the arc information to propose arcs in either direction. This is the same assumption as we made in Section 7.2 when searching the maze. This would result in the program:

```
go(X,X,T).
go(X,Y,T) :-
        (a(X,Z) ; a(Z,X)),
        legal(Z,T), go(Z,Y,[Z|T]).
```

Let's look now at a case of graph searching that we might find useful in practice. What if we have to plan a route for driving from one town to another? We might have a database of information about which roads go between which towns in the North of England, and how long they are:

```
a(newcastle,carlisle,58).
a(carlisle,penrith,23).
a(darlington,newcastle,40).
a(penrith,darlington,52).
a(workington,carlisle,33).
a(workington,penrith,39).
```

For the moment we can ignore the distances, and define a new predicate a as follows:

```
a(X,Y) :- a(X,Y,Z).
```

Given this definition of a, our existing graph searching procedure go will find possible ways that we can drive from any place in the graph to any other.

However, go has a deficiency: it does not tell us which route it has found when it finally succeeds. At the very least we might expect go to build up a list of the places to be visited in the correct order. Moreover, the program already has at hand the "trail", but in the reverse order to what we expect. We can use rev, defined in Section 7.5, to turn it the right way round again. Here is a new definition of go, which returns successful routes by means of a third argument:

```
go(Start,Dest,Route) :-
    go0(Start,Dest,[],R),
    rev(R,Route).

go0(X,X,T,[X|T]).
go0(Place,Y,T,R) :-
    legalnode(Place,T,Next),
    go0(Next,Y,[Place|T],R).

legalnode(X,Trail,Y) :-
    (a(X,Y) ; a(Y,X)), legal(Y,Trail).
```

Notice that we have used legalnode to represent the notion of what is a legal node to proceed to from another node, and that legal is defined as before. Here is an example of this program at work, finding a route from Darlington to Workington:

```
?- go(darlington,workington,X).
X=[darlington,newcastle,carlisle,penrith,workington]
```

Not the best route, perhaps, but it will find other routes if we ask for alternatives by backtracking.

This program has various deficiencies. The program is not fully in control of which path it should investigate next, because it is never in a position to survey the complete set of possibilities. The options that still remain to be considered are implicit in the backtracking structure of Prolog, rather than being explicit in a structure that the program can examine. Here is a revised version, which is more general-purpose. We shall see that simple modifications to this program can result in a variety of search behaviours.

```
go(Start,Dest,Route) :-
    go1([[Start]],Dest,R),
    rev(R,Route).

go1([First|Rest],Dest,First) :- First = [Dest|_].
go1([[Last|Trail]|Others],Dest,Route) :-
    findall([Z,Last|Trail],legalnode(Last,Trail,Z),
                                             List),
```

```
append(List,Others,NewRoutes),
go1(NewRoutes,Dest,Route).
```

Predicate legalnode is defined as before. Predicate go1 is given a list of routes under consideration together with the destination, and it returns the successful route in its last argument. The list of routes under consideration is simply all the paths that we have followed so far from the starting place. We hope we can extend one of these to make a path that gets to the destination. The paths are represented as lists of places in reverse order, so they function as "trails" as well.

When we start off, there is only one possible path we might want to extend. This is simply the path that starts at the starting place and doesn't go any further. If we start at Darlington, it will be [darlington]. If we now investigate paths going from Darlington to adjacent towns, there are two possible paths: [newcastle, darlington], and [penrith, darlington]. Since Workington is not on any of these, we must now decide which of these to extend. If we decide to look at the first one, we find that there is only one legal node adjacent to Newcastle (the last town on that path). So now we have a new path in addition to the Darlington-Penrith path: [carlisle, newcastle, darlington].

Our searcher, go1, keeps track of a whole list of paths that might be worth following. How does it decide which one to look at first? It simply chooses the *first one*. It then finds all possible ways to extend that path by one town at a time (using findall to build a list of all such extended paths) and puts them on the *front* of the list, to be considered next time around.

The resulting behaviour is that go1 will try all possible ways of extending the first path before it ever considers an alternative. This makes the strategy a version of depth first search. Incidentally, go1 considers routes in exactly the same order as go0. You might like to work out exactly why this is.

If we are interested in the shortest route from Darlington to Workington, the existing program does not seem to be much good. The first solution it finds is not the shortest one: indeed it is the longest one (in this case). We must alter the program so that it generates routes in order of length. If we change it so that it always extends shorter paths before considering longer paths, then it is bound to find the shortest path first (if we measure the length of a path by the number of towns on it). The resulting program will then perform a *breadth first* search. All we need to do is to put new alternatives on the *end* of the overall list of possibilities, instead of at the beginning as in the last example. We simply amend the second clause of go1 to read:

```
go1([[Last|Trail]|Others],Dest,Route) :-
    findall([Z,Last|Trail],legalnode(Last,Trail,Z),
                                              List),
    append(Others,List,NewRoutes),
    go1(NewRoutes,Dest,Route).
```

The amended program now finds possible routes from Darlington to Workington in the following order:

```
[darlington,penrith,workington]
[darlington,newcastle,carlisle,workington]
[darlington,penrith,carlisle,workington]
[darlington,newcastle,carlisle,penrith,workington]
```

We can simplify this program considerably if we are certain that there is always an answer to a query, and if we want only the first solution. Under such circumstances, we no longer need to check for loops in legalnode. See if you can work out why this is.

Unfortunately, the route that involves the smallest number of towns may not necessarily be the route with the least mileage. We have so far ignored the mileage information in our graph. If we add a few fictitious towns to our graph to obtain:

```
a(newcastle,carlisle,58).
a(carlisle,penrith,23).
a(townB,townA,15).
a(penrith,darlington,52).
a(townB,townC,10).
a(workington,carlisle,33).
a(workington,townC,5).
a(workington,penrith,39).
a(darlington,townA,25).
```

then the route of shortest mileage is actually generated last, because it involves travel through so many towns. What we need to do is to keep, with each path that may be extended, a record of how long that path is so far. We then always extend the path with the shortest mileage. This is called a *best first* search.

We shall now represent a path on the list of alternative paths as a structure of the form r(M,P), where M is the total length of the path in miles, and P is the list of places visited. Our modified predicate go3 now finds the shortest of the paths on its list of alternatives. The predicate shortest returns the shortest path on the list, and also returns the remaining paths on the list. Given the shortest path so far, predicate proceed finds all the legal extensions to the path, and adds them to the list. This in turn needs a new version of legalnode, which adds the distance to the next town to the distance computed so far. The entire program is:

```
go3(Routes,Dest,Route) :-
    shortest(Routes,Shortest,RestRoutes),
    proceed(Shortest,Dest,RestRoutes,Route).

proceed(r(Dist,Route),Dest,_,Route) :-
    Route = [Dest|_].
proceed(r(Dist,[Last|Trail]),Dest,Routes,Route) :-
    findall(
            r(D1,[Z,Last|Trail]),
            legalnode(Last,Trail,Z,Dist,D1),
            List),
    append(List,Routes,NewRoutes),
    go3(NewRoutes,Dest,Route).

shortest([Route|Routes],Shortest,[Route|Rest]) :-
    shortest(Routes,Shortest,Rest),
    shorter(Shortest,Route),
    !.
shortest([Route|Rest],Route,Rest).

shorter(r(M1,_),r(M2,_)) :- M1 < M2.

legalnode(X,Trail,Y,Dist,NewDist) :-
    (a(X,Y,Z) ; a(Y,X,Z)),
    legal(Y,Trail),
    NewDist is Dist + Z.
```

To use this program, we attempt to satisfy predicate go, defined as

```
go(Start,Dest,Route) :-
        go3([r(0,[Start])],Dest,R),
        rev(R,Route).
```

This new program successfully generates possible routes in the order of their actual mileage. You might like to alter it to tell how long the various routes are when it gives the answers.

We have hardly begun to look at the possible ways of organising graph searching. Information about how to search graphs using more effective heuristics than "best first" is available in books on Artificial Intelligence. For example: *Principles of Artificial Intelligence*, by Nils Nilsson, published in 1982 by Springer-Verlag; and *Artificial Intelligence*, (second edition) by Patrick Winston, published in 1984 by Addison-Wesley.

7.10 Sift the Two's and Sift the Three's

Sift the Two's and sift the Three's:
The Sieve of Erastosthenes.
When the multiples sublime,
The numbers that remain are Prime.

Anon.

A *prime number* is a number that has no whole number divisors except 1 and
itself. For instance, the number 5 is prime, but the number 15 is not, because
it has the whole number 3 as a divisor. One method for generating prime
numbers is called the Sieve of Erastosthenes. This method for sifting for
primes up to the integer N works as follows:

1. Put all the numbers between 2 and N into the "sieve".

2. Select and remove the smallest number remaining in the sieve.

3. Include this number in the primes.

4. Step though the sieve, removing all multiples of this number.

5. If the sieve is not empty, repeat steps 2 through 5.

To translate these rules into Prolog, we define a predicate integers to
generate a list of integers, a predicate sift to examine each element of the
sieve, and a predicate remove to create a new sieve by removing multiples of
the selected number from the sieve. This new sieve is passed back to sift.
The predicate primes is defined such that the goal primes(N,L)
instantiates L to the list of primes lying in the range from 1 to N inclusive:

```
primes(Limit,Ps) :-
      integers(2,Limit,Is),
      sift(Is,Ps).

integers(Low,High,[Low|Rest]) :-
      Low =< High,
      !,
      M is Low+1,
      integers(M,High,Rest).
integers(_,_,[]).

sift([],[]).
sift([I|Is],[I|Ps]) :-
      remove(I,Is,New),
      sift(New,Ps).
```

```
remove(P,[],[]).
remove(P,[I|Is],[I|Nis]) :-
    not(0 is I mod P),
    !,
    remove(P,Is,Nis).
remove(P,[I|Is],Nis) :-
    0 is I mod P,
    !,
    remove(P,Is,Nis).
```

Continuing in this arithmetical vein, here are Prolog programs for the recursive formulation of Euclid's algorithms for finding the greatest common divisor and the least common multiple of a pair of integers. The goal gcd(I,J,K) succeeds when the greatest common divisor of I and J is K. The goal lcm(I,J,K) succeeds when the least common multiple of I and J is K:

```
gcd(I,0,I).
gcd(I,J,K) :- R is I mod J, gcd(J,R,K).
lcm(I,J,K) :- gcd(I,J,R), K is (I*J)/R.
```

Notice that due to the way of computing remainders, these predicates are not "reversible". Variables I and J must be instantiated in order for the predicates to work

Exercise 7.10: The three numbers x, y, and z are said to form a *Pythagorean triple* if the square of z is equal to the sum of the squares of x and y (that is, if $z^2 = x^2 + y^2$). Write a program to generate Pythagorean triples. Define a predicate pythag such that asking

```
?- pythag(X,Y,Z).
```

and asking for alternative solutions gives us as many different Pythagorean triples as we dare. Hint: Make use of predicates such as is_integer of Chapter 4.

7.11 Symbolic Differentiation

In Mathematics, symbolic differentiation is an operation that converts a given arithmetic expression into another arithmetic expression called the *derivative*. Suppose U stands for an arithmetic expression which may contain a variable x. The derivative of U with respect to x is written as dU/dx, and is defined recursively by applying some conversion rules to the expression U. Two boundary conditions appear first, and the arrow is read "is converted to"; U and V stand for expressions, and c stands for a constant:

$\mathrm{d}c/\mathrm{d}x \to 0$

$\mathrm{d}x/\mathrm{d}x \to 1$

$\mathrm{d}(-U)/\mathrm{d}x \to -(\mathrm{d}U/\mathrm{d}x)$

$\mathrm{d}(U+V)/\mathrm{d}x \to \mathrm{d}U/\mathrm{d}x + \mathrm{d}V/\mathrm{d}x$

$\mathrm{d}(U\text{-}V)/\mathrm{d}x \to \mathrm{d}U/\mathrm{d}x - \mathrm{d}V/\mathrm{d}x$

$\mathrm{d}(cU)/\mathrm{d}x \to c(\mathrm{d}U/\mathrm{d}x)$

$\mathrm{d}(UV)/\mathrm{d}x \to U(\mathrm{d}V/\mathrm{d}x) + V(\mathrm{d}U/\mathrm{d}x)$

$\mathrm{d}(U/V)/\mathrm{d}x \to \mathrm{d}(UV^{-1})/\mathrm{d}x$

$\mathrm{d}(U^c)/\mathrm{d}x \to cU^{c-1}(\mathrm{d}U/\mathrm{d}x)$

$\mathrm{d}(\log_e U)/\mathrm{d}x \to U^{-1}(\mathrm{d}U/\mathrm{d}x)$

This set of conversion rules is easily translated to Prolog, because we can represent arithmetic expressions as structures, and use operators as the functors of the structures. We can also take advantage of the pattern-matching that occurs when a goal matches against the head of a rule. Let us consider a goal d (E , X , F) which succeeds when the derivative of expression E with respect to constant X is the expression F. Although the +, -, *, and / operators have built-in declarations, we shall have to declare a "^" operator, where X^Y means x^y. Operator declarations are used simply to make the syntax of expressions easier to read. For example, the following questions might be asked of d after it is defined:

```
?- d(x+1,x,X).
X = 1+0

?- d(x*x-2,x,X).
X = x*1+1*x-0
```

Notice that simply transforming one expression into another using the rules does not necessarily render the result in a simplified form, but a simplifier can be written as a separate procedure (Section 7.12). The differentiation program consists of the extra operator declarations plus a line-by-line translation of the above conversion rules into Prolog clauses:

```
?- op(300,yfx,^).

d(X,X,1) :- !.
d(C,X,0) :- atomic(C).
d(-U,X,-A) :- d(U,X,A).
d(U+V,X,A+B) :- d(U,X,A), d(V,X,B).
d(U-V,X,A-B) :- d(U,X,A), d(V,X,B).
d(C*U,X,C*A) :- atomic(C), C \= X, d(U,X,A), !.
```

```
d(U*V,X,B*U+A*V)  :- d(U,X,A),  d(V,X,B).
d(U/V,X,A)  :- d(U*V^(-1),X,A).
d(U^C,X,C*U^(C-1)*W)  :- atomic(C),  C \= X,  d(U,X,W).
d(log(U),X,A*U^(-1))  :- d(U,X,A).
```

Notice the two places where the cuts occur. The first cut ensures that the derivative of a variable with respect to itself matches *only* the first clause, eliminating the second clause as a possibility. Secondly, there are two clauses for multiplication, the first one dealing with a special case. If the special case succeeds, the general case must be eliminated as a possibility.

As pointed out above, the solutions generated by this program are far from simplified. For example, any occurrence of x*1 may as well be written as x and any occurrence of, for example x*1+1*x-0 may as well be written as 2*x. The next section describes an algebraic simplifier that can be used to simplify arithmetic expressions in very much the same way as the derivatives were derived above.

7.12 Mapping Structures and Transforming Trees

If we copy a structure component-by-component to form a new structure, we say that we are *mapping* one structure into another. It is usual to make a slight modification to each component as we copy it, as was done when we changed one sentence into another sentence in Chapter 3. In that example, sometimes we wanted to copy a word in the sentence exactly as it appeared in the original sentence, and sometimes we wanted the new copy to be a changed word. We used the following program to *map* the first argument of alter into its second argument:

```
alter([],[]).
alter([A|B],[C|D])  :- change(A,C),  alter(B,D).
```

Since mapping is such a general-purpose operation, we can define a predicate maplist such that the goal maplist(P,L,M) succeeds by applying the predicate P to each element of a list L to form a new list M. We assume that P has two arguments, such that the first argument is the "input" element, and the second argument is the modified element to be inserted into M:

```
maplist(_,[],[]).
maplist(P,[X|L],[Y|M])  :-
     Q =.. [P,X,Y],  call(Q),  maplist(P,L,M).
```

There are several points to note about this definition. First, the definition consists of a boundary condition (the first clause) and a general recursive case (the second clause). The second clause uses the "=.." operator, pronounced "univ", to form a goal from the given predicate (P), the input element (X), and the variable that P is assumed to instantiate to form the modified element (Y). Next, an attempt is made to satisfy Q, which will result in Y being instantiated, forming the head of the second argument to this call of maplist. Finally, the recursive call maps the tail into the tail.

The predicate alter can be replaced by using maplist. Assuming that change is defined as in Chapter 3, maplist would be used as follows:

```
?- maplist(change,[you,are,a,computer],Z).
Z=[i,[am,not],a,computer]
```

A simplification of maplist results in applist, which simply applies some predicate, assumed to have one argument, to each member of a list. No new list is created:

```
applist(_,[])
applist(P,[X|L]) :-
      Q =.. [P,X], call(Q), applist(P,L).
```

Notice that the predicate printstring of Chapter 5 could have been replaced by a goal of the form applist(put,L), where L is the string to be printed.

Mapping is not restricted to lists, but can be defined for any kind of structure. For example, consider arithmetic expressions made up of functors such as * and +, each having two arguments. Suppose we wanted to map one expression into another, removing all multiplications by 1 in the process. One way to describe this algebraic simplification would be to define a predicate s such that s(Op,La,Ra,Ans) means that for an expression consisting of an operator Op with a left argument La and right argument Ra, a simplified form is the expression Ans. The facts for removing multiplications by 1 would look like this, with two facts accounting for the commutativity of multiplication:

```
s(*,X,1,X).
s(*,1,X,X).
```

So, given an expression of the form 1*X, this table of simplifications could tell us to map it into whatever X is. Let us see how we can use this in a program.

To simplify an expression E using such a table of simplification rules, we need to first simplify the left-hand argument of E, then simplify the right-hand argument of E, and then see if the simplified result is in our table. If it is, we make the new expression whatever the table indicates. At the "leaves" of the expression tree there are integers or atoms, so we should use the built-in predicate atomic as a boundary condition to simplify leaves into themselves. As above, we can use "=.." to separate E into its functor and components:

```
simp(E,E) :- atomic(E), !.
simp(E,F) :-
      E =.. [Op, La, Ra],
      simp(La,X),
      simp(Ra,Y),
      s(Op,X,Y,F).
```

So, simp maps expression E into expression F, using the facts found in a simplification table s. What happens if no simplification can be made? To prevent s(Op,X,Y,F) failing, we must have a "catchall" rule at the end of each operator's part of the simplification table. The following simplification table includes rules for addition and multiplication, and shows the catchall rule for each operator included:

```
s(+,X,0,X).
s(+,0,X,X).
s(+,X,Y,X+Y).    /* catchall for + */
s(*,_,0,0).
s(*,0,_,0).
s(*,1,X,X).
s(*,X,1,X).
s(*,X,Y,X*Y).    /* catchall for * */
```

With the "catchall" rules present, there is now a choice of how to simplify some expressions. For instance, given 3+0, we can either use the first fact, or we can employ the "catchall" for +. Because of the way the facts are ordered, Prolog will always try the special case rules before the catchalls. Thus the first solution to simp will always be a true simplification (if there is one). However, alternative solutions will not be in the simplest possible form.

Another simplification used in computer-aided algebra is known as constant folding. The expression 3*4+a can have the constants 3 and 4 "folded" to form the expression 12+a. The folding rules can be added to the appropriate parts of the simplification table above. The rule for addition is

```
s(+,X,Y,Z) :- integer(X), integer(Y), Z is X+Y.
```

The rules for the other arithmetic operations are similar.

In commutative operations such as multiplication and addition, the simplifications described above may have different effects on expressions that are written differently but are algebraically equivalent. For example, if a folding rule is available for multiplication, then the simp predicate will faithfully map 2*3*a into 6*a, but a*2*3 or 2*a*3 will be mapped into themselves. To see why this is, think about what the expressions look like as trees:

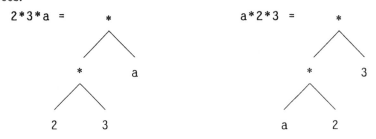

2*3*a =   a*2*3 =

The first tree can have its bottom-most multiplication folded from 2*3 into 6, but the second tree has no sub-tree that can be folded. Because multiplication is commutative, adding the following rule to the table will suffice for this particular case:

```
s(*,X*Y,W,X*Z) :- integer(Y), integer(W), Z is Y*W.
```

A more general algebra system can be constructed simply be adding more s clauses, instead of adding more "programming" to simp.

7.13 Manipulating Programs

Many of the built-in predicates discussed in this book can in fact be defined in Prolog using simpler built-in predicates. In this section we give a few such definitions. These may be of use to the programmer whose Prolog system is lacking in certain respects, but they are in any case of interest as examples of Prolog programming. Perhaps they may inspire you to develop rather different versions of these predicates for your own use.

We can use clause to define a version of the listing predicate. Let us define list1 such that satisfying the goal list1(X) will print out the clauses in the database whose heads match X. Because the definition of list1 will involve using clause with X as its first argument, we will have to require that X is sufficiently instantiated that the principal functor is known. Here is the definition of list1:

```
list1(X) :-
     clause(X,Y),
     output_clause(X,Y), write('.'), nl, fail.
list1(X).

output_clause(X,true) :- !, write(X).
output_clause(X,Y) :- write((X :- Y)).
```

When an attempt is made to satisfy a goal list1(X), the first clause causes a search for a clause whose head matches X. If one is found, that clause is printed out and then a failure is generated. Backtracking will reach the clause goal and find another clause, if there is one. And so on. When there are no more clauses to be found, the clause goal will be unable to be resatisfied, and so will fail. At this point, the second clause for list1 will be chosen, and so the goal will succeed. As a "side effect", all the appropriate clauses will have been printed out. The definition of output_clause specifies how the clauses will be printed. It looks for the special case of the body true and in this case just writes out the head. Otherwise, it writes out the head and the body, constructed with the functor ":-". Notice the use of the "cut" here to say that the first rule is the only valid possibility if the body is true. Because this example relies on backtracking, the cut is essential here.

The built-in predicate clause can also be used to write a Prolog interpreter in Prolog. That is, we can define what it is to run a Prolog program by something which is itself a Prolog program. Here is the definition of a predicate interpret, such that interpret(X) succeeds as a goal exactly when X succeeds as a goal. Predicate interpret is similar to the built-in call, but is more restricted because it does not deal with cuts or built-in predicates.

```
interpret(true) :- !.
interpret((G1,G2)) :- !, interpret(G1), interpret(G2).
interpret(Goal) :-
     clause(Goal,MoreGoals), interpret(MoreGoals).
```

The first two clauses deal with the special cases of the goal true, and a goal which is a conjunction. The last clause covers a simple goal. The procedure is to find a clause whose head matches the goal, and then interpret the goals in the body of that clause. Note that the above definition will not cope with programs using built-in predicates, because such predicates do not have clauses in the usual sense.

Here is a simplified definition of the predicate consult. Of course, consult is provided as a built-in predicate in most Prolog systems, but it is interesting to see how it can be defined in Prolog.

```
consult(File) :-
     seeing(Input),
     see(File),
     repeat,
     read(Term),
```

```
        process(Term),
        seen,
        see(Input),
        !.
    process(Term) :- end_of_file_mark(Term), !.
    process((?- Q)) :- !, call(Q), !, fail.
    process(Clause) :- assertz(Clause), fail.
```

There are several interesting points about this definition. First, the goal seeing(Input) and its partner see(Input) are there to ensure that the current input file will not be changed after the consult from what it was before. Second, we have used the predicate end_of_file_mark without defining it. It is supposed to succeed only if its argument is instantiated to the term used to represent an end of file (which would be encountered by read). Different Prolog implementations use different terms to represent "end of file", and so end_of_file_mark would have to be defined differently for different implementations. One possible definition is:

```
    end_of_file_mark(end_of_file).
```

The point of the definition of process is to cause an appropriate action to be taken for each term read from the input file. A process goal only succeeds when its argument is the end of file mark. Otherwise, a failure occurs after the appropriate action, and backtracking goes back to the repeat goal. Notice the importance of the "cut" at the end of the consult definition. This cuts out the choice introduced by the repeat. A final point: if a term read from the file represents a question (second clause for process), an attempt is made to satisfy the appropriate goal immediately using the call predicate (Section 6.7).

As an example of the use of retract, here is the definition of a useful predicate called retractall. When the goal retractall(X) is satisfied, all the clauses whose heads match X are removed from the database. Because the definition uses retract, X cannot be uninstantiated, for otherwise the predicate of the clause could not be determined. In the definition we must deal with the two cases of a clause whose head matches X: a fact and a rule. We provide different arguments to retract to access the two types of clauses. The definition exploits the property that retract backtracks until all clauses matching its argument are removed from the database.

```
    retractall(X) :- retract(X), fail.
    retractall(X) :- retract((X :- Y)), fail.
    retractall(_).
```

As an example of the predicate `retractall` in use, here is a definition in Prolog of the predicate `reconsult`. The purpose of `reconsult` is similar to `consult`, but any clauses read supersede existing clauses for the same predicate, rather than add to them (see Section 6.1).

```
reconsult(File) :-
    retractall(done(_)),
    seeing(Old),
    see(File),
    repeat,
    read(Term),
    try(Term),
    seen,
    see(Old),
    !.

try(X) :- end_of_file_mark(X), !.
try((?- Goals)) :- !, call(Goals), !, fail.
try(Clause) :-
    head(Clause,Head),
    record_done(Head),
    assertz(Clause),
    fail.

record_done(Head) :- done(Head), !.
record_done(Head) :-
    functor(Head,Func,Arity),
    functor(Proc,Func,Arity),
    asserta(done(Proc)),
    retractall(Proc),
    !.

head((A :- B), A) :- !.
head(A,A).
```

This definition looks similar to `consult`, with `try` taking the place of `process`. The main difference is `record_done`. When the first clause for a given predicate appears in a file, all the clauses in the database for that predicate must be removed before the new one is added. We must not remove clauses when later ones for that predicate appear, because then we will be removing clauses that have just been read in. How can we determine whether a clause is the first one in the file for its predicate? The answer is that we keep a record in the database of the predicates for which we have found clauses in the file. This is done though predicate `done`. When the first clause for a predicate, for instance `foo` with two arguments is read from the database, the existing clauses are removed, and the new clause is added to the database. In addition, the fact

```
done(foo(_,_)).
```

is added. When a later clause for predicate `foo` is read from the file, we will be able to see that the old clauses have already been removed, and so we avoid removing new clauses. It is important for the definition that we do not add something like

```
done(foo(a,X)).
```

because then the argument of `done` will not necessarily match the head of a clause for `foo`. The pair of goals

```
...,functor(Head,Func,Arity),functor(Proc,Func,Arity),...
```

instantiates `Proc` to a structure having the same functor as the head `Head`, but with variables as its arguments (see Section 6.5).

Chapter 8

Debugging Prolog Programs

By this point you will have used and modified many of the example programs described earlier, and you will have written programs of your own. It is now relevant to consider what to do when your program does not behave as intended. Such problems with programs are known as "bugs", and the process of removing bugs from programs is known as "debugging". We believe that a convenient approach to programming is what could be described as "preventative programming". To paraphrase an old proverb, "an ounce of careful programming is worth a pound of debugging". In this chapter we shall attempt to describe some techniques for debugging, but we shall start with a discussion of how to try to prevent bugs from infesting your programs. We realise that such a problem is unsolved in general, but we simply wish to convey some informal techniques that have helped other Prolog programmers.

As with any creative activity, whether musical composition, literature, or architecture, computer programming offers a multitude of methods for expressing how to *represent* and *manipulate* the objects and relationships that are found in a particular problem. In general, there will be a number of ways to represent or manipulate some item of information in a program. Every time the programmer decides to use one of the ways in the program, we say that the programmer has made a *design decision.*

Novices faced with the task of making design decisions for the first time often feel confused. An understanding of the choices available will help them, and it is important for a tutor to explain programming techniques in general. This is because the art of making design decisions in programming is a discipline in its own right. We attempted to give the flavour of this problem in Section 1.1 when we discussed the different ways to interpret clauses. This is a matter of *representing* objects and relationships. Also, in Section 7.7 the problem also became apparent when we described three different ways to sort a list of objects. This is a matter of different ways to *manipulate* objects and relationships.

We hope that this book provides help about making design decisions in two ways. First, by containing a number of example programs, it should convey some idea of the solutions that practising programmers have obtained. Second, this chapter should provide some advice and direction that is specific to Prolog.

8.1 Laying out Programs

Assuming that the programmer has decided how to represent and manipulate the objects and relationships in the problem, the next step is to ensure that the layout and syntax of the program is clear and easily read. The collection of clauses for a given predicate is called a *procedure*. In the examples in this book, you may have noticed that each clause in a procedure has started on a new line, and there is one blank line between procedures. For example, one way to define the set equality predicate (representing sets as lists) is to use three predicates, each of which is defined by a two-line procedure:

```
eqset(X,X) :- !.
eqset(X,Y) :- eqlist(X,Y).

eqlist([],[]).
eqlist([X|L1],L2) :- delete(X,L2,L3), eqlist(L1,L3).

delete(X,[X|Y],Y).
delete(X,[Y|L1],[Y|L2]) :- delete(X,L1,L2).
```

This is not necessarily the best definition of set equality, but it points out how to lay out procedures. Notice that the clauses for each procedure are grouped together, and procedures are separated by a blank line. Notice also that the body of each rule is short enough to fit on one line. Another convention that is adopted by many Prolog programmers is to write each clause on a single line if the entire clause will fit on a line. Otherwise, write the head of the clause and the ":-" on the first line, and write each goal of a conjunction indented on a separate line. For example, a program to generate all permutations of a list:

```
permute([],[]).
permute(L,[H|T]) :-
      append(V,[H|U],L),
      append(V,U,W),
      permute(W,T).
```

The definition uses a backtracking append, so that another permutation Y is generated from X each time an attempt is made to re-satisfy permute(X,Y). What we should notice here is the way the conjuncts in the second clause are laid out on the page.

The main point is to decide on consistent conventions, whatever the conventions may be. In general, it is wise to add comments, to group terms appropriately, to use round brackets when in doubt about operator precedences, and to use plenty of white space (spaces and blank lines) in consistent ways. Comments should indicate how the arguments of a structure (or clause) are interpreted: what order they come in, and what data structures (constants or structures) are expected to fill each argument. Also, it is wise to write comments on the way that variables are expected to become instantiated as the clause becomes satisfied.

For more global organisation of the program, it is helpful to divide the program into reasonably self-contained parts, for example, where all of the list processing procedures would appear in the same file. A Prolog procedure that uses more than about five to ten rules may be hard to read, so consider whether it can be broken up naturally by the definition of some subsidiary predicates. If a program uses many facts, such as the simplification rules in Section 7.12, then all of the facts should belong together in the same file. A lot of facts is generally easier to read than a lot of rules, and although even a few rules may be difficult to understand, many pages of a particular fact can be understood because the semantics of facts are less complex.

Another issue that affects the ease in which Prolog programs can be read is the use of semicolon ("or") and exclamation ("cut"). The problems with excessive use of the "cut" were introduced in Chapter 4. You should always consider whether it may be worthwhile avoiding a ";" by defining extra clauses. For instance, the following program:

```
nospy(X) :-
    check(X,Functor,Arity,A), !,
    ( spypoint(_,Functor,A), !,
    ( deny(spypoint(Head,Functor,Arity),_),
    makespy(Head,Body),deny(Head,Body),
    write('Spy-point on '), prterm(Functor,Arity),
    write(' removed.'), nl,
    fail    ; true )  ;  write('There is no spy-point
    on '),  write(X), put(46), nl  ), !.
```

is an example of what *not* to do. It is much harder to understand than:

```
nospy(X) :-
        check(X,Functor,Arity,A), !,
        try_remove(X,Functor,Arity,A).

try_remove(_,Functor,Arity,A) :-
        spypoint(_,Functor,A), !,
        remove_spy(Functor,Arity,A).

try_remove(X,_,_,_) :-
        write('There is no spy-point on '),
        write(X), put(46), nl, !.

remove_spy(Functor,Arity,A) :-
        deny(spypoint(Head,Functor,Arity),_),
```

```
        makespy(Head,Body),
        deny(Head,Body),
        write('Spy-point on '),
        prterm(Functor,Arity),
        write(' removed.'), nl, fail.
remove_spy(_,_,_).
```

which does exactly the same thing. When you really do want to use "or", it is helpful to arrange the conjunction of goals so that the "or" stands out from the rest of the goals, and to place brackets around the goals so that the scope of the "or" is made explicit.

Throughout this book we have emphasised the importance of thinking of many problems in terms of boundary conditions together with a general rule. Whenever possible, we write boundary conditions before all the other clauses of a procedure. This makes it easy to see what the boundary conditions are, and also provides some measure of protection against circular definitions. However, there are some cases where it is desirable to place the boundary condition after the other clauses of a procedure. Obviously, "catchall" rules, as seen several times previously, need to be placed at the end of the procedure.

When reading a Prolog procedure, it is helpful to look each time for the following key properties of the procedure.

- Look at how each predicate and variable in the procedure is *spelled*. Mis-spelling is a common mistake.

- Look for the *number of components* of each functor that is mentioned in the procedure. Ensure if the number of components (and their order) is consistent with your design decisions.

- Locate all of the *operators* in the clauses, and determine their precedence, associativity, and where their arguments are. You can determine this from operator declarations and the presence of brackets. When in doubt, add extra brackets. Also, to check whether an operator behaves in the way you expect, try printing out some sample terms using display.

- Notice the *scope* of each variable, and locate all the like-named variables within the scope. Notice which variables will "share" when one of them becomes instantiated. Notice whether variables in the head of the clause appear in the body of the clause.

- Try to determine what variables are instantiated or uninstantiated at the time the clause will be used.

- Locate the clause(s) that constitute the boundary condition(s). Determine whether all the conceivable boundary conditions have been accounted for.

Once you can "dissect" a procedure in this way, your understanding of the procedure will improve.

8.2 Common Errors

In this section we list a number of problems that both beginning and experienced Prolog programmers encounter. The problems fall into two categories: errors of *syntax*, and errors of *control flow*.

Once the programmer has decided what program to write, and how to lay it out on the printed page (or terminal display screen), there is the problem of getting the program into a file or typing it straight into the top level of a Prolog system. The main problem encountered here is ensuring that the *syntax* of the program is correct. Here we list a number of common syntactic errors. If these errors are not detected by the programmer, Prolog may provide an error message when an attempt is made to consult the program.

- A common syntax error is forgetting to add the dot "." at the end of a clause. A dot must also always follow any term that is read by the read predicate. You must also leave at least one "white space" character after the dot. So beware of ending a file with the dot of the last clause — make sure that there is a RETURN at the very end.

- Some special characters belong in pairs. There are the round brackets "(" and ")" for grouping terms, the square brackets "[" and "]" for the list notation, and the curly brackets "{" and "}" for the grammar rule notation (Chapter 9). Also, the double quote """" for denoting strings, and the single quote "'" for atoms, belong in pairs. The composite brackets "/*" and "*/" surround comments. Ensure that there are neither too few or too many of each kind of bracket.

- Beware of mis-spelled words, especially the names of built-in predicates. These can cause unexpected failures, because mis-spelled predicates are unlikely to match with any clauses in the database. Or, they may unexpectedly match with clauses that happen to have the same name as the mis-spelled one.

- Operators are another source of possible errors. Use round brackets when in doubt, to make the associativity of an operator explicit. Use display to experiment with the operators you have defined.

When considering the list notation, test yourself on the following questions and answers:

- How do [a,b,c] and [X|Y] match? *(X is instantiated to a, and Y is instantiated to [b,c]).*

- Do [a] and [X|Y] match? *(Yes. X is instantiated to a, and Y is instantiated to [ ]).*

- Do [ ] and [X|Y] match? *(no).*

- Is [X,Y|Z] meaningful? *(yes).*

- Is [X|Y,Z] meaningful? *(no).*

- Is [X|[Y|Z]] meaningful? *(Yes, it is the same as [X,Y|Z]).*

- How do [a,b] and [A|B] match? *(A is instantiated to a, and B is instantiated to [b]).*

- Is there more than one way to match them? *(No, never).*

When dealing with lists, or any other structure for that matter, it is important to stress the helpfulness of the "tree diagrams" that we introduced in Chapter 2.

Even if you are certain that a program is free from syntax errors, the program can still exhibit unexpected behaviour when an attempt is made to satisfy goals in the program. Typical symptoms are a program which seems to run without stopping (an "infinite loop"), the response **no** appearing unexpectedly, or variables being instantiated to unexpected terms. Usual sources of such errors are:

- Circular definitions, which were mentioned in Chapter 3.

- Not enough boundary conditions, or some other underspecification of the problem.

- Useless procedures that redefine built-in predicates.

- Supplying the wrong number of arguments to a functor. This is not considered a syntax problem because the number of arguments of a functor depends on what the functor is used for.

- Unexpectedly reaching the end of a file when using the read predicate.

One particularly insidious type of error is demonstrated by the following program to test list equality:

```
eq([],[]).
eq([X|L],M) :- del(X,M,N), eq(L,N),

del(X,[X|Y],Y).
del(X,[Y|L1],[Y|L2]) :- del(X,L1,L2).
```

Do you see the mistake? The second clause of eq is terminated by a comma. Although this is probably a typing error, the above program has *legal syntax* because the term following the comma is taken as the next goal! The above program is *identical* to the following program, which is certainly not a program to test list equality:

```
eq([],[]).
eq([X|L],M) :- del(X,M,N), eq(L,N), del(X,[X|Y],Y).

del(X,[Y|L1],[Y|L2]) :- del(X,L1,L2).
```

A variation on this theme is the following:

```
eq([],[]).
eq([X|L],M) :- del(X,M,N). eq(L,N).

del(X,[X|Y],Y).
del(X,[Y|L1],[Y|L2]) :- del(X,L1,L2).
```

Do you see the mistake? The second clause of eq has its goals separated by a dot. Again, this is likely to be a typing error, but the program as typed above has legal syntax, and is identical to the following, which again is not what was intended:

```
eq([],[]).
eq([X|L],M) :- del(X,M,N).
eq(L,N).

del(X,[X|Y],Y).
del(X,[Y|L1],[Y|L2]) :- del(X,L1,L2).
```

Beware of the following fallacies about the nature of backtracking:

Fallacy: One of the reasons for backtracking is so that Prolog can return to a previous match and do it again in some other way. *Fact:* When Prolog searches the database in an attempt to match a goal against something in the database (a fact or the head of a rule), the match either succeeds or fails. Prolog does not backtrack to a "match" and try to match another way, because there is only one way to match a particular goal with a particular clause in the database.

Fallacy: The list notation [X|Y] can match against any segment of a list, and can take apart lists in several different ways. The behaviour of append(X,Y,[a,b,c,d]) is due to this. *Fact:* In [X|Y], X matches only the head of a list, and Y matches only the tail. The append goals are able to find different partitions of lists because of backtracking, not because of matching.

8.3 The Tracing Model

There are various ways of looking at the method by which Prolog attempts to satisfy goals. We have introduced a model in terms of the "flow of satisfaction" through boxes representing goals. Here we present the model of Prolog execution used by a number of debugging aids, such as the trace facility. This model is largely due to our colleague Lawrence Byrd. You should be familiar with this model before you start to use the Prolog debugging facilities.

When the trace facility is used, the Prolog system prints out information about the sequence of goals in order to show where the program has reached in its execution. However, in order to understand what is happening, it is important to understand when and why the goals are printed. In a conventional programming language, the key points of interest are the entries to and exits from functions. But Prolog permits non-deterministic programs to be written, and this introduces the complexities of backtracking. Not only are clauses entered and exited, but backtracking can suddenly reactivate them in order to generate an alternative solution. Furthermore, the cut goal "!" indicates which goals are committed to having only one solution. One of the major confusions that novice programmers face is what actually occurs when a goal fails and the system suddenly starts backtracking. We hope this has been adequately explained in the previous chapters. However, the previous chapters discussed not only control flow, but also how variables are instantiated, how goals match against clause heads in the database, and how subgoals are satisfied. The tracing model describes the execution of Prolog programs in terms of four kinds of *events* that occur:

CALL. A CALL event occurs when Prolog starts trying to satisfy a goal. In our diagrams, this is when an arrow enters a box from the top.

EXIT. An EXIT event occurs when some goal has just been satisfied. In our diagrams, this is when the arrow emerges from the bottom of a box.

REDO. A REDO event occurs when the system comes back to a goal, trying to re-satisfy it. In our diagrams, this is when the arrow retreats back into a box from the bottom.

FAIL. A FAIL event occurs when a goal fails. If our diagrams, this is when the arrow retreats upwards out of a box.

The debugging aids tell us about when events of these four kinds occur in the execution of our programs. These events will take place for all of the various goals that Prolog considers during the execution. So that we can distinguish which events are happening to which goals, each goal is given a unique integer identifier, its *invocation number*. Below we shall show some goals together with their invocation numbers in square brackets.

Let us now take a look at an example. Consider the following definition of the predicate descendant:

```
descendant(X,Y) :- offspring(X,Y).
descendant(X,Z) :- offspring(X,Y), descendant(Y,Z).
```

This piece of program derives descendants of a person, provided that there are offspring facts in the database, such as

```
offspring(abraham,ishmael).
offspring(abraham,isaac).
offspring(isaac,esau).
```

The first clause of descendant states that Y is a descendant of X if Y is an offspring of X, and the second clause states that Z is a descendant X if Y is an offspring of X and if Z is a descendant of Y. We shall consider the question:

```
?- descendant(abraham,Answer), fail.
```

and we shall follow the control flow to see when the various kinds of events occur. It is important that you try to follow the trace we are about to look at by thinking about the flow of satisfaction entering and leaving the boxes for the goals. We will periodically display the current state in diagram form.

The first goal in the question is followed by a fail. This purpose of this is to force all possible backtracking behaviour out of the descendant goal. The question as a whole can therefore never succeed. However, the point of this trace is to observe the execution flow induced by the failure of the second goal (the fail). We begin with (as yet unentered) boxes for the two goals:

```
descendant(abraham,Answer)
```

```
fail
```

The first event is that the descendant goal is CALLed. This is invocation number 1 (shown in square brackets).

```
[1] CALL: descendant(abraham,Answer)
[2] CALL: offspring(abraham,Answer)
```

We have matched the first clause of the descendant procedure and this results in a CALL of a goal for offspring. The situation is now as follows, with the arrow moving downwards:

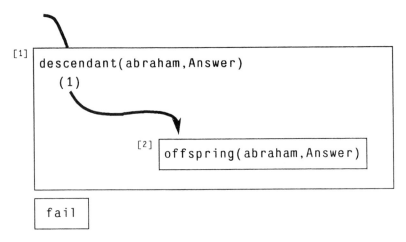

We continue:

    [2] EXIT: offspring(abraham,ishmael)

Immediate success on the first clause, and so the goal EXITs.

    [1] EXIT: descendant(abraham,ishmael)

And thus we have satisfied the first descendant clause.

    [3] CALL: fail
    [3] FAIL: fail
    [1] REDO: descendant(abraham,ishmael)

Then we try to satisfy fail, and, as might be expected, this goal FAILs. The arrow retreats back out of the fail box and back into the descendant box above. Here is a picture of where we are now. The arrow is moving upwards.

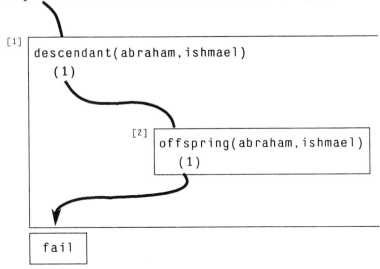

Continuing:

```
[2] REDO: offspring(abraham,ishmael)
[2] EXIT: offspring(abraham,isaac)
```

An alternative clause is chosen for the offspring goal, and so the arrow can move down out of this box again.

```
[1] EXIT: descendant(abraham,isaac)
[4] CALL: fail
[4] FAIL: fail
[1] REDO: descendant(abraham,isaac)
```

Again, fail causes us to reject this solution and to start backtracking. Notice that this was a completely new invocation of fail (we entered it afresh from the "top").

```
[2] REDO: offspring(abraham,isaac)
[2] FAIL: offspring(abraham,Answer)
```

This time, offspring cannot offer us another match and so we continue backtracking, the arrow retreating upwards out of the offspring box.

```
[5] CALL: offspring(abraham,Y)
```

What has happened here is that we have chosen the second descendant clause and this is a completely new offspring invocation corresponding to the first subgoal:

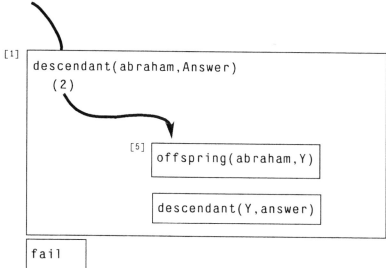

The arrow is now moving downwards again. Continuing:

```
[5] EXIT: offspring(abraham,ishmael)
[6] CALL: descendant(ishmael,Answer)
```

This provides a solution with which we now recursively call descendant.
This gives us a new invocation of descendant.

```
[7] CALL: offspring(ishmael,Answer)
[7] FAIL: offspring(ishmael,Answer)
[8] CALL: offspring(ishmael,Y2)
[8] FAIL: offspring(ishmael,Y2)
[6] FAIL: descendant(ishmael,Answer)
```

Ishmael has no offspring (in this example), and so the offspring subgoals
in both descendant clauses fail, thus failing the descendant goal.

```
[5] REDO: offspring(abraham,ishmael)
```

Back we go for an alternative.

```
[5] EXIT: offspring(abraham,isaac)
[9] CALL: descendant(isaac,Answer)
[10] CALL: offspring(isaac,Answer)
[10] EXIT: offspring(isaac,esau)
```

We get a new invocation of descendant and the offspring subgoal
succeeds:

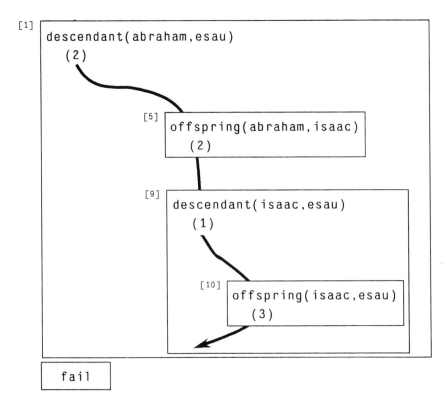

Continuing:

```
[9]  EXIT:  descendant(isaac,esau)
[1]  EXIT:  descendant(abraham,esau)
[11] CALL:  fail
[11] FAIL:  fail
[1]  REDO:  descendant(abraham,esau)
[9]  REDO:  descendant(isaac,esau)
```

This provides a final solution to the initial question, but the fail forces backtracking again and so back we come along the REDO paths.

```
[10] REDO:  offspring(isaac,esau)
[10] EXIT:  offspring(isaac,jacob)
[9]  EXIT:  descendant(isaac,jacob)
[1]  EXIT:  descendant(abraham,jacob)
```

The offspring subgoal has another alternative which produces another result for the initial descendant goal. As can be seen, this is Abraham's last possible descendant, however there is a certain amount of work left to be done. Let us continue to follow the control flow as it backtracks unsuccessfully back to the beginning.

```
[12] CALL:  fail
[12] FAIL:  fail
[1]  REDO:  descendant(abraham,jacob)
[9]  REDO:  descendant(isaac,jacob)
[10] REDO:  offspring(isaac,jacob)
[10] FAIL:  offspring(isaac,Answer)
[13] CALL:  offspring(isaac,Y3)
```

We are now trying the second clause for descendant.

```
[13] EXIT:  offspring(isaac,esau)
[14] CALL:  descendant(esau,Answer)
```

Recur again.

```
[15] CALL:  offspring(esau,Answer)
[15] FAIL:  offspring(esau,Answer)
[16] CALL:  offspring(esau,Y4)
[16] FAIL:  offspring(esau,Y4)
[14] FAIL:  descendant(esau,Answer)
[13] REDO:  offspring(isaac,esau)
[13] EXIT:  offspring(isaac,jacob)
[17] CALL:  descendant(jacob,Answer)
```

Try jacob.

```
[18] CALL: offspring(jacob,Answer)
[18] FAIL: offspring(jacob,Answer)
[19] CALL: offspring(jacob,Y5)
[19] FAIL: offspring(jacob,Y5)
[17] FAIL: descendant(jacob,Answer)
[13] REDO: offspring(isaac,jacob)
[13] FAIL: offspring(isaac,Y3)
[9] FAIL: descendant(isaac,Answer)
[1] FAIL: descendant(abraham,Answer)
```

no

And that's the end of that. We hope that this exhaustive example has provided an understanding of the control flow involved in the execution of a Prolog program. You should have noticed that for any goal there is always only one CALL and FAIL, although there may be arbitrarily many REDOs and corresponding EXITs. In the next section, we look at the trace messages for a more complicated example: append.

Exercise 8.1: In the above model, no mention is made of how the cut goal "!" is handled. Extend the model to account for the action of cut.

8.4 Tracing and Spy Points

When you find that your program doesn't work (because it generates an error, just says "no" or produces the wrong answer), you will want to find out quickly where the mistakes are so that you can correct them. This section describes a set of built-in predicates that allow you to "watch" your program running. Using these, you can give your program the same task again, and watch to see where it starts going wrong. What you will see is when the various events of the tracing model take place, as we saw with descendant in the last section. The exact facilities that the debugging predicates provide will depend on the particular Prolog implementation, but the following should give some guide about the sorts of options, so that you can make sense of what your system provides. In any case, you are strongly advised to consult the documentation for your Prolog system before you start using these facilities.

The basic principle behind tracing and spy points is that the programmer is informed about the satisfaction of certain goals that arise in the running of his program. The programmer can decide, first, what goals he wishes to be informed about, and second, how much he wants to interact with their satisfaction. The first decision involves deciding what combination of exhaustive tracing and spy points he will use. Basically, exhaustive tracing involves information being given about *all* goals, and spy points enable the programmer to get only information about certain predicates that he has specified. However, these options can be mixed in various ways. Section 6.13 outlines the relevant built-in predicates that are of use here. To set a spy point on a predicate, we use predicate spy (and to remove a spy point, we use nospy). To start exhaustive tracing, we use trace (and to turn it off, we use notrace).

The second decision involves deciding on the level of *leashing* that is to be used. In unleashed tracing, information about the goals is displayed on the terminal and the program keeps on running. In leashed tracing, as well as the information being displayed, the programmer is asked at each point which option to take. It may then be possible to specify changes in the level of tracing, alterations from the normal flow of the program and various other options. Your Prolog system may provide an independent choice of leashed or unleashed tracing for each of the four kinds of events:

- When an attempt is first made to satisfy a goal: when the goal is encountered for the first time (a CALL event),

- When a goal has successfully been satisfied (an EXIT event),

- When an attempt is about to be made to re-satisfy a goal (a REDO event), and

- When a goal is about to fail, because all attempts to re-satisfy it have failed (a FAIL event).

For instance, a reasonable choice would be to specify that CALL and REDO events are leashed and EXIT and FAIL events are unleashed. We gave a more detailed description of these four events in the satisfaction of goals in Section 8.3.

Now let us consider the information that is given to you when an event occurs for a goal you are interested in. First of all, the goal itself is shown, together with an indication of which kind of event has occurred and perhaps an invocation number. If tracing for this event type is unleashed, this is all that is provided. Otherwise, Prolog will also ask you to specify one of a set of options about what should be done next. A session with exhaustive, unleashed tracing would look something like:

```
?- [user].

append([],Y,Y).
append([A|B],C,[A|D]) :- append(B,C,D).
```

```
/* type the end of file character here */

yes
?- append([a],[b],X).

CALL append([a],[b],_43)
CALL append([],[b],_103)
EXIT append([],[b],[b])
EXIT append([a],[b],[a,b])

X = [a,b] ;

REDO append([a],[b],[a,b])
REDO append([],[b],[b])
FAIL append([],[b],_103)
FAIL append([a],[b],_43)

no
?- append(X,Y,[a]).

CALL append(_37,_38,[a])
EXIT append([],[a],[a])

X = [], Y = [a] ;

REDO append([],[a],[a])
CALL append(_93,_38,[])
EXIT append([],[],[])
EXIT append([a],[],[a])

X = [a], Y = [] ;

REDO append([a],[],[a])
REDO append([],[],[])
FAIL append(_93,_38,[])
FAIL append(_37,_38,[a])

no
```

Here, all four events for all goals are being shown on the terminal. However, the programmer is not given any chance to make the program pause at any point, change the amount of tracing half way through, or affect the way it runs in any other way. These facilities are what leashed tracing provides.

Before we go on to discuss leashed tracing, we should make some remarks about how Prolog shows your goals when you are tracing. Now, actually the way your goals are shown by the tracing facilities is not necessarily the same as if they were output using write. This is because you are allowed to provide your own special purpose definitions for showing the goals in your program. You can use this facility to output some of the common structures used in your program in ways that are clearer or more concise than write would normally produce. The way the facility works is as follows. The standard way of printing your goals is actually by using the built-in predicate print, with one argument. Predicate print works as if it is defined as follows:

```
print(X) :- portray(X), !.
print(X) :- write(X).
```

Now, the predicate portray is not a built-in predicate, and so you can provide clauses for it yourself. If your clauses allow the goal portray(X) to be satisfied for one of your goals X, then it will be assumed that that provides all the necessary output. Otherwise, the goal will be output using write instead. So if for some reason you did not want to ever see the third arguments of append goals, you could make sure of this by providing the clause:

```
portray(append(A,B,C)) :-
        write('append('), write(A), write(','),
        write(B), write(','),
        write('<foo>)').
```

Whenever a goal X involving append occurs, this clause will cause the goal portray(X) to succeed, and so it will provide the only output. For a goal involving any other predicate, portray(X) will fail, and X will be output using write. If the above clause was in the database, part of the above example session would look like the following:

```
?- append([a],[b],X).

CALL append([a],[b],<foo>)
CALL append([],[b],<foo>)
EXIT append([],[b],<foo>)
EXIT append([a],[b],<foo>)

X = [a,b] ;

REDO append([a],[b],<foo>)
REDO append([],[b],<foo>)
FAIL append([],[b],<foo>)
FAIL append([a],[b],<foo>)

no
```

Now for a discussion of leashed tracing. If you have specified leashed tracing for events of some type you will be asked to specify what should be done next

when an event of this type occurs. This will look something like the
following at the terminal:

```
?- append([a],[b],X).
```

CALL append([a],[b],_43) ?

The program stops after typing out the "**?**". You are now supposed to reply
by specifying one of a set of possible options. If the option you specify
involves the program continuing as usual, it will then run on as far as the
next leashed event for a predicate being traced, and again ask you, with
something like:

CALL append([],[b],_103) ?

There is likely to be an option to display a list of available options at the
terminal. Here are some of the options that may be available:

8.4.1 Examining the goal.

The first set of options involve looking at the goal in various ways. As we
have seen, the standard is for a goal to be shown using print, which gives
your portray clauses a chance to show things in a special way. However,
you may start to have doubts about the correctness of your portray clauses,
or just want to see a goal written in the normal way for a change. Hence
Prolog will allow you to either write or display the current goal as a
possible option. In this case, the program will not run any further, but you
will be asked for another option that will specify how the program should
continue. A typical interaction might be:

```
?- append([a],[b],X).
```

CALL append([a],[b],<foo>) ? write
CALL append([a],[b],_103) ?

Usually you will only want to use write as an alternative way of looking at
a goal. You might want to use display when the goal involves many
operators, and you have forgotten what their various precedences are. In
such a case, display will enable you to see the nesting of functors
unambiguously.

8.4.2 Examining the Ancestors.

The *ancestors* of a goal are those goals to which its satisfaction will
eventually contribute. In our box diagrams, these are the goals whose boxes
enclose the goal under consideration. Thus every goal has an ancestor which
is one of the goals in the original question, the one that it is helping to
satisfy. Also, whenever a rule is used, each of the goals introduced by the
rule body has as an ancestor the goal that matched the rule head. Let us look

at some examples of ancestors. Consider the following simple program to reverse a list (described in Section 7.5):

```
rev([],[]).
rev([H|T],L) :- rev(T,Z), append(Z,[H],L).

append([],X,X).
append([A|B],C,[A|D]) :- append(B,C,D).
```

If we ask the initial question:

```
?- rev([a,b,c,d],X).
```
                                                                (A)

then, because of the second clause of rev, there will be two subgoals to satisfy. Each of these has the goal in the question as its immediate ancestor. The subgoals are:

```
rev([b,c,d],Z)
```
                                                                (B)
```
append(Z,[a],X)
```
                                                                (C)

Since the second clause will be used again to satisfy (B), again two subgoals will be introduced.

```
rev([c,d],Z1)
```
                                                                (D)
```
append(Z1,[a],Z)
```
                                                                (E)

Each of (D) and (E) has both (A) and (B) as ancestors. Note that goal (C) is not an ancestor of these, because they are only contributing immediately to the satisfaction of (B), which contributes to the satisfaction of (A). Goals (D) and (E) are not contributing in any way to the satisfaction of (C). When the satisfaction of this question has progressed fairly far, a goal of the form:

```
append([c],[b],Y)
```

will appear. At this stage, the goal and its ancestors might be displayed as follows:

```
rev([a,b,c,d],_46)
```
                                                           (Goal A)
```
rev([b,c,d],[d|_50])
```
                                                           (Goal B)
```
append([d,c],[b],[d|_51])
append([c],[b],_52)
```

Before you read any further, you should make sure that you understand why these are all ancestors of the goal, and why there are not any more ancestors. There is one peculiarity with the way the ancestors are shown here, which may be reflected in your Prolog system. There are two possible ways of printing out an ancestor: as it was when an attempt was first made to satisfy it, or as it stands now, with any variables as they are now instantiated. Here we have adopted the second course. When the goal (B) was first encountered, the second argument of rev was uninstantiated. However, that argument is shown with a value in the ancestor list. This is because by now the variable that was in that position has become instantiated. By now we have found out that the first element of the reverse of [b , c , d] is d.

By looking at the ancestors of the current goal, you can get a fair idea what your program is up to, and why is is doing what it is. One of the options that a Prolog system may provide at a leashed event for a goal is for some of the current ancestors to be printed out. So if your program seems to be spending a lot of time somewhere and you suspect that it may be in a loop, a good strategy is to interrupt the execution, turn on full tracing and then take a look at the ancestors to see where you are.

8.4.3 Altering the degree of tracing

Another set of options that may be available at a leashed event concerns changing how much tracing is going on. Some of the more coarse controls that you can exercise are:

- Removing all spy points. This has the same effect as invoking the goal nodebug (Section 6.13).

- Turning exhaustive tracing off. This has the same effect as invoking the goal notrace (Section 6.13).

- Turning exhaustive tracing on. This has the same effect as invoking the goal trace (Section 6.13).

With all of these, your program will subsequently carry on running until it reaches a goal that you wish to trace, given your new conditions. Depending on what version of Prolog you use, more local controls of tracing may be available. These help you quickly to get over bits of the program's execution that are of little interest, so that you can concentrate on where the bugs seem to be. Possible options here are:

- "creep": Carry on with the program, doing exhaustive tracing, until you are prompted again (at the next leashed event).

- "skip": Carry on with the program, and produce no trace messages at all until another event occurs involving the current goal.

- "leap": Carry on with the program, producing no trace messages until either a spy point is reached or an event occurs involving the current goal.

The first of these is what you will want to use if you want to follow the program closely at this point. The second is used when you are not worried about how a certain goal is satisfied, and just want to move on quickly to what happens afterwards. The third is used when there may be a lot of uninteresting work going on in the satisfaction of a goal, but somewhere in the middle a goal that is of interest (which has a spy point) will occur. Hence you want to ignore everything until either that spy point is reached or (if the program is faulty) if the current goal succeeds or fails without ever reaching the spy point. Here is an example of the use of "creep" and "skip". Let us assume that there is a bug in the naïve sort program given in Section 7.7, but that we are confident that our program to generate permutations is all right. If you remember, the definition of sort started as follows:

```
sort(X,Y) :- permutation(X,Y), sorted(Y), !.
```

We can use the "skip" option to avoid having to look at the gory details of how permutation works, and produce a trace that starts as follows:

```
CALL sort([3,6,2,9,20],_45) ? creep
CALL permutation([3,6,2,9,20],_45) ? skip
EXIT permutation([3,6,2,9,20],[3,6,2,9,20]) ? creep
CALL sorted([3,6,2,9,20]) ? creep
CALL sorted(0,[3,6,2,9,20]) ? creep
CALL 0<3 ?
  .
  .
  .
```

8.4.4 Altering the satisfaction of the goal

The following options enable you to alter how your program works. You can use these to repeat things that you want to look at in more detail, avoid choices which you know to be irrelevant and force the program to consider choices that it might not otherwise find. These can greatly speed up debugging, because they mean that you can subject the difficult parts of the program to repeated scrutiny without having to run the whole thing again.

- "retry": If you specify the option "retry" at an event for some goal, Prolog will go back to where it was when it originally CALLed the goal. Everything will be exactly as it was when the goal was first encountered (except for any additions to the database that may have been made). Hence you can look at what happens in the satisfaction of the goal once again. A common technique is to combine the use of the "retry" and "skip" options. If you are not sure whether a bug occurs in the satisfaction of some goal, you can "skip" over its satisfaction to start with. This means that you will not have to wade through lots of output about a goal that is satisfied completely correctly. If there is a bug, and the goal either fails or produces the wrong result, you can afterwards use the "retry" option to go back and look more closely.

- "or": This option is just like the ";" you type in to ask for alternative solutions to a question. If you are at an EXIT for a goal, you can also ask for alternatives. So if you know that the first answer found will not allow the rest of the program to succeed, you can immediately ask for another solution to be found. This means that you will be able to get quicker to the part of the program that has the bug. The alternative would be to have to watch the eventual failure after the first alternative was found.

- "fail": This is mainly to be used at a CALL event for a goal. If you know that the goal is going to fail eventually, and the goal is of no interest to you, you can cause it to fail immediately by using this option.

Here is an example of these various options being used to move around the satisfaction of the question:

```
?- member(X,[a,b,c]), member(X,[d,c,e]).
CALL member(_44,[a,b,c]) ? creep
EXIT member(a,[a,b,c]) ? or
REDO member(a,[a,b,c]) ? creep
CALL member(_44,[b,c]) ? fail
FAIL member(_44,[b,c]) ? creep
FAIL member(_44,[a,b,c]) ? retry
CALL member(_44,[a,b,c]) ? creep
EXIT member(a,[a,b,c]) ? creep
CALL member(a,[d,c,e]) ? fail
FAIL member(a,[d,c,e]) ? creep
REDO member(a,[a,b,c]) ? creep
CALL member(_44,[b,c]) ? creep
EXIT member(b,[b,c]) ? or
REDO member(b,[b,c]) ? creep
CALL member(_44,[c]) ? fail
FAIL member(_44,[c]) ? retry
CALL member(_44,[c]) ? creep
EXIT member(c,[c]) ? creep
EXIT member(c,[b,c]) ? creep
EXIT member(c,[a,b,c]) ? creep
CALL member(c,[d,c,e]) ? creep
CALL member(c,[c,e]) ? creep
EXIT member(c,[c,e]) ? creep
EXIT member(c,[d,c,e]) ? or
REDO member(c,[d,c,e]) ? creep
REDO member(c,[c,e]) ? creep
CALL member(c,[e]) ? creep
CALL member(c,[]) ? creep
FAIL member(c,[]) ? creep
FAIL member(c,[e]) ? creep
```

```
FAIL member(c,[c,e]) ? retry
CALL member(c,[c,e]) ? creep
EXIT member(c,[c,e]) ? creep
EXIT member(c,[d,c,e]) ? creep
```

8.4.5 Other Options

Other options that may be open to you at a leashed event are:

- "break": This causes the current execution to be suspended and a new copy of the Prolog interpreter to be made available to you. You can use this to ask questions about what clauses you have, to set spy points, or anything else that you want. When you exit from the interpreter (by typing the end-of-file character), your previous program will be resumed.

- "abort": This causes all your current running programs to be abandoned, and you get "thrown back" to the Prolog interpreter, ready to give the next question.

- "halt": This causes you to leave Prolog completely. You might want to use this as soon as you discover a bug, because you want to edit a file that contains the bug-ridden program.

8.4.6 Summary

In conclusion then, there are three things to think about when you start to look at your program as it runs:

1. Which goals do you want to look at? If you look at everything (use exhaustive tracing with trace), you may become overwhelmed by the amount of information that appears on your terminal. On the other hand, if you just look at what happens to a few predicates (setting spy points with spy), you may miss where the program is going wrong. The best solution is probably a compromise, with careful use of spy points to narrow down the search, and then exhaustive tracing at the end to isolate the bug.

2. How much do you want to control the program's progress from the terminal? If you have all event types unleashed, you will have no control at all over the program, which will rapidly run past the faulty bits before you can notice and look in more detail. On the other hand, if you have all event types leashed, you will get thoroughly fed up telling the program to keep going at each event.

3. Do you want to provide special output facilities for your goals? This will be useful if some of the goals will contain huge structures of little interest, which will only distract from the arguments that you are really interested in. In this case, you can provide a portray facility that suppresses this information.

8.5 Fixing Bugs

When you have watched your faulty program working and discovered something wrong with it, you will want to fix the bug and try the program again. Assuming that your program is of a reasonable size, you will already have it stored in disc files. At this point, you will need to use an editor program to change what is in those files. There are two possibilities now:

- Your Prolog system may allow you to use an editor and then return to Prolog with exactly the same database as before. You may be able to do this directly, by using an appropriate built-in predicate. Alternatively, Prolog may allow you to save the current state of the database in a special file and then restore it again later. You then save your current state, exit from Prolog, change your program, run Prolog again and restore the previous database state. Having returned to where you were before, but with one or more program files changed, all you need to do is reconsult these files to supersede the old definitions with new ones.

- If your Prolog system does not allow you to return to a previous state after using an editor, after changing your program files you will have to run Prolog and consult all your program files from scratch.

You can make this process easier by having a single file containing commands to Prolog to consult all the files of your program. You can then read in the whole program by just asking Prolog to consult the first file. For instance, if you asked Prolog to consult a file containing:

```
?- [file1,file2,file3].
?- [file4,file5,file6].
```

then as a result each of file1, file2, file3, file4, file5, file6 will be read in.

In some circumstances, the change to your program may seem so minimal that you can enter it from the terminal, by a consult(user) or reconsult(user). However, you should beware of doing this too often. If you are not careful, you will forget all the little changes you have made this way and run across the same bugs when you run your program in a later session. Also, since you will want eventually to incorporate the changes into your program files, it is rather a waste to have to type them in at the terminal as well. So do not be tempted into entering clauses from the terminal by the prospect of getting the program to work quickly.

To show how consult and reconsult can be used to change a program from the terminal, here is a small example session where this is done. The session starts with the programmer having no clauses in the database.

```
?- append([a,b,c,d],[e],X).
no

?- consult(user).
append([A|B],C,[A|D]) :- append(A,C,D).
append([],X,X).
reverse([],[]).
reverse([A|B],C) :- reverse(B,D), append(D,[A],C).
/* the end of file character is typed here */
yes

?- reverse([a,b,c,d,e],X).
no

?- append([a,b,c,d,e],[f],X).
no

?- append([],[a,b,c],X).
X = [a,b,c]
yes

?- reconsult(user).
append([A|B],C,[A|D]) :- append(B,C,D).
/* the end of file character is typed here */
yes

?- reverse([a,b,c,d],X).
no

?- consult(user).
append([],X,X).
/* the end of file character is typed here */
yes

?- reverse([a,b,c,d,e],X).
X = [e,d,c,b,a]
yes
```

In this session, a particularly careless programmer starts by entering clauses for the predicates append and reverse from the terminal. Of course, he could have typed these into a file first and then told Prolog to consult that file, but for an example of this small size that might not have been worthwhile. Unfortunately, there is a mistake in the first clause for append. The goal contains an A where there should be a B. This mistake is revealed when the system cannot answer the append and reverse questions. Somehow, the programmer realises that the definition of append is wrong (in a real session, this would probably happen after use was made of the debugging aids). So he decides to supersede his existing definition with a new one, using reconsult. Unfortunately, in the new definition, he forgets to specify the boundary condition (the [ ] case). So the program still does not work. At this point, the original two-clause definition of append has been replaced by a new one-clause definition, which is not complete. The programmer sees what he has done, and can rectify the situation by simply adding a new clause to the existing definition. This is achieved with another use of consult. The program now works.

In conclusion, when you are making changes to a program, exercise the same care that you take when you write the first version of a program. Make sure that what you add is still compatible with your conventions about which variables should be instantiated when and what arguments are used for what purposes. Above all, take the opportunity to look over the program again: there may be some other mistakes in it!

Chapter 9
Using Prolog Grammar Rules

9.1 The Parsing Problem

Sentences in a language such as English are much more than just arbitrary sequences of words. We cannot string together any set of words and make a reasonable sentence. At the very least, the result must conform to what we consider to be grammatical.

A grammar for a language is a set of rules for specifying what sequences of words are acceptable as sentences of that language. It specifies how the words must group together into phrases and what orderings of these phrases are allowed. Given a grammar for a language, we can look at any sequence of words and see whether it meets the criteria for being an acceptable sentence. If the sequence is indeed acceptable, the process of verifying this will have established what the natural groups of words are and how they are put together. That is, it will have established something of the underlying structure of the sentence.

A particularly simple kind of grammar is known as a "context free" grammar. Rather than give a formal definition of what such a thing is, we will illustrate it by means of a simple example. The following might be the start of a grammar of English sentences:

```
sentence --> noun_phrase, verb_phrase.

noun_phrase --> determiner, noun.

verb_phrase --> verb, noun_phrase.
verb_phrase --> verb.

determiner --> [the].

noun --> [apple].
noun --> [man].

verb --> [eats].
verb --> [sings].
```

The grammar consists of a set of rules, here shown one to a line. Each rule specifies a form that a certain kind of phrase can take. The first rule says that a sentence consists of a phrase called a noun_phrase followed by a phrase called a verb_phrase. These two phrases are what are commonly known as the subject and predicate of the sentence:

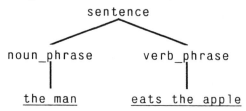

To see what a rule in a context free grammar means, read "X --> Y" as saying "X can take the form Y", and read "X, Y" as saying "X followed by Y." Thus, the first rule can be read as:

A sentence can take the form: a noun_phrase followed by a verb_phrase.

This is all very well, but what is a noun_phrase and what is a verb_phrase? How are we to recognise such things and to know what constitute grammatical forms for them? The second, third and fourth rules of the grammar go on to answer these questions. For instance,

A noun_phrase can take the form: a determiner followed by a noun.

Informally, a noun phrase is a group of words that names a thing (or things). Such a phrase contains a word, the "noun", which gives the main class that the thing belongs to. Thus "the man" names a man, "the program" names a program and so on. Also, according to this grammar, the noun is preceded by a phrase called a "determiner":

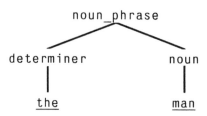

Similarly, the internal structure for a verb_phrase is described by the rules. Notice that there are two rules for what a verb_phrase is. This is because there are two possible forms. A verb_phrase can contain a noun_phrase, as in "the man eats the apple", or it need not, as in "the man sings."

What are the other rules in the grammar for? These express how some phrases can be made up in terms of actual words, rather than in terms of smaller phrases. The things inside square brackets name actual words of the language, so that the rule:

```
determiner --> [the].
```

can be read as:

> A determiner can take the form: the word the.

Now that we have got through the whole of the grammar, we can begin to see what sequences of words are actually grammatical sentences according to it. This is a very simple grammar and needs extending in many ways, especially as it will only accept sentences formed out of five different words. If we wish to investigate whether a given sequence of words is actually a sentence according to these criteria, we need to apply the first rule to ask,

> Does the sequence decompose into two phrases, such that the first is an acceptable noun_phrase and the second is an acceptable verb_phrase?

Then in order to test whether the first phrase is a noun phrase, we need to apply the second rule, asking,

> Does it decompose into a determiner followed by a noun?

and so on. At the end, if we succeed, we will have looked at all the phrases and sub-phrases of the sentence, as specified by the grammar, and will have established a structure like, for instance:

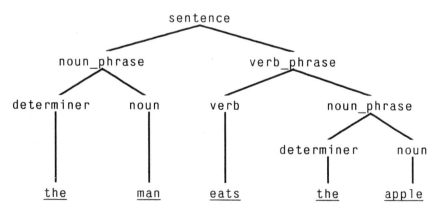

This diagram showing the phrase structure of the sentence is called a *parse tree* for the sentence.

We have seen how having a grammar for a language means that we can construct parse trees to show the structure of sentences of the language. The

problem of constructing a parse tree for a sentence, given a grammar, is what
we call the *parsing problem*. A computer program that constructs parse trees
for sentences of a language we shall call a parser.

This chapter illustrates how the parsing problem can be formulated in
Prolog, and introduces the Prolog grammar rule formalism, which makes it
rather more convenient to write parsers in Prolog. The ideas are not
confined to applications concerned with the syntax of natural languages.
Indeed, the same techniques apply to any problem where we are presented
with an ordered sequence of items that seem to fall into natural groups and
where the arrangement of these groups can be specified by a set of rules.
However, for the sake of simplicity the rest of the chapter will concentrate on
the problem of parsing English sentences and the generalisation to other
fields will be left to you.

9.2 Representing the Parsing Problem in Prolog

The primary structure that we are talking about in discussing the parsing
problem is the sequence of words whose structure is to be determined. We
expect to be able to isolate subsequences of this structure as being various
phrases accepted by the grammar, and to show in the end that the whole
sequence is acceptable as a phrase of type sentence. Because a standard
way of representing a sequence is as a list, we shall represent the input to the
parser as a Prolog list. What about the representation of the words
themselves? For the moment, there seems to be no point in giving the words
internal structure. All we want to do is compare words with one another.
Hence it seems reasonable to represent them as Prolog atoms.

Let us develop a program to see if a given sequence of words is a sentence
according to the grammar shown above. In order to do this, it will have to
establish the underlying structure of the sentences it is given. We will later
on consider how to develop a program that remembers this structure and
displays it to us, but for now it will be easier if we ignore this extra
complexity. Since the program involves testing to see if something is a
sentence, let us define a predicate sentence. The predicate will only need
one argument, and we will give it a meaning as follows:

> sentence(X) means that:
> > X is a sequence of words forming a grammatical sentence.

So we anticipate asking questions such as:

> ?- sentence([the,man,eats,the,apple]).

This will succeed if "the man eats the apple" is a sentence and fail otherwise.

It is rather unfortunate that we have to specify sentences artificially by giving lists of Prolog atoms. For a more serious application, we would probably want to be able to type English sentences at the terminal in the normal way. In Chapter 5, we saw how a predicate read_in can be defined so that we can convert a sentence typed in to a list of Prolog atoms. We could obviously build this into our parser to allow a more natural means of communication with the program's user. However, we will ignore these "cosmetic" matters for now and concentrate on the real problem of parsing.

What is involved in testing to see whether a sequence of words is a sentence? Well, according to the first rule of the grammar, the task decomposes into finding a noun_phrase at the beginning of the sequence and then finding a verb_phrase in what is left. At the end of this, we should have used up exactly the words of the sequence, no more and no less. Let us introduce the predicates noun_phrase and verb_phrase to express the properties of being a noun phrase or verb phrase, so that:

noun_phrase(X) means that: sequence X is a noun phrase.

Also,

verb_phrase(X) means that: sequence X is a verb phrase.

We can put together a definition of sentence in terms of these predicates. A sequence X is a sentence if it decomposes into two subsequences Y and Z, where Y is a noun_phrase and Z is a verb_phrase. Since we are representing sequences as lists, we already have available the predicate append for decomposing one list into two others. So we can write:

```
sentence(X) :-
     append(Y,Z,X), noun_phrase(Y), verb_phrase(Z).
```

Similarly,

```
noun_phrase(X) :-
     append(Y,Z,X), determiner(Y), noun(Z).

verb_phrase(X) :-
     append(Y,Z,X), verb(Y), noun_phrase(Z).
verb_phrase(X) :- verb(X).
```

Notice that the two rules for verb_phrase give rise to two clauses for our predicate, corresponding to the two ways of verifying that a sequence is a verb_phrase. Finally, we can easily deal with the rules that introduce words:

```
determiner([the]).
```

```
noun([apple]).
noun([man]).

verb([eats]).
verb([sings]).
```

So our program is complete. Indeed, this program will successfully tell us which sequences of words are sentences according to the grammar. However, before we consider the task complete, we should have a look at what actually happens when we ask questions about some example sequences. Consider just the sentence clause:

```
sentence(X) :-
        append(Y,Z,X), noun_phrase(Y), verb_phrase(Z).
```

and a question:

```
?- sentence([the,man,eats,the,apple]).
```

Variable X in the rule will be instantiated (to [the, man, eats, the, apple]), but Y and Z will be uninstantiated, so the goal will generate a possible pair of values for Y and Z such that when Z is appended to Y the result is X. On backtracking, it will generate all the possible pairs, one at a time. The noun_phrase goal will only succeed if the value for Y actually is an acceptable noun_phrase. Otherwise it will fail, and append will have to propose another value. So the flow of control for the first part of the execution will be something like:

1. The goal is sentence([the, man, eats, the, apple]).

2. Decompose the list into two lists Y and Z. The following decompositions are possible:
```
        Y = [],    Z = [the,man,eats,the,apple]
        Y = [the],    Z = [man,eats,the,apple]
        Y = [the,man],    Z = [eats,the,apple]
        Y = [the,man,eats],    Z = [the,apple]
        Y = [the,man,eats,the],    Z = [apple]
        Y = [the,man,eats,the,apple],    Z = []
```

3. Choose a possibility for Y and Z from the above list of possibilities, and see if Y is a noun_phrase. That is, try to satisfy noun_phrase(Y).

4. If Y is a noun_phrase, then succeed (and then look for a verb_phrase). Otherwise, go back to Step 3 and try another possibility.

There seems to be a lot of unnecessary searching in this approach. The goal append(Y,Z,X) generates a large number of solutions, most of which are useless from the point of view of identifying noun phrases. There must be a more directed way of getting to the solution. As our grammar stands, a noun_phrase must have precisely two words in it, and so we might think of using this fact to avoid searching among possible decompositions of the sequence. The trouble is that this state of affairs may not stay true if we change the grammar. Even a small change in the rules for determiner could affect the possible lengths of noun phrases and hence affect the way in which the presence of noun phrases would be tested. In designing the program it would be nice to retain some modularity. If we wish to change one clause, it should not necessarily have ramifications for the whole program.

So, the heuristic about the length of noun phrases is too specific to be built into the program. Nevertheless, we can see it as a specific case of a general principle. If we wish to select a subsequence that is a noun phrase, then we can look at the properties of noun phrases to restrict what kinds of sequences are actually proposed. If the noun phrase definition is liable to change, we cannot do this, unless we hand over the whole responsibility to the noun_phrase clauses. Since it is the noun_phrase clauses that express what the properties of noun phrases are, why not expect them to decide how much of the sequence is to be looked at? Let us require the noun_phrase clauses to decide how much of the sequence is to be consumed, and what is to be left for the verb_phrase definition to work on.

This discussion leads us to consider a new definition for the noun_phrase predicate, this time involving two arguments:

noun_phrase(X,Y) is true if
> there is a noun phrase at the beginning of sequence X
> and the part of the sequence left after the noun phrase is Y.

So we might expect these questions:

```
?- noun_phrase([the,man,saw,the,cat],[saw,the,cat]).
?- noun_phrase([the,apple,sings],[sings]).
```

to succeed. We must now revise the definition of noun_phrase to reflect this change of meaning. In doing this, we must resolve how the sequence taken up by a noun phrase decomposes into a sequence taken up by a determiner followed by a sequence taken up by a noun. We can again delegate the problem of how much of the sequence is taken up to the clauses for the embedded phrases, giving the following:

```
noun_phrase(X,Y) :- determiner(X,Z), noun(Z,Y).
```

So a noun_phrase exists at the beginning of sequence X if we can find a determiner at the front of X, leaving behind Z, and we can then find a noun at the front of Z. The amount of the sequence left behind by the whole noun phrase is the same as that left behind after the noun. Expressed diagramatically:

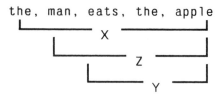

In order for this to work, we will have to adopt a similar convention with determiner and noun as we did with noun_phrase.

This clause tells us how the problem of finding a sequence that is a noun phrase decomposes into finding subsequences that is a determiner followed by one which is a noun. Similarly, the problem of finding a sentence decomposes into finding a noun phrase followed by a verb phrase. This is all very abstract. None of this tells us how many words are actually consumed in the determiner, noun phrase or sentence. The information must be built up from our version of the rules that actually introduce English words. We can again express these as Prolog clauses, but this time we need to add an extra argument, to give for example:

```
determiner([the|X],X).
```

This rule expresses the fact that one can find a determiner at the front of a sequence beginning with the word the. Moreover, the determiner only takes up the first word of the sequence, and leaves the rest behind.

In fact, we can add an extra argument to every predicate that recognises a kind of phrase, to express how that kind of phrase "uses up" some of the words of a sequence and leaves the rest. In particular, for consistency, it would be sensible to do this with the sentence predicate. How does the initial goal that we give to the program look now? We must decide on what two arguments to give to sentence in the question. The arguments indicate the sequence that it starts from and the sequence it is to leave behind. The first of these is obviously the same as the argument we gave to sentence before. Moreover, since we want to find a sentence that occupies the whole of the sequence, we want nothing left after the sentence has been found. We want only the empty sequence to be left. Hence we must give the program a goal like:

```
?- sentence([the,man,eats,the,apple],[]).
```

Let us now see how the complete grammar looks after we have rewritten it with the above discussion in mind:

```
sentence(S0,S) :-
        noun_phrase(S0,S1),
        verb_phrase(S1,S).

noun_phrase(S0,S) :- determiner(S0,S1), noun(S1,S).

verb_phrase(S0,S) :- verb(S0,S).
verb_phrase(S0,S) :- verb(S0,S1), noun_phrase(S1,S).

determiner([the|S],S).

noun([man|S],S).
noun([apple|S],S).

verb([eats|S],S).
verb([sings|S],S).
```

So we now have a more efficient version of our program to recognise
sentences accepted by the grammar. It is a pity, though, that the code looks
more messy than that of the previous version. All the extra arguments seem
to clutter it up unnecessarily. We shall now see how to cope with this
problem.

9.3 The Grammar Rule Notation

The Prolog grammar rule notation was developed as an aid to people writing
parsers using the techniques we have just described. The notation makes the
code easier to read, because it suppresses information that is not interesting.
Because the notation is more concise than ordinary Prolog, there is also less
chance of making silly typing mistakes if you use grammar rules for writing
your parsers.

Although the grammar rule notation is self-contained, it is important to
realise that it is only a shorthand for ordinary Prolog code. You can use
grammar rules either because they are built-in to your Prolog system
already, or because there is a library package that enables you to use a
special form of consult. In either case, the way that the system handles
grammar rules is to recognise them when they are input and then translate
them into ordinary Prolog. So your grammar rules end up as ordinary Prolog
clauses, although naturally looking a bit different from what you typed in.

The actual notation is built around the notation for context-free
grammars that we introduced at the beginning of this chapter. In fact, if the
grammar as presented there (reproduced below) were given to Prolog, it
would be translated into clauses exactly the same as what we ended up with
as the final version of the parsing program:

```
sentence --> noun_phrase, verb_phrase.

noun_phrase --> determiner, noun.
```

```
verb_phrase --> verb.
verb_phrase --> verb, noun_phrase.

determiner --> [the].

noun --> [man].
noun --> [apple].

verb --> [eats].
verb --> [sings].
```

The actual grammar rules are Prolog structures, with main functor "-->", which is declared as an infix operator. All the Prolog system has to do is check whether a term read in (in a consult or similar) has this functor, and if so translate it into a proper clause.

What is involved in this translation? First of all, every atom that names a kind of phrase must be translated into a predicate with two arguments. One argument is for the sequence provided, and the other is for the sequence left behind, as in our program above. Second, whenever a grammar rule mentions phrases coming one after another, it must be arranged that that the arguments reflect the fact that what is left behind by one phrase forms the input to the next. Finally, whenever a grammar rule mentions that a phrase can be realised as a sequence of subphrases, the arguments must express the fact that the amount of words consumed by the whole phrase is the same as the total consumed by the subphrases mentioned on the right of the "-->". These criteria ensure, for instance, that:

```
sentence --> noun_phrase, verb_phrase.
```

translates into:

```
sentence(S0,S) :-
          noun_phrase(S0,S1), verb_phrase(S1,S).
```

or, in English,

> There is a sentence between S0 and S if: there is a noun phrase between S0 and S1, and if there is a verb phrase between S1 and S.

Finally, the system has to know how to translate those rules that introduce actual words. This involves inserting the words into the lists forming the arguments of the predicates, so that, for instance,

```
determiner --> [the].
```

translates into:

```
determiner([the|S],S).
```

Once we have expressed our parsing program as grammar rules, how do we specify the goals that we want it to work at? Since we now know how grammar rules translate into ordinary Prolog, we can express our goals in

Prolog, adding the extra arguments ourselves. The first argument to add is the list of words that is to be looked at, and the second is the list that is going to be left, which is normally the empty list, [ ]. So, we can specify goals such as:

```
?- sentence([the,man,eats,the,apple],[]).
?- noun_phrase([the,man,sings],X).
```

As an alternative, some Prolog implementations provide a built-in predicate phrase which simply adds the extra arguments for you. The predicate phrase is defined by:

phrase(P,L) is true if: list L can be parsed as a phrase of type P.

So we could replace the first of the above goals by the alternative:

```
?- phrase(sentence,[the,man,eats,the,apple]).
```

Note that the definition of phrase involves the whole list being parsed, with the empty list being left. Therefore we could not replace the second goal above by a use of phrase.

If your Prolog implementation does not provide phrase already defined, you can easily provide a clause for it, as follows:

```
phrase(P,L) :- Goal =.. [P,L,[]], call(Goal).
```

Note, however, that this definition will not be adequate when we consider more general grammar rules in the next section.

Exercise 9.1: You may wish to define in Prolog a procedure translate, such that translate(X,Y) is true if X is a grammar rule (of the kind we have encountered in this section) and Y is the term representing the corresponding Prolog clause. This is quite a hard exercise. Procedures that are much like translate are provided by the Prolog system, either built-in or as library programs, but it may help you to understand what translation process is involved if you actually write translate.

9.4 Adding Extra Arguments

The grammar rules we have considered so far are only of a fairly restricted kind. In this section we will consider one useful extension, which allows phrase types to have extra arguments. This "extension" is still part of the standard grammar rule facility that Prolog provides.

We have seen how an occurrence of a phrase type in a grammar rule translates to the use of a Prolog predicate with two extra arguments. So the rules we have seen so far give rise to a lot of two-argument predicates. Now Prolog predicates can have any number of arguments, and we may sometimes want to have extra arguments used in our parsers, apart from the ones dealing with the consumption of the input sequence. The grammar rule notation supports this.

Let us look at an example where extra arguments may be useful. Consider the problem of "number agreement" between the subject and verb of a sentence. Sequences like

★ The boys eats the apple.
★ The boy eat the apple.

are not grammatical English sentences, even though they might be allowed by a simple extension of our grammar (the "★" is a convention used to denote an ungrammatical sentence). The reason they are not grammatical is that if the subject of a sentence is singular then the sentence must also use the singular form of the verb. Similarly, if the subject is plural, the plural form of the verb must be used. We could express this in grammar rules by saying that there are two kinds of sentences, singular sentences and plural sentences. A singular sentence must start with a singular noun phrase, which must have a singular noun, and so on. We would end up with a set of rules like the following:

```
sentence --> singular_sentence.
sentence --> plural_sentence.

noun_phrase --> singular_noun_phrase.
noun_phrase --> plural_noun_phrase.

singular_sentence -->
    singular_noun_phrase, singular_verb_phrase.

singular_noun_phrase -->
    singular_determiner, singular_noun.

singular_verb_phrase --> singular_verb, noun_phrase.
singular_verb_phrase --> singular_verb.

singular_determiner --> [the].

singular_noun --> [boy].

singular_verb --> [eats].
```

and also a whole lot of rules for plural phrases. This is not very elegant, and obscures the fact that singular and plural sentences have a lot of structure in common. A better way is to associate an extra argument with phrase types, according to whether they are singular or plural. Thus sentence(singular) names a phrase which is a singular sentence and, in general, sentence(X) a sentence of plurality X. The rules about number agreement then amount to consistency conditions on the values of these arguments. The plurality of the subject noun phrase must be the same as that of the verb phrase, and so on. Rewriting the grammar in this way, we get:

```
sentence --> sentence(X).

sentence(X) --> noun_phrase(X), verb_phrase(X).

noun_phrase(X) --> determiner(X), noun(X).

verb_phrase(X) --> verb(X).
verb_phrase(X) --> verb(X), noun_phrase(Y).

noun(singular) --> [boy].
noun(plural) --> [boys].

determiner(_) --> [the].

verb(singular) --> [eats].
verb(plural) --> [eat].
```

Note the way in which we can specify the plurality of the. This word could introduce a singular or a plural phrase, and so its plurality is compatible with anything. Also note that in the second rule for verb_phrase the naming of the variables expresses the fact that the plurality of a verb phrase (the thing that must agree with the subject) is taken from that of the verb, and not that of the object, if there is one.

We can introduce arguments to express other important information as well as number agreement. For instance, we can use them to keep a record of constituents that have appeared outside their "normal" position, and hence deal with the phenomena that linguists call "movement". Or we can use them to record items of semantic significance, for example to say how the meaning of a phrase is composed of the meanings of the subphrases. We will not investigate these any more here, although Section 9.6 gives a simple example of incorporating semantics into the parser. However, one point should be noted here. Linguists may be interested to know that once we introduce extra arguments into grammar rules, we cannot guarantee that the language defined by the grammar is still context-free, although it often will be.

An important use of extra arguments is to return a parse tree as a result of the analysis. In Chapter 3 we saw how trees can be represented as Prolog structures, and we will now make use of that in extending the parser to make a parse tree. Parse trees are helpful because they provide a structural representation of a sentence. It is convenient to write programs that process this structural representation in a way analogous to processing the arithmetic formulae and lists in Chapter 7. The new program, given a grammatical sentence like:

```
The man eats the apple.
```

will generate a structure like this:

```
sentence(
```

```
noun_phrase(
            determiner(the),
            noun(man)),
verb_phrase(
            verb(eats),
            noun_phrase(
                        determiner(the),
                        noun(apple))
            )
)
```

as a result. In order to make it do this, we only need to add an extra argument to each predicate, saying how the tree for a whole phrase is constructed from the trees of the various sub-phrases. Thus we can change the first rule to:

```
sentence(X,sentence(NP,VP))  -->
     noun_phrase(X,NP), verb_phrase(X,VP).
```

This says that if we can find a sequence constituting a noun phrase, with parse tree NP, followed by a sequence constituting a verb phrase, with parse tree VP, then we have found a sequence constituting a complete sentence, and the parse tree for that sentence is sentence(NP,VP). Or, in more procedural terms, to parse a sentence one must find a noun phrase followed by a verb phrase, and then combine the parse trees of these two constituents, using the functor sentence to make the tree for the sentence.

It is only coincidental that we have named the grammar rule sentence as well as the sentence node of the parse tree. We could have used, say, s to name the parse tree node instead. Note that the X arguments are just the number agreement arguments used earlier, and that the decision to put the tree generating arguments after rather then before them was arbitrary. If you have any difficulty understanding this extension, it helps to see that this is all just a shorthand for an ordinary Prolog clause:

```
sentence(X,sentence(NP,VP),S0,S)  :-
     noun_phrase(X,NP,S0,S1),
     verb_phrase(X,VP,S1,S).
```

where S0, S1 and S stand for parts of the input sequence. We can introduce tree-building arguments throughout the grammar in a routine way. Here is an excerpt from what is produced if we do this (number agreement arguments being left out for clarity):

```
sentence(sentence(NP,VP))  -->
     noun_phrase(NP), verb_phrase(VP).

verb_phrase(verb_phrase(V))  --> verb(V).
```

```
noun(noun(man)) --> [man].
verb(verb(eats)) --> [eats].
```

The translation mechanism needed to deal with grammar rules with extra arguments is a simple extension of the one described before. Previously a new predicate was created for each phrase type, with two arguments to express how the input sequence was consumed. Now it is necessary to create a predicate with two more arguments than are mentioned in the grammar rules. By convention, these two extra arguments are added as the last arguments of the predicate (although this may vary between Prolog systems). Thus the grammar rule:

```
sentence(X) --> noun_phrase(X), verb_phrase(X).
```

translates into:

```
sentence(X,S0,S) -->
        noun_phrase(X,S0,S1), verb_phrase(X,S1,S).
```

When we want to invoke goals involving grammar rules from the top level of the interpreter or from ordinary Prolog rules, we must explicitly add the extra arguments. Thus appropriate goals involving this definition of sentence would be:

```
?- sentence(X,[a,clergyman,eats,a,cake],[]).
?- sentence(X,[every,bird,sings,and,pigs,can,fly],L).
```

Exercise 9.2: Write a new version of phrase that allows grammar rules with extra arguments, so that one can provide goals such as:

```
?- phrase(sentence(X),[the,man,sings]).
```


9.5 Adding Extra Tests

So far in our parser, everything mentioned in the grammar rules has had to do with how the input sequence is consumed. Every item in the rules has had something to do with those two extra argument positions that are added by the grammar rule translator. So every goal in the resulting Prolog clause has been involved with consuming some amount of the input. Sometimes we may want to specify Prolog goals that are not of this type, and the grammar rule formalism allows us to do this. The convention is that any goals enclosed inside curly brackets {} are to be left unchanged by the translator.

Let us look at some examples of where it would be beneficial to use this facility, in improving the "dictionary" of the parser, that is, the parser's knowledge about words of the language. First, consider the overhead involved in introducing a new word into the program with both sets of extra arguments. If we wished to add the new noun banana, for instance, we would have to add at least the rule:

```
noun(singular,noun(banana)) --> [banana].
```

which amounts to:

```
noun(singular,noun(banana),[banana|S],S).
```

in ordinary Prolog. This is a lot of information to specify for each noun, especially when we know that every noun will only occupy one element of the input list and will give rise to a small tree with the functor noun. A much more economical way would be to express the common information about all nouns in one place and the information about particular words somewhere else. We can do this by mixing grammar rules with ordinary Prolog. We express the general information about how nouns fit into larger phrases by a grammar rule, and then the information about what words are nouns in ordinary clauses. The solution that results looks like:

```
noun(S,noun(N)) --> [N], {is_noun(N,S)}.
```

where the normal predicate is_noun expresses which words are nouns and whether they are singular or plural:

```
is_noun(banana,singular).
is_noun(bananas,plural).
is_noun(man,singular).
```

Let us look carefully at what this grammar rule means. It says that a phrase of type noun can take the form of any single word N (a variable is specified in the list) subject to a restriction. The restriction is that N must be in our is_noun collection, with some plurality S. In this case, the plurality of the phrase is also S, and the parse tree produced consists just of the word N underneath the node noun. Why does the goal is_noun(N,S) have to be put inside curly brackets? Because it expresses a relationship that has nothing to do with the input sequence. If we were to leave out the curly brackets, it would be translated to something like is_noun(N,S,S1,S2), which would never match our clauses for is_noun. Putting it inside the curly brackets stops the translation mechanism from changing it, so that our rule will be correctly translated to:

```
noun(S,noun(N),[N|Seq],Seq) :- is_noun(N,S).
```

In spite of this change, our treatment of individual words is still not very elegant. The trouble with this technique is that we will have to have to write two is_noun clauses for every new noun that is introduced — one for the singular form, and one for the plural form. This is unnecessary, because for most nouns the singular and plural forms are related by a simple rule:

> If X is the singular form of a noun, then the word formed by adding an "s" on the end of X is the plural form of that noun.

We can use this rule about the form of nouns to revise our definition of noun. The revisions will give a new set of conditions that the word N must satisfy in order to be a noun. Because these conditions are about the internal structure of the word, and do not have anything to do with the consumption of the input sequence, they will appear within curly brackets. We are representing English words as Prolog atoms, and so considerations about how words decompose into letters translate into considerations about the characters that go to make up the appropriate atoms. So we will need to use the predicate name in our definition. The amended rule looks as follows:

```
noun(plural,noun(RootN)) -->
     [N],
     {(name(N,Plname),
     append(Singname,"s",Plname),
     name(RootN,Singname),
     is_noun(RootN,singular))} .
```

Of course, this expresses a general rule about plurals that is not always true (for instance, the plural of "fly" is not "flys"). We will still have to express the exceptions in an exhaustive way. Notice that the double-quote notation is used to represent the character "s" as a member of a list. We need now only specify is_noun clauses for the singular forms of regular nouns. Note that under the above definition the item inserted into the parse tree will be the "root" noun, rather than the inflected form. This may be useful for subsequent processing of the tree. Note also the syntax of curly brackets. This may differ slightly between different Prolog implementations, but the safest thing is to surround multiple goals inside curly brackets with an extra pair of round brackets and to leave a space between any curly bracket and the final ".".

In addition to knowing about curly brackets, most Prolog grammar rule translators will know about certain other goals that are not to be translated normally. Thus it is not normally necessary to enclose "!"s or disjunctions (";") of goals involving the input sequence inside curly brackets.

9.6 Summary

We shall now summarise the syntax of grammar rules as described so far. We shall then indicate some of the possible extensions to the basic system and some of the interesting ways that grammar rules can be used. The best way to describe the syntax of grammar rules is by grammar rules themselves. So here is an informal definition. Note that it is not completely rigorous, because it neglects the influence of operator precedences on the syntax.

```
grammar_rule --> grammar_head, ['-->'], grammar_body.
grammar_head --> non_terminal.
grammar_head --> non_terminal, [','], terminal.
```

```
grammar_body --> grammar_body, [','], grammar_body.
grammar_body --> grammar_body, [';'], grammar_body.
grammar_body --> grammar_body_item.

grammar_body_item --> ['!'].
grammar_body_item --> ['{'], prolog_goals, ['}'].
grammar_body_item --> non_terminal.
grammar_body_item --> terminal.
```

This leaves several items undefined. Here are definitions of them in English. A non_terminal indicates a kind of phrase that may occupy part of the input sequence. It takes the form of a Prolog structure, where the functor names the category of the phrase and the arguments give extra information, like the number class, the meaning, etc. A terminal indicates a number of words that may occupy part of the input sequence. It takes the form of a Prolog list (which may be [ ] or a list of any determinate length). The items of the list are Prolog items that are to match against the words as they appear in the order given. prolog_goals are any Prolog goals. They can be used to express extra tests and actions that constrain the possible analysis paths taken and indicate how complex results are built up from simpler ones.

When translated into Prolog, prolog_goals are left unchanged and non_terminals have two extra arguments inserted after the ones that appear explicitly, corresponding to the sequence provided to and the sequence left behind by the phrase. The terminals appear within the extra arguments of the non_terminals. When a predicate defined by grammar rules is invoked at the top level of the interpreter or by an ordinary Prolog rule, the two extra arguments must be provided explicitly.

The second rule for grammar_head in the above mentions a kind of grammar rule that we have not met before. Up to now, our terminals and non-terminals have only been defined in terms of how they consume the input sequence. Sometimes we might like to define things that insert items into the input sequence (for other rules to find). For instance, we might like to analyse an imperative sentence such as:

Eat your supper.

as if there were an extra word you inserted:

You eat your supper.

It would then have a nice noun phrase/verb phrase structure, which conforms to our existing ideas about the structure of sentences. We can do this by having a grammar that looks in part like:

```
sentence --> imperative, noun_phrase, verb_phrase.

imperative, [you] --> [].
imperative --> [].
```

There is only one rule here that deserves mention. The first rule for imperative actually translates to:

```
imperative(L,[you|L]).
```

So this involves a sequence being returned that is longer than the one originally provided. In general, the left-hand side of a grammar rule can consist of a non-terminal separated from a list of words by a comma. The meaning of this is that in the parsing, the words are inserted into the input sequence after the goals on the right-hand side have had their chance to consume words from it.

Exercise 9.3: The definition given for grammar rules, even if made complete, would not constitute a useful parser, given a sequence of tokens as its input. Why?

Finally, we present an example (taken from Pereira and Warren's paper in the journal *Artificial Intelligence* Volume 13) of grammar rules used to obtain the meaning of sentences directly, without an intermediate parse tree. The following rules translate from (a restricted number of) English sentences into a representation of their meaning in Predicate Calculus. For a description of Predicate Calculus and our notation for it, the reader is referred to Chapter 10. As an example of the program at work, the meaning obtained for "every man loves a woman" is the structure:

```
all(X,(man(X) -> exists(Y,(woman(Y) & loves(X,Y))))))
```

Here are the grammar rules:

```
?- op(500,xfy,&).
?- op(600,xfy,->).
sentence(P) -->
    noun_phrase(X,P1,P), verb_phrase(X,P1).
noun_phrase(X,P1,P) -->
    determiner(X,P2,P1,P),
    noun(X,P3),
    rel_clause(X,P3,P2).
noun_phrase(X,P,P) --> proper_noun(X).
verb_phrase(X,P) -->
    trans_verb(X,Y,P1), noun_phrase(Y,P1,P).
verb_phrase(X,P) --> intrans_verb(X,P).
rel_clause(X,P1,(P1&P2)) -->
    [that], verb_phrase(X,P2).
rel_clause(_,P,P) --> [].
```

```
determiner(X,P1,P2, all(X,(P1->P2))) --> [every].
determiner(X,P1,P2, exists(X,(P1&P2))) --> [a].

noun(X,man(X)) --> [man].
noun(X,woman(X)) --> [woman].

proper_noun(john) --> [john].

trans_verb(X,Y,loves(X,Y)) --> [loves].

intrans_verb(X,lives(X)) --> [lives].
```

In this program, arguments are used to build up structures representing the meanings of phrases. For each phrase, it is the last argument that actually specifies the meaning of that phrase. However, the meaning of a phrase may depend on several other factors, given in the other arguments. For instance, the verb lives gives rise to a proposition of the form lives(X), where X is something standing for the person who lives. The meaning of lives cannot specify in advance what X will be. The meaning has to be applied to some specific object in order to be useful. The context in which the verb is used will determine what this object is. So the definition just says that, for any X, when the verb is applied to X, the meaning is lives(X). A word like every is much more complicated. In this case, the meaning has to be applied to a variable and two propositions containing that variable. The result is something that says that, if substituting an object for the variable in the first proposition yields something true then substituting that same object for the variable in the second proposition will also yield something true.

Exercise 9.4: Read and understand this program. Try running the program, giving it goals like

```
?- sentence(X,[every,man,loves,a,woman],[]).
```

What meaning does the program generate for the sentence "every man that lives loves a woman", "every man that loves a woman lives"? The sentence "Every man loves a woman" is actually ambiguous. There could either be a single woman that every man loves, or there could be a (possibly) different woman that each man loves. Does the program produce the two possible meanings as alternative solutions? If not, why not? What simple assumption has been made about how the meanings of sentences are built up?

Chapter 10
The Relation of Prolog to Logic

The programming language Prolog was invented by Alain Colmerauer and his associates around 1970. It was a first attempt at the design of a practical programming language that would enable a programmer to specify his tasks in logic, instead of in terms of conventional programming constructs about *what* the machine should do *when*. This motivation explains the name of the programming language, for "Prolog" stands for *Pro*gramming in *Log*ic.

In this book we have emphasised mainly how one can use Prolog as a tool for doing practical tasks, and we have not discussed the ways in which Prolog is a step towards the ultimate goal of a "logic programming" system. In this chapter, we intend to redress this imbalance somewhat by considering briefly how Prolog is related to logic and the extent to which Prolog programming is really like "programming in logic".

10.1 Brief Introduction to Predicate Calculus

If we wish to discuss how Prolog is related to logic, we must first of all establish what we mean by logic. Logic was originally devised as a way of representing the form of arguments, so that it would be possible to check in a formal way whether or not they were valid. Thus we can use logic to express propositions, the relations between propositions and how one can validly *infer* some propositions from others. The particular form of logic that we will be talking about here is called the Predicate Calculus. We will only be able to say a few words about it here. For a good basic introduction to logic, consult *Logic*, by Wilfrid Hodges, published by Penguin Books, 1977. For a more detailed treatment, you can consult *Introduction to Mathematical Logic* by Elliott Mendelson, published in 1964 by Van Nostrand Reinhold, or any of the other books that deal with Symbolic Logic. Another text that may be of interest is *Symbolic Logic and Mechanical Theorem Proving*, by Chin Liang Chang and Richard Char-Tung Lee, published in 1973 by Academic Press.

If we wish to express propositions about the world, we must be able to describe the objects that are involved in them. In Predicate Calculus, we represent objects by *terms*. A term is of one of the following forms:

- A *constant symbol*. This is a symbol that stands for a single individual or concept. We can think of this as a Prolog atom, and we will use the Prolog syntax. So greek, agatha, and peace are constant symbols.

- A *variable symbol*. This is a symbol that we may want to stand for different individuals at different times. Variables are really only introduced in conjunction with quantifiers, which are discussed below. We can think of them as Prolog variables and will use the Prolog syntax. Thus X, Man, and Greek are variable symbols.

- A *compound term*. A compound term consists of a *function symbol*, together with an ordered set of terms as its *arguments*. The idea is that the compound term represents some individual that depends on the individuals represented by the arguments. The function symbol represents how the first depends on the second. For instance, we could have a function symbol standing for the notion of "distance" and two arguments. In this case, the compound term stands for the distance between the objects represented by the arguments. We can think of a compound term as a Prolog structure with the function symbol as the functor. We will write Predicate Calculus compound terms using the Prolog syntax, so that, for instance, wife(henry) might mean Henry's wife, distance(point1,X), might mean the distance between some particular point and some other place to be specified, and classes(mary,dayafter(W)) might mean the classes that Mary teaches on the day after some day W to be specified.

Thus in Predicate Calculus the ways of representing objects are just like the ways available in Prolog.

In order to express propositions about objects we must be able to express relationships between objects. We do this with *predicate symbols*. An *atomic proposition* consists of a predicate symbol, together with an ordered sequence of terms as its arguments. This is just like the kind of thing that can appear as a Prolog goal. So, for example, the following are atomic propositions: human(mary), owns(X,donkey(X)), likes(Man,wine). In Prolog, a structure can serve either as a goal, or as an argument to another structure, or both. This is not the case in Predicate Calculus, where a rigid separation is made between function symbols, which are functors that are used to construct arguments, and predicate symbols, which are functors that are used to construct propositions.

We can make compound propositions from atomic propositions in various ways. It is here that we begin to find things that do not have direct analogues in Prolog. There are several ways in which we can make more complicated propositions out of simpler ones. First, we can use the *logical connectives*. These are ways of expressing the familiar notions "not", "and", "or", "implies" and "is equivalent to". The following table summarises the connectives and their meanings. In this summary, α and β are meant to represent any propositions. We give both the traditional Predicate Calculus syntax and the syntax that we shall use in programs because it is easy to type on an ordinary computer terminal.

Connective	PC Syntax	Our Syntax	Meaning
Negation	$\neg \alpha$	~α	"not α"
Conjunction	$\alpha \wedge \beta$	α & β	"α and β"
Disjunction	$\alpha \vee \beta$	α # β	"α or β"
Implication	$\alpha \supset \beta$	α -> β	"α implies β"
Equivalence	$\alpha \equiv \beta$	α <-> β	"α is equivalent to β"

Thus, for example,

```
man(fred) # woman(fred)
```

could be used to represent the proposition that Fred is a man or Fred is a woman;

```
man(john) -> human(john)
```

might represent the proposition that John's being a man implies his being human (if John is a man then he is human). The notions of implication and equivalence are sometimes a little hard to grasp at first. We say that α implies β if, whenever α is true so is β. We say that α is equivalent to β if α is true in exactly those circumstances when β is true. In fact, these notions can be defined in terms of "and", "or", and "not", for:

α -> β	means the same as	(~α) # β
α <-> β	means the same as	(α & β) # (~α & ~β)
α <-> β	also means the same as	(α -> β) & (β -> α).

So far, we have not made it clear what it means when variables appear inside a proposition. In fact, the meaning is only defined when such variables are introduced by quantifiers. Quantifiers provide a means of talking about sets of individuals and what is true of them. Predicate Calculus provides two quantifiers. If *v* represents any variable and *P* any proposition, we can summarise them as follows:

PC Syntax	Our Syntax	Meaning
$\forall v.P$	all(v,P)	"P is true whatever v stands for"
$\exists v.P$	exists(v,P)	"there is something that v can stand for such that P is true"

The first of these is called the *universal quantifier* because it talks about everything in the Universe ("for all v, . . ."). The second is called the *existential quantifier* because it talks about the existence of some object(s) ("there exists v such that . . ."). As examples of uses of the quantifiers, for instance,

```
all(X, man(X) -> human(X) )
```

means that, whatever X we choose, if X is a man then X is a human. We can read it as, "for all X, if X is a man, then X is human." Or, in English, simply "every man is human." Similarly,

```
exists(Z, father(john,Z) & female(Z) )
```

means that there is something that Z can stand for such that John is the father of Z and Z is female. We can read it as "there exists a Z such that John is the father of Z and Z is female", or in English, simply "John has a daughter". Here are some more complicated Predicate Calculus formulae for your amusement:

```
all(X, animal(X) -> exists(Y,motherof(X,Y)) )
all(X, pcform(X) <-> (atomic(X) # compound(X))) .
```

10.2 Clausal Form

As we saw in the last section, Predicate Calculus formulae expressed in terms of -> (implication) and <-> (equivalence) can be rewritten in terms of & (conjunction), # (disjunction) and ˜ (negation). In fact, there are many more identities of this form, and we would not sacrifice any expressive power if we were to completely avoid using #, ->, <->, and exists(X,P), for instance. As a result of the redundancy, there are many ways of writing down the same proposition. If we wish to carry out formal manipulations on Predicate Calculus formulae, this turns out to be very inconvenient. It is much nicer if everything we want to say can only be expressed in one way. So we will now consider how a Predicate Calculus proposition can be translated into a special form, *clausal form*, where there are fewer ways of saying the same thing. In fact, it will turn out that a Predicate Calculus proposition in clausal form is very much like a set of Prolog clauses. So an

investigation of clausal form is essential for an understanding of the relation
between Prolog and logic.

In Appendix B we give a Prolog program that automatically translates a
Predicate Calculus formula into clausal form. There is one difference
between our discussion here and the actual program in Appendix B. To
make certain manipulations easier, PC variables are represented as atoms
when given as input to the program. Thus, when using the program in
Appendix B to process, for example, the formula

    (person(X) # ~mother(X,Y)) # ~person(Y)   ,

it will be necessary to write this as

    (person(x) # ~mother(x,y)) # ~person(y)   .

The conversion of a Predicate Calculus formula into normal form has six
main stages.

Stage 1. Removing Implications.

We start by replacing occurrences of -> and <-> in accordance with the
definitions given in Section 10.1. As a result of this definition, we would
expect:

    all(X,man(X)->human(X))

to be transformed to:

    all(X, ~man(X) # human(X)) .

Stage 2. Moving negation inwards

This stage is involved with cases where "~" is applied to a formula that is not
atomic. If such a case is detected, an appropriate rewrite is made. Thus, for
instance,

    ~ (human(caesar) & living(caesar))

is transformed to

    ~ human(caesar) # ~ living(caesar)

and

    ~ all(Y,person(Y))

is transformed to:

    exists(Y,~ person(Y)) .

The validity of this stage results from the following identities:

˜(α & β)	means the same as	(˜α) # (˜β)
˜exists(v,P)	means the same as	all(v,˜P)
˜all(v,P)	means the same as	exists(v,˜P)

After Stage 2, negation will only appear in our formulae applied directly to atomic formulae. We call an atomic proposition, or an atomic proposition preceded by a "˜" a *literal*. The next few stages will treat literals as single items, and the significance of which literals are negated will only be important at the end.

Stage 3. Skolemising

The next stage involves removing the existential quantifiers. This is done by introducing new constant symbols, *Skolem constants*, in the place of the variables introduced by the existential quantifiers. Instead of saying that there exists an object with a certain set of properties, one can create a name for one such object and simply say that it has the properties. This is the motivation behind introducing Skolem constants. Skolemising does more damage to the logical properties of a formula than the other transformations we discuss. Nevertheless, it has the following important property. There is an interpretation for the symbols of a formula that makes the formula true if and only if there is an interpretation for the Skolemised version of the formula. For our purposes, this form of equivalence is enough. Thus, for example,

```
exists(X, female(X) & motherof(X,eve) )
```

is changed by Skolemisation to

```
female(g197) & motherof(g197,eve)
```

where g197 is some new constant not used elsewhere. Constant g197 represents some female whose mother is Eve. It is important that we use a different symbol from any used previously, because

```
exists(X, female(X) & motherof(X,eve) )
```

is not saying that some particular person is Eve's daughter, but only that there is such a person. It may turn out that g197 will correspond to the same person as some other constant symbol, but that is extra information that is not conveyed by this proposition.

When there are universal quantifiers in a formula, Skolemisation is not quite so simple. For instance, if we Skolemised

```
all(X, human(X) -> exists(Y,motherof(X,Y)) )
```

("every human has a mother") to

```
all(X, human(X) -> motherof(X,g2) )
```

we would be saying that every human has the *same* mother — the thing denoted by g2. When there are variables introduced by universal quantifiers, Skolemisation must instead introduce function symbols, to express how what exists *depends* on what the variables are chosen to stand for. Thus the above example should Skolemise to

```
all(X, human(X) -> motherof(X,g2(X)) ) .
```

In this case, the function symbol g2 corresponds to the function in the world that, given any person, returns as its value the mother of that person.

Stage 4. Moving universal quantifiers outwards.

This stage is very simple. We just move any universal quantifiers to the outside of the formula. This does not affect the meaning. As an example,

```
all(X, man(X) -> all(Y,woman(Y)->likes(X,Y)) )
```

is transformed to

```
all(X,all(Y, man(X) -> (woman(Y)->likes(X,Y)) )) .
```

Since every variable in the formula is now introduced by a universal quantifier at the outside of the formula, the quantifiers themselves no longer provide any extra information. So we can abbreviate the formula by simply leaving the quantifiers out. We just need to remember that every variable is introduced by an implicit quantifier that we have left out. Thus we can now represent:

```
all(X,alive(X) # dead(X))
  & all(Y,likes(mary,Y) # impure(Y))
```

as:

```
(alive(X) # dead(X)) & (likes(mary,Y) # impure(Y)) .
```

The formula means that, whatever X and Y we choose, either X is alive or X is dead, and either Mary likes Y or Y is impure.

Stage 5. Distributing "&" over "#".

At this stage, our original Predicate Calculus formula has changed a lot. We no longer have any explicit quantifiers, and the only connectives left are & and # (apart from where literals are negated). We now put this in a special normal form, *conjunctive normal form*, where conjunctions no longer appear inside disjunctions. Thus we can convert the whole formula into a bundle of &'s, where the things joined together are either literals or literals joined by #'s. Suppose A, B, and C stand for literals. We can make use of the following identities:

$$(A \ \& \ B) \ \# \ C \qquad \text{is equivalent to} \qquad (A \ \# \ C) \ \& \ (B \ \# \ C)$$
$$(A \ \# \ B) \ \& \ C \qquad \text{is equivalent to} \qquad (A \ \& \ C) \ \# \ (B \ \& \ C)$$

As an example of what happens, the formula:

```
holiday(X) #
          (work(chris,X) & (angry(chris) # sad(chris)))
```

(For every X, either X is a holiday, or, both Chris works on X and Chris is angry or sad) is equivalent to:

```
(holiday(X) # work(chris,X)) &
          (holiday(X) # (angry(chris) # sad(chris)))
```

(For every X, first, X is a holiday or Chris works on X, and second, either X is a holiday or Chris is angry or sad).

Stage 6. Putting into clauses

The formula we have now is in general made up of a collection of &'s relating things which are either literals or composed of literals by #'s. Let us look first at the top level of this, not looking in detail at the #'s. We might have something like:

$$(A \ \& \ B) \ \& \ (C \ \& \ (D \ \& \ E))$$

where the letters stand for complex propositions, but having no &'s in them. Now all this nesting of structure is unnecessary, because all the propositions

$$(A \ \& \ B) \ \& \ (C \ \& \ (D \ \& \ E))$$
$$A \ \& \ ((B \ \& \ C) \ \& \ (D \ \& \ E))$$
$$(A \ \& \ B) \ \& \ ((C \ \& \ D) \ \& \ E)$$

mean the same thing. Although structurally the formulae are different, they have the same meaning. This is because, if I assert that some set of propositions are all true, then it does not matter how I group them together when I do so. It does not matter, for instance, whether I say "A is true, and so are B and C" or "A and B are true, and so is C". So the bracketing is unnecessary to the meaning. We can just say (informally):

$$A \ \& \ B \ \& \ C \ \& \ D \ \& \ E \ .$$

Secondly, the order in which we write these formulae also does not matter. It does not matter whether I say "A is true and so is B" or "B is true and so is A". They both mean the same. Finally, we do not really need to specify the &'s between the formulae, because we know in advance that the top level of the formula is made up with &'s. So, really, we can be much more concise about the import of the formula we are given just by saying that it consists of the *set* $\{A, B, C, D, E\}$. By calling this a set, we are saying that the order does not matter. The set $\{A, B, C, D, E\}$ is exactly the same as $\{B, A, C, E, D\}$, $\{E, D, B, C, A\}$, and so on. The formulae that end up in this set, when we convert a formula to Clausal form, are called *clauses*. So any Predicate Calculus formula is equivalent (in some sense) to a set of clauses.

Let us now look in more detail at what these clauses are actually like. We said that they are made up of literals joined together by disjunctions. So in general, if the letters V through Z stand for literals, a clause will be something like:

```
((V # W) # X) # (Y # Z) .
```

Now we can do the same trick that we played with the top level of the formula. Once again the bracketing is irrelevant to the meaning, and the order is also unimportant. So we can simply say that the clause is the set of literals $\{V, W, X, Y, Z\}$ (implicitly disjoined).

Now our original formula has reached clausal form. Moreover the rules used for this have not altered whether there is an interpretation that makes it true or not. The clausal form consists of a collection of clauses, each of which is a collection of literals. A literal is either an atomic formula or a negated atomic formula. This form is quite concise, since we have left out things like implicit conjunctions, disjunctions and universal quantifiers. We must obviously remember the conventions about where these have been missed out when we look to see what something in clausal form means.

Let us look at some formulae (as they would be produced by Stage 5) to see what they look like in clausal form. First of all, look the example used before:

```
(holiday(X) # work(chris,X)) &
       (holiday(X) # (angry(chris) # sad(chris))) .
```

This gives rise to two clauses. The first contains the literals:

```
holiday(X), work(chris,X)
```

and the second contains the literals:

```
holiday(X), angry(chris), sad(chris)   .
```

As another example, the formula:

```
(person(adam) & person(eve)) &
       ((person(X) # ~mother(X,Y)) # ~person(Y))
```

gives rise to three clauses. Two of them contain one literal each,

```
person(adam)
```

and

```
person(eve)  .
```

The other one has three literals:

```
person(X), ~mother(X,Y), ~person(Y)  .
```


To bring this section to a close, let us just consider one more example, and the various stages as it is translated into clausal form. We start with the formula:

```
all(X, all(Y,person(Y)->respect(Y,X)) -> king(X))
```

which says that, if everybody respects somebody then that person is a king (For every X, if every Y that is a person respects X, then X is a king). When we remove implications (Stage 1) we get:

```
all(X, ~(all(Y,~person(Y) # respects(Y,X))) # king(X))
```

Moving negation inwards (Stage 2) leads us to:

```
all(X, exists(Y,person(Y) & ~respects(Y,X)) # king(X))
```

Next, Skolemising (Stage 3) translates this to:

```
all(X, (person(f1(X)) & ~respects(f1(X),X)) # king(X))
```

where f1 is a Skolem function. Now comes the stage of removing universal quantifiers (Stage 4), which leads to:

```
(person(f1(X)) & ~respects(f1(X),X)) # king(X) .
```

We now put this into conjunctive normal form (Stage 5), where conjunctions do not appear within disjunctions, thus:

```
(person(f1(X)) # king(X)) &
    (~respects(f1(X),X) # king (X)) .
```

This amounts (stage 6) to two clauses. The first has the two literals:

```
person(f1(X))      king(X)
```

and the second has the literals:

```
~respects(f1(X),X)      king(X)  .
```


10.3 A Notation for Clauses

We need a way of writing something down in clausal form, and this is what we will now present. First of all, something in clausal form is a collection of clauses. As good a convention as any is to write down the clauses one after the other, remembering that the order is actually irrelevant. Within a clause there is a collection of literals, some negated and some not negated. We will adopt the convention of writing the unnegated literals first and the negated ones second. The two groups will be separated by the sign ": -". The unnegated literals will be written separated by ;'s (remembering, of course, that the order is not important), and the negated literals will be written without their ˜'s and separated by commas. Finally, a clause will be terminated by a full stop. In this notation, a clause with the n negated literals $˜Q_1, ˜Q_2, ..., ˜Q_n$ and the m unnegated literals $P_1, P_2, ..., P_m$ would be written as:

$$P_1; \ P_2; ..., P_m :- \ Q_1, \ Q_2, ..., \ Q_n \ .$$

Although we have introduced our convention for writing out clauses as something arbitrary, it actually has some mnemonic significance. If we write a clause including the disjunctions, with the negated literals separated from the unnegated ones, it will look something like:

$$(P_1 \# P_2 \# ... \# P_m) \# (˜Q_1 \# ˜Q_2 \# ... \# ˜Q_n)$$

which is equivalent to:

$$(P_1 \# P_2 \# ... \# P_m) \# ˜(Q_1 \& Q_2 \& ... \& Q_n)$$

which is equivalent to:

$$(Q_1 \& Q_2 \& ... \& Q_n) \ -> \ (P_1 \# P_2 \# ... \# P_m) \ .$$

If we write "," for "and", and ";" for "or", and ":-" for "is implied by" (following the Prolog convention), the clause naturally comes out as:

$$P_1 ; P_2 ; ... ; P_m :- \ Q_1, \ Q_2, ..., \ Q_n \ .$$

Given these conventions, the formula about Adam and Eve:

```
(person(adam) & person(eve)) &
    ((person(X) # ~mother(X,Y)) # ~person(Y))
```

comes out as:

```
person(adam) :- .
person(eve) :- .
person(X) :- mother(X,Y), person(Y).
```

This is beginning to look rather familiar. This really looks like a Prolog definition for what it is to be a person. However, other formulae give rise to more puzzling things. The example about holidays ends up as:

```
holiday(X); work(chris,X) :- .
holiday(X); angry(chris); sad(chris) :- .
```

which does not so obviously correspond to something in Prolog. We shall see why this is in a later section.

In Appendix B we present a Prolog program to print out clauses in this special notation. Written according to our convention, the clauses produced at the end of the last section come out as:

```
person(f1(X)); king(X) :- .
king(X) :- respects(f1(X),X).
```

10.4 Resolution and Proving Theorems

Now that we have got a way of putting our Predicate Calculus formulae into a nice tidy form, we should consider what we can do with them. An obvious thing to investigate, when we have a collection of propositions, is whether anything interesting *follows from* those propositions. That is, we may investigate what *consequences* the propositions have. We shall call those propositions that we are taking as true for the sake of argument our *axioms* or *hypotheses*, and those propositions that we find to follow from them our *theorems*. This is consistent with the terminology used to describe one view of Mathematics: a view which sees the work of a mathematician as involving the derivation of more and more interesting theorems from some exact axiomatisation of what sets and numbers are. In this section, we will look briefly at the activity of deriving interesting consequences from our given propositions, that is, we will look at the activity of *theorem proving*.

There was a great deal of activity in the 1960's as people began to investigate the possibility that digital computers could be programmed to prove theorems automatically. It was this area of scientific endeavour, which is still progressing healthily, that gave rise to the ideas behind Prolog. One of the fundamental breakthroughs made at this time was the discovery of the *resolution principle* by J. Alan Robinson, and its application to mechanical theorem proving. Resolution is a *rule of inference*. That is, it tells us how one proposition can follow from others. Using the resolution principle, we can prove theorems in a purely mechanical way from our axioms. We only have to decide which propositions to apply it to, and valid conclusions will be produced automatically.

Resolution is designed to work with formulae in clausal form. Given two clauses related in an appropriate way, it will generate a new clause that is a consequence of them. The basic idea is that if the same atomic formula appears both on the left hand side of one clause and the right hand side of another, then the clause obtained by fitting together the two clauses, missing out the duplicated formula, follows from them. For example:

From:

```
sad(chris); angry(chris) :-
    workday(today), raining(today).
```

and:

```
unpleasant(chris) :- angry(chris), tired(chris).
```

follows:

```
sad(chris); unpleasant(chris) :-
    workday(today), raining(today), tired(chris).
```

In English, if today is a workday and it is raining, then Chris is sad or angry. Also, if Chris is angry and tired, he is unpleasant. Therefore, if today is a workday, it is raining and Chris is tired, then Chris is sad or unpleasant.

In fact, we have over-simplified in two ways here. Firstly, things are actually more complicated when the clauses contain variables. Now the two atomic formulae do not have to be identical, they only have to "match". Also, the clause that follows from the first two is obtained from the two fitted together (with the duplicated formula removed) by an extra operation. This operation involves "instantiating" the variables just enough so that the two matching formulae are identical. In Prolog terms, if we had the two clauses as structures and matched together the appropriate substructures, the result of fitting them together afterwards would be the representation of the new clause. Our second simplification is that in general resolution one is allowed to match *several* literals on a right hand side against several on a left hand side. Here, we shall only consider examples where one literal is chosen from each clause.

Let us look at one example of resolution involving variables:

```
(1)    person(f1(X)); king(X) :- .

(2)    king(Y) :- respects(f1(Y),Y).

(3)    respects(Z,arthur) :- person(Z).
```

The first two of these are what we obtained as the clausal form of our formula saying "if every person respects somebody then that person is a king". We have renamed the variables for ease of explanation. The third expresses the proposition that every person respects Arthur. Resolving (2) with (3) (matching the two respects literals), gives us:

```
(4)    king(arthur) :- person(f1(arthur)).
```

(Y in (2) matched with arthur in (3), and Z in (3) matched with f1(Y) in (2)). We can now resolve (1) with (4), to give:

(5)   king(arthur); king(arthur) :- .

This is equivalent to the fact that Arthur is a king.

In the formal definition of resolution, the process of "matching" that we have referred to informally is called *unification*. Intuitively, some atomic formulae are *unifiable* if, as Prolog structures, they can be matched together. Actually, we will see in a later section that the matching in most Prolog implementations is not exactly the same as unification.

How can we use resolution to try and prove a specific thing? One possibility is that we can keep on applying resolution steps to our hypotheses and look to see if what we want appears. Unfortunately, we cannot guarantee that this will happen, even if the proposition we are interested in really does follow from the hypotheses. In the above example, for instance, there is no way of deriving the simple clause king(arthur) from the clauses given, even though it is clearly a consequence. So must we conclude that resolution is not powerful enough for what we want? Fortunately, the answer is "no", for we can rephrase our aims in such a way that resolution is guaranteed to be able to solve our problem if it is possible.

The important formal property that Resolution has is that of being *refutation complete*. This means that, if a set of clauses are *inconsistent* then Resolution will be able to derive from them the *empty clause*:

:- .

Also, since Resolution is *correct*, it will only be able to derive the empty clause in this circumstance. A set of formulae is inconsistent if there is no possible interpretation for the predicates, constant symbols and function symbols that makes them simultaneously express true propositions. The empty clause is the logical expression of *falsity* — it represents a proposition that cannot possibly be true. So Resolution can be guaranteed to tell us when our formulae are inconsistent by deriving this clear expression of contradiction.

How can these particular properties of resolution help us? Well, it is a fact that

If the formulae $\{A_1, A_2, ..., A_n\}$ are consistent, then formula B is a consequence of formulae $\{A_1, A_2, ..., A_n\}$ exactly when the formulae $\{A_1, A_2, ..., A_n, \neg B\}$ are inconsistent.

So, if our hypotheses are consistent, we just need to add to them the clauses for the negation of what we want to prove. Resolution will derive the empty clause exactly when the proposition follows from the hypotheses. We call the clauses that we add to the hypotheses the *goal statements*. Note that the goal statements do not look in any way different from the hypotheses — all of them are just clauses. So, if we are presented with a set of clauses A_1, A_2, ..., A_n, and are told that the task is to show them to be inconsistent, we cannot actually tell whether this is in order to show that:

$\neg A_1$ follows from A_2, ..., A_n, or that
$\neg A_2$ follows from A_1, A_3, ..., A_n, or that
$\neg A_3$ follows from A_1, A_2, A_4, ..., A_n,
etc.

It is a matter of emphasis which statements we actually consider to be the goal statements, because in a Resolution system all these tasks are equivalent.

In our example about Arthur being king, it is easy to see how we can obtain the empty clause if we add the goal statement:

(6)   :- king(arthur).

(this is the clause for ˜king(arthur)). We saw before how the clause

(5)   king(arthur); king(arthur) :- .

was derived from the hypotheses. Resolving (5) with (6) (matching either of the atomic formulae in (5)), we obtain:

(7)   king(arthur) :- .

Finally, resolving (6) with (7) gives us:

:- .

So resolution has shown that as a consequence, Arthur is a king.

The completeness of Resolution is a nice mathematical property. It means that if some fact follows from our hypotheses, we should be able to prove its truth (by showing the inconsistency of its negation and the hypotheses) using Resolution. However, when we say that Resolution will be able to derive the empty clause, we mean that there is a sequence of Resolution steps, each involving axioms or clauses derived in previous steps, which ends in the production of a clause with no literals. The only trouble is to find the sequence of steps. For, although Resolution tells us how to derive a consequence from two clauses, it does not tell us either how to decide which clauses to look at next or which literals to "match". Usually, if we have a large number of hypotheses, there will be many possibilities for each. Moreover, each time we derive a new clause, it too becomes a candidate to take part in further resolutions. Most of the possibilities will be irrelevant for the task at hand, and if we are not careful we may spend so much time on irrelevances that we will never find the solution path.

Many refinements of the original resolution principle have been proposed, to address these issues. The next section considers some of these.

10.5 Horn Clauses

We shall look now at refinements designed for resolution when all the clauses are of a certain kind — when they are *Horn clauses*. A Horn clause is a clause with at most one unnegated literal. It turns out that, if we are using a clausal theorem prover to determine the values of computable functions, it is only strictly necessary to use Horn clauses. Because resolution with Horn clauses is also relatively simple, they are an obvious choice as the basis of a theorem prover which provides a practical programming system. Let us consider briefly what Resolution theorem proving looks like if we restrict ourselves to Horn Clauses.

First, there are two kinds of Horn Clauses: those with one unnegated literal and those with none. Let us call these two types *headed* and *headless* Horn Clauses. The two types are exemplified by the following (remember that we write the unnegated literals on the left hand side of the ": -"):

```
bachelor(X) :- male(X), unmarried(X).
:- bachelor(X).
```

In fact, when we consider sets of Horn Clauses (including goal statements), we need only consider those sets where all but one of the clauses are headed. That is, any soluble problem (theorem-proving task) that can be expressed in Horn Clauses can be expressed in such a way that:

- There is one headless clause
- All the rest of the clauses are headed

Since it is arbitrary how we decide which clauses are actually the goals, we can decide to view the headless clause as the goal and the other clauses as the hypotheses. This has a certain naturalness.

Why do we only have to consider collections of Horn Clauses that conform to this pattern? First, it is easy to see that at least one headless clause must be present for a problem to be soluble. This is because the result of resolving two headed Horn Clauses is itself a headed Horn Clause. So, if all the clauses are headed, we will only be able to derive other headed clauses. Since the empty clause is not headed, we will not be able to derive it. The second claim — that only one headless clause is needed — is slightly more difficult to justify. However, it turns out that, if there are several headless clauses among our axioms, any Resolution proof of a new clause can be converted into a proof using at most one of them. Therefore, if the empty clause follows from the axioms, it follows from the headed ones together with at most one of the headless ones.

10.6 Prolog

Let us now summarise how Prolog fits into this scheme of things. As we saw before, some of our formulae turned into clauses that looked remarkably like Prolog clauses, whereas others looked somewhat peculiar. Those that turned into Prolog-like clauses were, in fact, those whose translation was into Horn clauses. When we write a Horn clause according to our conventions, at most one atomic formula appears on the left of the ": -". In general, clauses may have several such formulae (these correspond to the literals which are unnegated atomic formulae). In Prolog, we can express directly only the Horn clauses. The clauses of a Prolog program correspond to headed Horn clauses in a certain kind of theorem prover. What in Prolog corresponds to the goal statement? Quite simply, the Prolog question:

$$?\text{-}\ A_1,\ A_2,\ ...,\ A_n.$$

corresponds exactly to the headless Horn Clause:

$$:\text{-}\ A_1,\ A_2,\ ...,\ A_n.$$

We saw in the last section that, for any problem we want to solve with Horn Clauses, it suffices to have exactly one headless clause. This corresponds to the situation in Prolog, where all the clauses of the "program" are headed and only one (headless) goal is considered at any one time.

A Prolog system is based on a resolution theorem prover for Horn clauses. The particular strategy that it uses is a form of *linear input resolution*. When this strategy is used, the choice of what to resolve with what at any time is restricted as follows. We start with the goal statement and resolve it with one of the hypotheses to give a new clause. Then we resolve that with one of the hypotheses to give another new clause. Then we resolve that with one of the hypotheses, and so on. At each stage, we resolve the clause last obtained with one of the original hypotheses. At no point do we either use a clause that has been derived previously or resolve together two of the hypotheses. In Prolog terms, we can see the latest derived clause as the conjunction of goals yet to be satisfied. This starts off as the question, and hopefully ends up as the empty clause. At each stage, we find a clause whose head matches one of the goals, instantiate variables as necessary, remove the goal that matched and then add the body of the instantiated clause to the goals to be satisfied. Thus, for instance, we can go from:

```
:- mother(john,X), mother(X,Y).
```
and
```
mother(U,V) :- parent(U,V), female(V).
```
to:
```
:- parent(john,X), female(X), mother(X,Y).
```

In fact, Prolog's proof strategy is even more restricted than general linear input resolution. In this example, we decided to match the first of the literals in the goal clause, but we could equally well have matched the second. In Prolog, the literal to be matched is always selected in the same way: it is always the first one in the goal clause. In addition, the new goals derived from the use of a clause are placed at the *front* of the goal clause. This just means that Prolog finishes satisfying a subgoal before it goes on to try anything else.

So much for what happens when Prolog has decided what clause to match against the first goal. But how does it organise the investigation of alternative clauses to satisfy the same goal? Basically, Prolog adopts a *depth-first* strategy, rather than a *breadth-first* one. This means that it only considers one alternative at a time, following up the implications under the assumption that the choice is correct. For each goal, it chooses the clauses in a fixed order, and it only comes to consider the later ones if all the earlier ones have failed to lead to solutions. The alternative strategy would be one where the system kept track of alternative solution paths simultaneously. It would then move around from one alternative to another, following it up for a short time and then going on to something else. This latter, breadth-first, strategy has the advantage that, if a solution exists, it will be found. The Prolog depth-first strategy can get into "loops" and hence never follow up some of the alternatives. On the other hand, it is much simpler and less space-consuming to implement on a conventional computer.

Finally, a note about how Prolog matching sometimes differs from the unification used in Resolution. Most Prolog systems will allow you to satisfy goals like:
```
equal(X,X).
?- equal(foo(Y),Y).
```
that is, they will allow you to match a term against a subterm of itself. In this example, foo(Y) is matched against Y, which appears within it. As a result, Y will stand for foo(Y), which is foo(foo(Y)) (because of what Y stands for), which is foo(foo(foo(Y))), and so on. So Y ends up standing

for some kind of infinite structure. Note that, whereas they may allow you to construct something like this, most Prolog systems will not be able to write it out at the end. According to the formal definition of Unification, this kind of "infinite term" should never come to exist. So Prolog does not act correctly as a Resolution theorem prover in this respect. In order to make it do so, we would have to add a check that a variable cannot be instantiated to something containing itself. Such a check, an *occur check*, would be straightforward to implement, but would slow down the execution of Prolog programs considerably. Since it would only affect very few programs, most implementors have simply left it out.

10.7 Prolog and Logic Programming

In the last few sections, we have seen how Prolog is based on the idea of a theorem prover. As a result of this, we can see that our programs are rather like our hypotheses about the world, and our questions are rather like theorems that we would like to have proved. So programming in Prolog is not so much like telling the computer what to do when, but rather like telling it what is true and asking it to try and draw conclusions. The idea that programming should be like this is an appealing one, and has led many people to investigate the notion of *logic programming*, that is, programming in logic as a practical possibility. This is supposed to contrast with using a conventional programming language such as FORTRAN or LISP, where one specifies tasks much more clearly in terms of what the computer should do and when it should do it.

The advantages of logic programming should be that computer programs are easier to read. They should not be cluttered up with details about *how* things are to be done — they will be more like specifications of *what* a solution will look like. Moreover, if a program is rather like a specification of what it is supposed to achieve, it should be relatively easy, just by looking at it (or, perhaps, by some automatic means) to check that it really does do what is required. In summary, the advantages of a logic programming language would result from programs having a *declarative* semantics as well as a *procedural* one. We would know *what* a program computes, rather than *how* it computes it. We will not be able to look at logic programming in general here. The interested reader is referred to Robert Kowalski's book *Logic for Problem Solving* published by North Holland in 1979, and Christopher Hogger's book *Introduction to Logic Programming* published by Academic Press in 1984.

Let us briefly look at Prolog as a candidate logic programming language, and see how well it shapes up. First, it is clear that some Prolog programs do represent logical truths about the world. If we write:

```
mother(X,Y) :- parent(X,Y), female(Y).
```

we can see this as saying what it is to be a mother (it is to be a female parent). So this clause expresses a proposition that we are hypothesising to be true, as well as saying how to *show* that somebody is a mother. Similarly, the clauses:

```
append([],X,X).
append([A|B],C,[A|D]) :- append(B,C,D).
```

say what it is for one list to be concatenated to the front of another. If the empty list is put on the front of some list X, then the result is just X. On the other hand, if a non-empty list is appended on the front of a list, then the head of the result is the same as the head of the list being put on the front. Also, the tail of the result is the same list as would be obtained by appending the tail of the first list onto the front of the second. These clauses can definitely be seen as expressing what is true about the append relation, as well as (perhaps) how one should actually set about appending two lists together.

So much for some Prolog programs, but what possible logical meaning can we give to clauses like these?

```
member1(X,List) :- var(List), !, fail.
member1(X,[X|_]).
member1(X,[_|List]) :- member1(X,List).

print(0) :- !.
print(N) :- write(N), N1 is N-1, print(N1).

noun(N) :-
    name(N,Name1), append(Name2,[115],Name1),
    name(RootN,Name2), noun(RootN).

implies(Assum,Concl) :-
    asserta(Assum),
    call(Concl),
    retract(Concl).
```

The problem comes with all those "built-in" predicates that we use in our Prolog programs. A goal such as var(List) does not say anything about lists or membership, but refers to a state of affairs (some variable being uninstantiated) that may hold at some time during the proof. The "cut" similarly says something about the proof of a proposition (which choices may be ignored), rather than about the proposition itself. These two "predicates" can be regarded as ways of expressing *control information* about how the proof is to be carried out. Similarly, something like write(N) does not have any interesting logical properties, but presupposes that the proof will have reached a certain state (with N instantiated) and initiates a communication with the programmer at his terminal. The goal name(N,Name1) is saying something about the internal structure of what, in Predicate Calculus, would be an indivisible symbol. In Prolog, we can convert symbols to character strings, convert structures to lists and convert structures to clauses. These operations violate the simple self-contained nature of Predicate Calculus propositions. In the last example, the use of asserta means that the rule is talking about adding something to the set of axioms. In logic, each fact or rule states an independent truth, independent of what other facts and rules there may be. Here we have a rule that violates that principle. Also, if we use this rule, we will be in a position of having a different set of axioms at different times of the proof! Finally, the fact that the rule envisages Conc1 being used as a *goal* means that a logical variable is being allowed to stand for a proposition appearing in an axiom. This is not something that could be expressed in Predicate Calculus at all, but is reminiscent of what higher-order logic can provide.

Given these examples, we can see that some Prolog programs can only be understood in terms of what happens when and how they tell the system what to do. As an extreme case, the program for gensym given in Chapter 7 can hardly be given any declarative interpretation at all.

So does it make sense to regard Prolog as a logic programming language at all? Can we really expect any of the advantages of logic programming to apply to our Prolog programs? The answer to both these questions is a qualified "yes", and the reason is that, by adopting an appropriate programming style, we can still extract some advantages from the relation of Prolog to logic. The key is to decompose our programs into parts, confining the use of the non-logical operations to within a small set of clauses. As an example, we saw in Chapter 4 how some uses of the "cut" could be replaced with uses of not. As a result of such replacements, a program containing a number of "cuts" can be reduced to one with the "cut" only used once (in the definition of not). Use of the predicate not, even though it does not capture exactly the logical "¬", enables one to recapture part of the underlying logical meaning of a program. Similarly, confining the use of the predicates asserta and retract to within the definitions of a small number of predicates (such as gensym and findall) results in a program that is clearer overall than one where these predicates are used freely in all sorts of contexts.

The ultimate goal of a logic programming language has not, then, been achieved with Prolog. Nevertheless, Prolog provides a practical programming system that has some of the advantages of clarity and declarativeness that a logic programming language would offer. Meanwhile the work goes on to develop improved versions of Prolog that are truer to the logic than what we currently have available. Among the highest priorities of workers in this area is to develop a practical system that does not need the "cut" and has a version of not that exactly corresponds to the logical notion of negation.

For more information on the theory of logic programming, you should consult *Logic for Problem Solving*, by Robert Kowalski, published by North-Holland in 1979; and *Introduction to Logic Programming*, by Christopher Hogger, published by Academic Press in 1984.

Chapter 11
Projects in Prolog

This chapter contains a list of projects that you may wish to undertake in order to exercise your programming ability. Some of the projects are easy, but some may be appropriate as "term projects" as a part of a course in Prolog. The easier projects should be used to supplement the exercises in the previous chapters. The projects are in no particular order, although those in Section 11.2 are more open ended and ambitious, and will require some knowledge or background reading in various areas of artificial intelligence and computer science. A few of the projects assume knowledge about some particular field of study, so if you are not a mathematical physicist, do not feel discouraged if you cannot write a program to differentiate three dimensional vector fields.

A collection of Prolog programs is published in the report "How to solve it with Prolog", edited by H. Coelho, J.C. Cotta, and L.M. Pereira. The report is distributed by the Laboratório Nacional de Engenharia Civil, in Lisbon, Portugal. It contains over a hundred small examples, problems, and exercises in areas such as deductive reasoning over databases, natural language, symbolic equation solving, and so forth. The report is not intended to be tutorial in nature, and so the Prolog programs in it are presented with limited explanatory accompaniment.

11.1 Easier Projects

1. Define a predicate to "flatten" a list by constructing a list containing no lists as elements, but containing all of the atoms of the original list. For example, the following goal would succeed:

```
?- flatten([a,[b,c],[[d],[],e]], [a,b,c,d,e]).
```

There are at least six distinct ways to write this program.

2. Write a program to calculate the interval in days between two dates expressed in the form Day-Month, assuming they refer to the same year which is not a leap year. Notice that "-" is simply the infix form of a 2-ary functor. For example, the following goal would succeed:

```
interval(3-march, 7-april, 35).
```

3. In Chapter 7 sufficient information is given to construct programs to differentiate and simplify arithmetic expressions. Extend these programs so they will handle expressions containing trigonometric functions, and if you desire, differential geometry operators such as div, grad, and curl.

4. Write a program to produce the negation of a propositional expression. Propositional expressions are built up from atoms, the unary functor not, and binary functors and, or, and implies. Provide suitable operator declarations for the functors, perhaps using the operator declarations ($\tilde{\ }$, &, #, and ->) in Chapter 10. The negated expression should be in simplest form, where not is only applied to atoms. For example, the negation of

```
p implies (q and not(r))
```

should be

```
p and (not(q) or r).
```

5. A concordance is a listing of words that occur in a text, listed in alphabetical order together with the number of times each word appears in the text. Write a program to produce a concordance from a list of words represented as Prolog strings. Recall that strings are lists of ASCII codes.

6. Write a program that understands simple English sentences having the following forms:

```
__ is a __ .
A __ is a __ .
Is __ a __ ?
```

The program should give an appropriate response (yes, no, ok, unknown), on the basis of the sentences previously given. For example,

```
John is a man.
ok
A man is a person.
ok
Is John a person?
yes
Is Mary a person?
unknown
```

Each sentence should be translated into a Prolog clause, which is then asserted or executed as appropriate. Thus, the translations of the preceding examples are:

```
man(john).
person(X) :- man(X).
```

```
?- person(john).
?- person(mary).
```

Use grammar rules if you find them appropriate. The top clause to control the dialogue might be:

```
talk :-
        repeat,
        read(Sentence),
        parse(Sentence,Clause),
        respond_to(Clause),
        Clause = stop.
```

7. The alpha-beta (α-β) algorithm is a method for searching game trees that is mentioned in many books on artificial intelligence programming. Implement the α-β algorithm in Prolog.

8. The N-queens problem is also widely discussed in programming texts. Implement a program to find all the ways of placing 4 queens on a 4×4 chessboard so that no queen attacks another. One way is to write a permutation generator, which then checks each permutation to ensure that it places the queens correctly.

9. Write a program that rewrites propositional expressions (Problem 4), replacing all occurrences of and, or, implies, and not by the single connective nand. The connective nand is defined by the following identity:

$$(\alpha \text{ nand } \beta) \equiv \neg(\alpha \wedge \beta)$$

10. One way of representing the positive whole numbers is as Prolog terms involving the integer 0 and the functor s with one argument. Thus, we represent 0 by itself, 1 by s(0), 2 by s(s(0)), and so on (each number is represented by the functor s applied to the representation of the number one less). Write definitions of the standard arithmetic operations addition, multiplication and subtraction, given this representation of numbers. For instance, you should define a predicate plus that exhibits the following behaviour:

```
?- plus(s(s(0)),s(s(s(0))),X).
X = s(s(s(s(s(0)))))
```

that is, $2+3=5$. For subtraction, you will have to introduce a convention for when the result of the operation is not a positive whole number. Also define the predicate "less than". What arguments need to be instantiated for your definitions to work? What happens in the other cases? How does this compare with the standard Prolog arithmetic operations? Try defining some more complicated arithmetic operations, like integer division and square root.

11.2 Advanced Projects

Although the projects in this section may seem open ended, all of them have been implemented in Prolog by various programmers around the world. Some of them are straightforward enhancements to programs discussed earlier, and some of them are completely new, and depend on knowledge of the artificial intelligence literature or computer science.

1. Given a map that describes roads that connect towns, write a progam that plans a route between two towns, giving a timetable of expected travel. The map data should include mileage, road conditions, estimated amount of other traffic, gradients, availability of fuel along various roads.

2. Only integer arithmetic operations are built into current Prolog systems. Write a package of programs to support arithmetic over rational numbers, represented either as fractions or as mantissa and exponent.

3. Write procedures to invert and multiply matrices.

4. Compiling a high-level computer language into a low-level language can be viewed as the successive transformation of syntax trees. Write such a compiler, first compiling arithmetic expressions. Then add control syntax (like if ... then ... else). The syntax of the assembly output is not crucial for this purpose. For example, the arithmetic expression x+1 could be "simplified" into the assembly language statement inc   x, where inc is declared as a unary operator. The problem of register allocation can be postponed by assuming that the code compiles into a form suitable for execution by a stack machine (0-address machine).

5. Devise a representation for complex board games such as Chess or Go, and understand how the pattern matching capabilities of Prolog might be used to implement strategies for these games.

6. Devise a formalism for expressing sets of axioms, say from Group Theory, Euclidean Geometry, Denotational Semantics, and investigate the problem of writing a theorem prover for these domains.

7. An interpreter for Prolog clauses can be written in Prolog (see Section 7.13). Write an interpreter that implements different semantics for Prolog execution, such as more flexible execution order (instead of left-to-right), perhaps using an "agenda" or other scheduling mechanism.

8. Consult the artificial intelligence literature on the area of generating plans to solve problems, and implement a plan generator.

9. Express in Prolog the problem of interpreting a line drawing in terms of some underlying scene. Features of the picture can be labelled with variables representing corresponding features of the scene. The picture then corresponds to a set of constraints these variables must satisfy.

10. Write a program, using Grammar Rules, to parse sentences of the form:

Fred saw John.
Mary was seen by John.
Fred told Mary to see John.
John was believed to have been seen by Fred.
Was John believed to have told Mary to see Fred?

11. A production rule system, used in artificial intelligence research, is a sequence of rules of the form "**if** *situation* **then** *action*." It has become fashionable within the artificial intelligence field to write "expert knowledge" in terms of production rules. For example, the following sentences are typical of those used in actual production systems that have been implemented:

Pharmacology: If agent X is a quaternary ammonium salt and an anti-arhythmic, and agent Y is a salicylate, then X and Y will interact to produce increased absorption by ion pair formation.

Playing chess: If the black king can move adjacent to the black knight and the distance from the white king to the knight is greater than one square, then the knight is safe.

Medicine: If the site of the culture is blood, and the gram stain of the organism is negative, and the morphology of the organism is a rod, and the patient is a compromised host, then there is a 60% chance that the infecting organism is *Pseudomonas aeruginosa*.

Write a Prolog program to interpret a set of production rules. Consider some domain such as identifying plants or animals from identifying characteristics. For example, a rule from botany would read:

If a plant has a square stem, paired leaves, two-lipped hooded flowers, and fruit consisting of four tiny nuts enclosed in the calyx, then it belongs to the family *Labiatae*.

So, if the program asked the question "Does the flower have a square stem?", then we would rule out the possibility that it belongs to the family *Labiatea* by answering "no".

12. Write a program to translate some corpus of English sentences into Predicate Calculus.

13. Write a program to prove theorems in Predicate Calculus.

14. Write a program to act as a simulated psychiatrist that makes a reply based on key words in the input, rather like the program in Chapter 3 that changed keywords in a sentence into other words. A typical dialogue might be (computer replies shown in boldface):

What is your problem?
This is too much work.
What else do you regard as too much work?
Writing letters.
I see. Please continue.
Also washing my mother's car.
Tell me more about your family.
Why should I?
Why should you what?
⋮

Here the appropriate key words were this is, mother, and why. The lack of appropriate keyword evoked the response **I see. Please continue.**

15. Write a program that parses sentences about happenings in an office building, such as "Smith will be in his office at 3 pm for a meeting". You might wish to use Grammar Rules to capture the "business English" language. The program should then print out a "summary" of the sentence telling who, what, where, and when; such as follows:

```
who:    smith
where:  office
when:   3 pm
what:   meeting
```

The summary could be represented as assertions in the database, so that questions could be asked:

```
Where is Smith at 3 pm?
```
where: office
what: meeting

16. Write a natural language interface to the filing system of your computer to answer questions such as:

How many files does David own?
Does Chris share PROG.MAC with David?
When did Bill change the file VIDEO.C?

The program must be able to interrogate various parts of the filing system such as ownership and dates.

APPENDIX A. Answers to Selected Exercises

We include here suggested answers to some of the exercises that appear in the text. With most programming exercises, there is rarely a single correct answer, and you may well have a good answer that looks different from what we suggest. In any case, you should always try out your program on your local Prolog system, to see whether it really works. Even if you have written a correct program that is different, it may still be instructive to spend some time looking at an alternative approach to the same problem.

Exercise 1.3. Here are possible definitions of the family relationships.

```
is_mother(Mum) :- mother(Mum,Child).

is_father(Dad) :- father(Dad,Child).

is_son(Son) :- parent(Par,Son), male(Son).

sister_of(Sis,Pers) :-
        parent(Par,Sis), parent(Par,Pers),
        female(Sis), diff(Sis,Pers).

granpa_of(Gpa,X) :- parent(Par,X), father(Gpa,Par).

sibling(S1,S2) :-
        parent(Par,S1), parent(Par,S2), diff(S1,S2).
```

Note that we are using the predicate diff in the definition of sister_of and sibling. This prevents the system concluding that somebody can be a sister or sibling of themselves. You will not be able to define diff at this stage.

Exercise 5.2. The following program reads in characters (from the current input file) indefinitely, printing them out again with a's changed to b's.

```
go :- repeat, get0(C), deal_with(C), fail.

deal_with(97) :- !, put(98).
deal_with(X) :- put(X).
```

The "cut" in the first deal_with rule is essential (why?). 97 and 98 are the ASCII codes for a and b respectively.

Exercise 6.2. Why will the following definition of get not work if we have a get goal with an instantiated argument?

```
get(X) :- new_get(X), X>32.

new_get(X) :- repeat, get0(X).
```

Let's assume that we give Prolog the goal get(97) (is the next printing character an a?) when the very next character is in fact a b. To satisfy get(97), we try to satisfy new_get(97). The repeat goal succeeds, but then the goal get0(97) fails (the next character is not an a). Now backtracking occurs. The get0 goal cannot be resatisfied, but the repeat one can be. So repeat succeeds again, and an attempt is made to satisfy get0(97) again. This time, of course, the next character will be the one after the b. If this is not an a, the goal will fail, and repeat will succeed again. Then the next character will be looked at. And so on. What is actually happening is that the program is reading more and more characters until it finally finds one that matches with the argument. This is not what get was supposed to do. A good definition of get, which gets over this problem and also contains a "cut" to remove the repeat choice, follows:

```
get(X) :- repeat, get0(Y), 32<Y, !, X=Y.
```

Exercise 7.10. Here is a program that generates Pythagorean triples:

```
pythag(X,Y,Z) :-
        intriple(X,Y,Z),
        Sumsq is X*X + Y*Y, Sumsq is Z*Z.

intriple(X,Y,Z) :-
        is_integer(Sum),
        minus(Sum,X,Sum1), minus(Sum1,Y,Z).

minus(Sum,Sum,0).
minus(Sum,D1,D2) :-
        Sum>0, Sum1 is Sum-1,
        minus(Sum1,D1,D3), D2 is D3+1.

is_integer(0).
is_integer(N) :- is_integer(N1), N is N1 + 1.
```

The program uses the predicate intriple to generate possible triples of integers X, Y, Z. It then checks to see whether this triple really is a Pythagorean triple. The definition of intriple has to guarantee that all triples of integers will eventually be generated. It first of all generates an integer that is the sum of X, Y and Z. Then it uses a non-deterministic subtraction predicate, minus, to generate values of X, Y and Z from that.

Exercise 9.1. Here is the program for translating a simple grammar rule into Prolog. It is assumed here that the rule contains no phrase types with extra arguments, no goals inside curly brackets and no disjunctions or cuts.

```
?- op(1199,xfx,-->).
```

```
translate((P1-->P2),(G1:-G2)) :-
        left_hand_side(P1,S0,S,G1),
        right_hand_side(P2,S0,S,G2).
left_hand_side(P0,S0,S,G) :-
        nonvar(P0), tag(P0,S0,S,G).
right_hand_side((P1,P2),S0,S,G) :-
        !,
        right_hand_side(P1,S0,S1,G1),
        right_hand_side(P2,S1,S,G2),
        and(G1,G2,G).
right_hand_side(P,S0,S,true) :-
        islist(P),
        !,
        append(P,S,S0).
right_hand_side(P,S0,S,G) :- tag(P,S0,S,G).
tag(P,S0,S,G) :- atom(P), G =..[P,S0,S].
and(true,G,G) :- !.
and(G,true,G) :- !. and(G1,G2,(G1,G2)).
islist([]) :- !. islist([_|_]).
append([A|B],C,[A|D]) :- append(B,C,D).
append([],X,X).
```

In this program, variables beginning with P stand for phrase descriptions (atoms, or lists of words) in grammar rules. Variables beginning with G stand for Prolog goals. Variables beginning with S stand for arguments of the Prolog goals (which represent sequences of words). In case you are interested, there follows a program that will handle the more general cases of grammar rule translation. One way in which a Prolog system can handle grammar rules is to have a modified version of consult, in which a clause of the form A --> B is translated before it is added to the database. We have defined a pair of operators to act as curly brackets "{" and "}", but some Prolog implementations may have built-in definitions, so that the term {X} is another form of the structure '{}'(X).

```
?- op(1101,fx,'{').
?- op(1100,xf,'}').
?- op(1199,xfx,-->).

translate((P0-->Q0),(P:-Q)) :-
        left_hand_side(P0,S0,S,P),
```

```prolog
            right_hand_side(Q0,S0,S,Q1),
            flatten(Q1,Q).
left_hand_side((NT,Ts),S0,S,P) :- !,
            nonvar(NT),
            islist(Ts),
            tag(NT,S0,S1,P),
            append(Ts,S,S1).
left_hand_side(NT,S0,S,P) :-
            nonvar(NT), tag(NT,S0,S,P).

right_hand_side((X1,X2),S0,S,P) :- !,
            right_hand_side(X1,S0,S1,P1),
            right_hand_side(X2,S1,S,P2),
            and(P1,P2,P).
right_hand_side((X1;X2),S0,S,(P1;P2)) :-
            !, or(X1,S0,S,P1), or(X2,S0,S,P2).
right_hand_side({P},S,S,P) :- !.
right_hand_side(!,S,S,!) :- !.
right_hand_side(Ts,S0,S,true) :-
            islist(Ts),
            !,
            append(Ts,S,S0).
right_hand_side(X,S0,S,P) :- tag(X,S0,S,P).

or(X,S0,S,P) :-
            right_hand_side(X,S0a,S,Pa),
            ( var(S0a), S0a \== S, !,
                    S0=S0a, P=Pa; P=(S0=S0a,Pa) ).

tag(X,S0,S,P) :-
            X =.. [F|A], append(A,[S0,S],AX), P =.. [F|AX].

and(true,P,P) :- !.
and(P,true,P) :- !.
and(P,Q,(P,Q)).

flatten(A,A) :- var(A), !.
flatten((A,B),C) :- !, flatten1(A,C,R), flatten(B,R).
flatten(A,A).

flatten1(A,(A,R),R) :- var(A), !.
flatten1((A,B),C,R) :-
            !, flatten1(A,C,R1), flatten1(B,R1,R).
flatten1(A,(A,R),R).
```

```
islist([]) :- !.
islist([_|_]).

append([A|B],C,[A|D]) :- append(B,C,D).
append([],X,X).
```

Exercise 9.2. The definition of the general version of phrase is as follows:

```
phrase(Ptype,Words) :-
        Ptype =.. [Pred|Args],
        append(Args,[Words,[]],Newargs),
        Goal =.. [Pred|Newargs],
        call(Goal).
```

where append is defined as in Section 3.6.

APPENDIX B. Clausal Form Program Listings

As promised in Chapter 10, we shall illustrate the process of converting a formula to clausal form by showing fragments of a Prolog program for doing this. The top level of the program is as follows:

```
translate(X) :-
        implout(X,X1),          /* Stage 1 */
        negin(X1,X2),           /* Stage 2 */
        skolem(X2,X3,[]),       /* Stage 3 */
        univout(X3,X4),         /* Stage 4 */
        conjn(X4,X5),           /* Stage 5 */
        clausify(X5,Clauses),   /* Stage 6 */
        pclauses(Clauses).      /* Print out clauses */
```

This defines a predicate translate, such that if we give Prolog the goal translate(X), with X standing for a Predicate Calculus formula, the program will print out the formula's representation as clauses. In the program, we will represent Predicate Calculus formulae as Prolog structures, as we have indicated before. *Remember that Predicate Calculus variables will be represented by Prolog atoms*, as this makes certain manipulations easier. We can distinguish Predicate Calculus variables from constants by having some convention for their names. For instance, we could say that variable names always begin with one of the letters x, y, and z. In fact, in the program we will not need to know about this convention because variables are always introduced by quantifiers and hence are easy to detect. Only in reading the program's output will it be important for the programmer to remember which names were Predicate Calculus variables and which were constants.

First, we will need the following operator declarations for the connectives:

```
?- op(200,fx,~).
?- op(400,xfy,#).
?- op(400,xfy,&).
?- op(700,xfy,->).
?- op(700,xfy,<->).
```

It is important to note how we have defined these. In particular, "~" has a lower precedence than "#" and "&". To start with, we must make an important assumption. The assumption is that the variables have been renamed as necessary, so that the same variable is never introduced by more than one quantifier in the formula at hand. This is to prevent accidental name clashes in what follows.

The actual programming technique we use to implement the conversion to clausal form is tree transformation, as discussed in Sections 7.11 and 7.12. By representing the logical connectives as functors, Predicate Calculus formulae become structures that can be depicted as trees. Each of the six main stages of conversion into clausal form is a tree transformation that maps an input tree onto an output tree.

Stage 1 — Removing Implications

We define a predicate implout such that implout(X,Y) means that Y is the formula derived from X by removing implications.

```
implout((P <-> Q),((P1 & Q1) # (~P1 & ~Q1))) :-
        !, implout(P,P1), implout(Q,Q1).
implout((P -> Q),(~P1 # Q1)) :-
        !, implout(P,P1), implout(Q,Q1).
implout(all(X,P),all(X,P1)) :- !, implout(P,P1).
implout(exists(X,P),exists(X,P1)) :- !, implout(P,P1).
implout((P & Q),(P1 & Q1)) :-
        !, implout(P,P1), implout(Q,Q1).
implout((P # Q),(P1 # Q1)) :-
        !, implout(P,P1), implout(Q,Q1).
implout((~P),(~P1)) :- !, implout(P,P1).
implout(P,P).
```

Stage 2 — Moving Negation Inwards

We need to define two predicates here: negin and neg. Goal negin(X,Y) means that Y is the formula derived by applying the "negation inwards" transformation to the whole of X. This is the main thing we will ask questions about. Goal neg(X,Y) means that Y is the formula derived by applying the transformation to the formula ~X. With both of these, we assume that stage 1 has been carried out, and that we hence do not need to deal with -> and <->.

```
negin((~P),P1) :- !, neg(P,P1).
negin(all(X,P),all(X,P1)) :- !, negin(P,P1).
negin(exists(X,P),exists(X,P1)) :- !, negin(P,P1).
negin((P & Q),(P1 & Q1)) :-
        !, negin(P,P1), negin(Q,Q1).
negin((P # Q),(P1 # Q1)) :-
        !, negin(P,P1), negin(Q,Q1).
negin(P,P).

neg((~P),P1) :- !, negin(P,P1).
neg(all(X,P),exists(X,P1)) :- !, neg(P,P1).
```

```
neg(exists(X,P),all(X,P1)) :- !, neg(P,P1).
neg((P & Q),(P1 # Q1)) :- !, neg(P,P1), neg(Q,Q1).
neg((P # Q),(P1 & Q1)) :- !, neg(P,P1), neg(Q,Q1).
neg(P,(~P)).
```

Stage 3 — Skolemising

The predicate skolem has three arguments: corresponding to the original formula, the transformed formula and the list of variables that have been introduced so far by universal quantifiers.

```
skolem(all(X,P),all(X,P1),Vars) :-
        !, skolem(P,P1,[X|Vars]).
skolem(exists(X,P),P2,Vars) :-
        !,
        gensym(f,F),
        Sk =..[F|Vars],
        subst(X,Sk,P,P1),
        skolem(P1,P2,Vars).
skolem((P # Q),(P1 # Q1),Vars) :-
        !, skolem(P,P1,Vars), skolem(Q,Q1,Vars).
skolem((P & Q),(P1 & Q1),Vars) :-
        !, skolem(P,P1,Vars), skolem(Q,Q1,Vars).
skolem(P,P,_).
```

This definition makes use of two new predicates. Predicate gensym must be defined such that the goal gensym(X,Y) causes Y to be instantiated to a new atom built up from the atom X and a number. This is used to generate Skolem constants that have not been used before. Predicate gensym is defined in Section 7.8. The second new predicate that is mentioned is subst. We require subst(V1,V2,F1,F2) to be true if the result of substituting V2 for V1 every time it appears in the formula F1 is F2. The definition of this is left as an exercise for the reader, but it is similar to predicates defined in Sections 7.5 and 6.5.

Stage 4 — Moving Universal Quantifiers Outwards

After this point, of course, it will be necessary to be able to tell which Prolog atoms represent Predicate Calculus variables and which represent Predicate Calculus constants. We will no longer have the convenient rule that the variables are precisely those symbols introduced by quantifiers. Here is the program for moving out and removing the universal quantifiers:

```
univout(all(X,P),P1) :- !, univout(P,P1).
univout((P & Q),(P1 & Q1)) :-
        !, univout(P,P1), univout(Q,Q1).
```

```
univout((P # Q),(P1 # Q1)) :-
        !, univout(P,P1), univout(Q,Q1). univout(P,P).
```

These rules define the predicate univout so that univout(X,Y) means that the version of X with universal quantifiers moved out is Y.

It should be noted that our definition of univout assumes that this operation will only be applied after the first three stages are already complete. Hence it makes no allowance for implications or existential quantifiers in the formula.

Stage 5 — *Distributing & over #*

The actual program to put a formula into conjunctive normal form is rather more complicated than the last one. When it comes across something like (P # Q), where P and Q are any formulae, it must first of all put P and Q into conjunctive normal forms, P1 and Q1 say, and only then look to see if the formula as a whole is suitable for translation by one of the equivalences. The process must happen in this order, because it may happen that neither of P and Q has & at the top level, but one of P1 and Q1 does. Here is the program:

```
conjn((P # Q),R) :-
        !,
        conjn(P,P1), conjn(Q,Q1),
        conjn1((P1 # Q1),R).
conjn((P & Q),(P1 & Q1)) :-
        !, conjn(P,P1), conjn(Q,Q1).
conjn(P,P).

conjn1(((P & Q) # R),(P1 & Q1)) :-
        !, conjn((P # R),P1), conjn((Q # R),Q1).
conjn1((P # (Q & R)),(P1 & Q1)) :-
        !, conjn((P # Q),P1), conjn((P # R),Q1).
conjn1(P,P).
```

Stage 6 — *Putting into Clauses*

Here, now, is the last part of our program to put a formula in clausal form. We define first of all the predicate clausify, which involves building up an internal representation of a collection of clauses. The collection is represented as a list, where each clause is represented as a structure cl(A,B). In such a structure, A is the list of literals that are not negated, and B is the list of literals that are negated (but written without their ~'s). Predicate clausify has three arguments. The first is for the formula, as delivered by Stage 5. The second and third are for defining the list of clauses. Predicate clausify builds a list terminating in a variable, instead of the usual [ ], and returns this variable through the third argument. It is then

possible for other rules to add things to the end of the list by instantiating the
variable. One feature built into the program checks that the same atomic
formula does not appear both negated and unnegated within the same
clause. If this happens, the clause is not added to the list, because such a
clause is trivially true and contributes nothing. Also, it is checked that the
same literal does not appear twice within a clause.

```
clausify((P & Q),C1,C2) :-
        !, clausify(P,C1,C3), clausify(Q,C3,C2).
clausify(P,[cl(A,B)|Cs],Cs) :-
        inclause(P,A,[],B,[]), !.
clausify(_,C,C).

inclause((P # Q),A,A1,B,B1) :-
        !,
        inclause(P,A2,A1,B2,B1), inclause(Q,A,A2,B,B2).
inclause((~P),A,A,B1,B) :-
        !, notin(P,A), putin(P,B,B1).
inclause(P,A1,A,B,B) :- notin(P,B), putin(P,A,A1).

notin(X,[X|_]) :- !, fail.
notin(X,[_|L]) :- !, notin(X,L).
notin(X,[]).

putin(X,[],[X]) :- !.
putin(X,[X|L],L) :- !.
putin(X,[Y|L],[Y|L1]) :- putin(X,L,L1).
```

Printing out Clauses

We will now define a predicate pclauses which causes a formula
represented in this way to be displayed according to our notation.

```
pclauses([]) :- !, nl, nl.
pclauses([cl(A,B)|Cs]) :-
        pclause(A,B), nl, pclauses(Cs).

pclause(L,[]) :-
        !, pdisj(L), write('.').
pclause([],L) :-
        !, write(':- '), pconj(L), write('.').
pclause(L1,L2) :-
        pdisj(L1),
        write(' :- '), pconj(L2), write('.').

pdisj([L]) :- !, write(L).
pdisj([L|Ls]) :- write(L), write('; '), pdisj(Ls).
```

```
pconj([L]) :- !, write(L).
pconj([L|Ls]) :- write(L), write(', '), pconj(Ls).
```

APPENDIX C. Different Versions of Prolog

Prolog is by now available in many different versions in many different places. The differences that exist are due partly to the different kinds of computers available at the various computer installations. No two kinds of computer make it equally easy to write all kinds of programs, and this is reflected in the facilities that the various Prolog implementors have got around to providing. Even if two installations have the same kind of computer, they may still run different operating systems on them. The operating system is the program in overall control of the computer, with tasks such as ensuring that the available resources are divided fairly between the different people who want to use the computer. Some operating systems allow the programmer to use a wide range of the facilities supported by the computer, whereas others are more restrictive. This leads again to differences between Prolog systems. Finally, the people who actually construct Prolog systems often have differing ideas about what features are aesthetically pleasing and what facilities are most needed. As a result, no two Prolog systems are completely alike. This situation is unlikely to change very quickly, because new ideas and improvements for Prolog implementation are constantly being thought up.

In this book, we have presented a version of Prolog that does not correspond exactly to any existing system. Rather, it is supposed to represent a "core" Prolog that will have a lot in common with any system you might encounter. If you have mastered the ideas of this book, you should not have too much difficulty adapting to any Prolog system that comes along. For most Prolog systems, the examples in this book can be used without change. For a few systems, the syntax and some of the built-in predicates may be confusingly different, but underneath will be the same basic Prolog that has been described here.

The best way to get to know about your own Prolog system is to read the user's manual that is provided with it. This may well be somewhat terse and summary, but if you have a basic grounding in the language, it should not be too hard to work out how the system differs from what you know. This appendix mentions a few points that are worth looking out for, and also goes into more detail about two particular Prolog systems that are fairly widespread. However, we would like to emphasise the fact that many of the current Prolog systems are slowly changing, and there is really no substitute for looking at an up-to-date manual for your installation. Here are some of the things that are most likely to differ between Prolog implementations.

Syntax.

Everybody has his own idea about what forms of syntax are most natural and pleasing. Fortunately, the syntax of Prolog is quite simple, and so there is not much scope for variation. One matter of dispute is how one should distinguish variables from atoms. Here we have used names beginning with upper-case letters for variables and names beginning with lower-case letters for atoms. In addition, we have allowed atoms consisting of sequences of sign symbols like "*", "." and "=". Some Prolog systems have adopted the reverse convention as regards upper- and lower-case letters (in which variables begin with lower-case letters). Others distinguish variable names by starting them with a special character, such as "_PERSON" or "*PERSON". This is convenient for a system that does not distinguish between upper- and lower-case letters. Another area where there is scope for variation is in the notation for clauses — how is the head separated from the body, and how are the goals in the body separated? Also, how are questions distinguished? It may just be a matter of some other atoms instead of ":-", ",", and "?-". Or it may be more complicated. In one early system, the head and the goals of a clause were placed one after another, with a "+" in front of the head and a "-" in front of each of the goals. In summary, you may find clauses that look like any of the following, or are different again:

```
uncle(X,Z) :- parent(X,Y), brother(Y,Z).
Uncle(x,z) <- Parent(x,y) & Brother(y,z).
UNCLE(_X,_Z) :- PARENT(_X,_Y), BROTHER(_Y,_Z).
+UNCLE(*X,*Z) -PARENT(*X,*Y) -BROTHER(*Y,*Z).
((UNCLE X1 X3) (PARENT X1 X2) (BROTHER X2 X3))
uncle(X,Z): parent(X,Y); brother(Y,Z).
```

Arbitrary Bounds

Because of the way different computers organise their storage, it may be difficult for the Prolog implementor to allow certain things to grow to unlimited size. Some things that are liable to vary from computer to computer are the maximum size of Prolog integers, whether floating-point numbers are available, the maximum number of arguments that a functor can have, the maximum number of characters in an atom, the maximum number of clauses a predicate can have, and so on.

Environmental Features

Because of the differences between different operating systems, some Prolog systems may allow you to interrupt your program while it is running, edit a disc file without losing the current state of your Prolog session, maintain several simultaneously running Prolog programs, receive input from or send output to special devices. However, none of these can necessarily be provided in all systems, and so you can expect to find some variation here. As well as determining which of these facilities are available, the operating system of your computer will most likely attach special importance to certain characters that you type in. For instance, the character that you type to mark an "end of file" at the end of a `consult(user)` will vary between installations. Other characters may be interpreted as requests for information about the status of the machine or as requests to change characters already typed. Such features are not part of the Prolog system that you use, but are nevertheless important when you decide to actually use the system.

Compilation

Most Prolog systems work by storing your clauses in a form that is close to the original textual form. When a clause is used, such a system has to inspect the clause and decide what to do according to what form it has. Such a system is called an *interpreter*. Another possibility is for the system to translate from your clauses into instructions that can be directly executed by the machine. Such a system is called a *compiler*. Using a compiler, you have the advantage that your program is run directly, rather than having to go through an interpretation process. Hence you might expect your program to run quicker. On the other hand, since the textual form is normally no longer available with a compiler, you might expect not to have the same information available when you are debugging (for instance, you may not be able to ask for a listing of your clauses). In some systems, you may have the choice between compiling and interpreting your clauses. In this case, you must carefully weigh up what advantages each has to offer.

Particular Built-In Predicates

Whereas the basic flow of control will work just the same in most Prolog systems, the special built-in predicates may differ. Sometimes it will simply be that extra predicates are provided for facilities that are easy to provide on a particular computer. Sometimes the same basic facilities may be provided by predicates that have slightly different effects. For instance, it would be sufficient for a Prolog system to provide either `functor` and `arg`, or just

"=..". This is because the first two can be defined in terms of the last one and vice versa. You may have to work out how to use the facilities provided to mimic those that you are used to working with. Some Prolog systems may provide *libraries* of useful programs, providing optional facilities in addition to the built-in predicates. For instance, grammar rules may be provided as part of the basic system, or it may be possible to load in a Prolog program from a library that will provide these facilities.

Debugging Facilities

It is still a matter for research to determine what debugging facilities are most suitable for Prolog. Meanwhile different systems present different conceptions of what features are needed. It is hoped that our general introduction of Chapter 8 will equip the reader to cope with whatever he finds.

APPENDIX D. Edinburgh Prolog

In this appendix we describe briefly the Prolog system implemented at the University of Edinburgh by David Warren, Fernando Pereira, and Luis Pereira. This implementation has become a *de facto* standard, and implementations modelled on it are available for a variety of other computers ranging from the smallest microcomputer to the largest mainframe. The "core" Prolog presented in this book is also modelled on Edinburgh Prolog, but in this Appendix we will mention only the points where there are significant differences from "core" Prolog. We first show what a session with Edinburgh Prolog looks like, and then go into more detail about how this system differs from our "core" Prolog. Finally, we list derivatives of Edinburgh Prolog that are available for other computers.

Example Session

Here is what a programming session with Edinburgh Prolog is like. In this example, we show exactly what appears on the terminal in the session. We also make various extra comments about what is happening. Here is the example session:

We start at the monitor level of the TOPS-10 operating system, and we ask it to run Prolog.

```
r prolog
Prolog-10  version 3.3 Copyright (C) 1981 by D. Warren, F. Pereira and L. Byrd
| ?- likes(X,Y).
no
```

The header information is, of course, liable to change slightly between different versions of the system. The characters "| ?-" were printed by Prolog as a "prompt". This tells us that it expects a question at this point. We have asked a question, and the answer was no. Not surprising, since there are no facts in the database yet. Now we assume that there is a file 'test.pl', and we consult it:

```
| ?- ['test.pl'].
test.pl consulted   58 words    0.01 sec.
yes
```

To make Prolog read in clauses from a file, we give it a question consisting of the file name (as a Prolog atom) in list brackets. Here we have a file of clauses about people liking one another.

```
| ?- likes(john,bertrand).

no

| ?- likes(john,albert).

no
```

Just asking a few questions about who likes whom. Prolog cannot satisfy any of these.

```
| ?- listing(likes).

likes(john,alfred).
likes(alfred,john).
likes(bertrand,john).
likes(david,bertrand).
likes(john,_1) :- likes(_1,bertrand).
yes
```

To find out what clauses we have for a predicate, we ask a question about the special built-in predicate listing. This particular question causes Prolog to print out all our clauses for likes. Note that Prolog writes out uninstantiated variables as an underline followed by a number. The clause at the end of the database was written in the file as:

```
likes(john,X) :- likes(X,bertrand).
```

Continuing,

```
| ?- likes(john,X).
X = alfred ;
X = david ;
no
```

Here we have asked for alternative solutions to the question, by typing semicolon and RETURN. There were two possible solutions, and then Prolog could find no more.

```
| ?- likes(X,Y).
X = john, Y = alfred ;
X = alfred, Y = john ;
X = bertrand, Y = john ;
X = david, Y = bertrand ;
X = john, Y = david ;
no
```

This time, each solution involves seeing what two variables are instantiated to. Again, we ask for alternatives by typing semicolon and RETURN until there are no more solutions.

```
| ?- [user].
```

Now we ask Prolog to read in clauses from the file user. This causes clauses
to be read in from the terminal. These clauses will be added at the end of the
database. When it is reading clauses (rather than questions), Prolog prompts
with "|" rather than "| ?-".

```
| likes(timothy,bertrand).
| user consulted    10 words       0.03 sec.
yes
```

We told Prolog to stop reading clauses after the first one by typing control-Z
at that point. We could have typed in several facts and rules before typing
control-Z. Now Prolog has finished with that question and is expecting
another question again.

```
| ?- likes(john,X).
X = alfred ;
X = david ;
X = timothy ;
no
```

Again, we ask for alternatives. Note that the new clause has led to a new
solution that was not present when we asked this question before.

```
| ?- likes(bertrand,Y).
Y = john
yes
```

This just illustrates the other way we can deal with alternatives. Here, we
just typed RETURN after the first answer. This causes the question to
succeed, and Prolog is now waiting for another question again.

```
| ?- core      36864  (7680 lo-seg + 29184 hi-seg)
heap      2560 =  1573 in use +   987 free
global    1177 =    16 in use +  1161 free
local     1024 =    16 in use +  1008 free
trail      511 =     0 in use +   511 free
0.36 sec. runtime
```

In response to the last "| ?-", we typed control-Z, to indicate that we were
finished. Prolog printed out some statistical information, and now we are
back with the TOPS-10 monitor. A complete record of this session has been
recorded on the file 'prolog.log' in your main directory.

Syntax

The syntax of Edinburgh Prolog is essentially as we have described in this book. In fact, it is slightly less restrictive about valid atoms and variables than the rules we have given. Every example in this book should be valid according to Edinburgh Prolog syntax. One important point should be made about operators with high precedences. Because " , " is itself an operator, it is stipulated that to avoid ambiguity all terms written with operators with the same or higher precedence must be enclosed in brackets. This ensures that, for instance,

```
foo(a,b,c)
```

can only be interpreted as a structure with functor foo of three arguments, and not as, for instance, something equivalent to

```
foo(a,',' (b,c))
```

or

```
foo(',' (a,',' (b,c)))
```

If we wanted to write this last term, we could do it with

```
foo((a,b,c))
```

The rule about operators of high precedence only affects a few operators like " : - " and " ; ". It does mean that something like:

```
?- retract(parent(A,B) :- father(A,B)).
```

is syntactically incorrect in Edinburgh Prolog. We need to supply an extra pair of brackets to make it legal.

Edinburgh Prolog provides an alternative syntax, in case you are using a terminal or an operating system that does not provide lower-case letters as well as upper-case letters. In this syntax, variables are distinguished from atoms by starting with the character "_". A built-in predicate 'NOLC' is provided to cause Prolog to start using these alternative conventions. The predicate 'LC' enables you to switch back to the normal rules.

Finally, a small point. The functor " . " (with two arguments) is not predefined as an operator in Edinburgh Prolog. You can define it yourself if you wish, but this is unnecessary if you always use the special list notation for lists.

Arbitrary Bounds

Edinburgh Prolog, as originally implemented on the DECsystem-10 computer, does not provide many arbitrary bounds that you are likely to encounter in practice. Operator precedences must be between 1 and 1200, and are roughly as given in this book. Prolog integers must be in the range -131072 to 131071, although the evaluation of integer expressions is able to deal with intermediate results that are larger than this. Real (floating point) numbers are not provided.

Environmental Features

DECsystem-10 Prolog provides the very useful facility of logging. In the normal case, during a Prolog session, the system makes a copy of (most of) what appears on your computer terminal in a disc file called 'prolog.log'. After you have finished, you can look at this file and see exactly what happened in the session. The 'prolog.log' file provides a useful record of what your program did when and what changes you made in the course of running it. Built-in predicates are provided for turning the logging facility on and off, in case you do not want it to operate all the time.

It is possible to interrupt a running program in DECsystem-10 Prolog by typing the character control-C. The system prompts you for an action to be performed. The options include break, continue (carry on with the program), exit (from Prolog), trace and notrace. The last two options involve continuing with the program after the amount of tracing has been altered. The break option suspends the execution of your current program, and gives you a new "copy" of the Prolog system to interact with. When you exit the break, your program will continue running.

The DECSystem-10 end-of-file character is control-Z. Typing this causes an exit from Prolog, the end of a break or the end of a consult, according to what situation you are in. The built-in predicate read matches its argument with the atom end_of_file if it encounters an end of file.

DECsystem-10 Prolog provides various facilities to help you save time reading in your programs again and again. It is possible to store the "state" of the Prolog system, including its current database, in a disc file in such a way that the state can be restored much faster than it would take to read in the program and get it to the same state. Also, DECsystem-10 Prolog will automatically read any input you may have in a file 'prolog.ini' at the beginning of a session before taking input from the terminal.

If an error occurs when you are running DECsystem-10 Prolog, the system prints out a message to tell you what has gone wrong. Most kinds of error will then cause a simple failure of the goals that caused them, and so your program will carry on running. Some errors are, however, more serious, and the system will abandon all currently running programs and ask you for the next question.

Compilation

DECsystem-10 Prolog provides the option of selectively compiling some of your clauses. This can increase space and time efficiency considerably. A built-in predicate provides a facility like consult, except that the clauses of the file are compiled, not interpreted. Efficiency of compiled clauses can be increased by the use of mode declarations, which allow you to specify how the clauses will be used (in terms of which arguments will be instantiated at which times). There are some restrictions on which clauses are suitable for compilation. It is also necessary to make certain other declarations to the system in order that it can properly function with a mixture of compiled and interpreted clauses.

Differences in Built-In Predicates

DECsystem-10 Prolog provides all the built-in predicates we have discussed, and will also deal correctly with grammar rules encountered inside a normal consult. This section describes some of the differences from the descriptions we have given.

The effect of the display predicate is always to print its argument on the terminal, not to the current output as we described.

In our description of arithmetic expressions, we stated that an arithmetic expression is only evaluated when it appears as the second argument of is. In all other circumstances, a structure like "2+3" just stands for itself.

This is not the case in DECsystem-10 Prolog, where various other predicates also evaluate integer expressions appearing as arguments. Examples of this are the relational operators "<", "=<", etc., and the predicate put. Hence the following sequence will work in DECsystem-10 Prolog, but produce an error or a failure in our "core" Prolog:

```
?- 2+4 < 12*(2+8).
```

yes

As an extra twist, a structure which is a list consisting of a single number is considered to be an arithmetic expression with the same value as the number. Hence in DECsystem-10 Prolog:

```
?- X is [25].
```

X = 25
yes

Because of this combination of features, the output of single characters can be specified in a mnemonic way, for instance:

```
?- put("a"), put("b").
```

ab
yes

(remember that "a" is the list consisting solely of the character code for the first letter of the alphabet in its lower case form).

Syntax of negation. There is no predicate named not, but the prefix operator "\+" is used instead. There is no "not equals" predicate "\=".

Variables as goals. This is really a matter of syntax, rather than anything else. We have seen how it is possible to invoke the goal corresponding to what a Prolog variable stands for by using the predicate call. DECsystem-10 Prolog provides an alternative way of doing the same thing. Instead of putting a goal like

```
..., call(X), ...
```

in a clause, it is possible to just put the variable on its own as a goal:

```
..., X, ...
```

It is still possible to use the call version, and indeed the system converts any goal X to a goal call(X) when it uses asserta or assertz on a clause.

Arguments to retract. In DECsystem-10 Prolog, because of difficulties associated with variables as goals, there are some differences about how bodies of clauses must be specified in goals for retract. The problem is that when we ask:

```
?- retract((mother(A,B) :- C)).
```

we might be asking Prolog to remove a clause specifically like:

```
mother(A,B) :- C.
```

with a variable as a goal in the body, or we might be asking it to remove a clause for mother with any body, like for instance:

```
mother(X,Y) :- parent(X,Y), female(Y).
```

To remove the possibility of ambiguity in these cases, DECsystem-10 Prolog always starts by replacing uninstantiated variables standing for single or multiple goals in retract arguments by structures using call. So the question:

```
?- retract((mother(A,B):-C)).
```

is actually treated like:

```
?- retract((mother(A,B):-call(C))).
```

If we wanted to remove the first clause for mother regardless of its body, we could specify instead:

```
?- clause(mother(A,B),C), retract((mother(A,B):-C)).
```

In this case, the previous clause goal results in C becoming sufficiently instantiated to escape the transformation.

Extra Built-In Predicates

As well as the built-in predicates we have described, DECsystem-10 Prolog provides a multitude of other facilities.

A *conditional form* makes it possible to provide goals that look like the following:

```
..., (likes(john,X) -> wooden(X); plastic(X)),...
```

The idea of such a complex goal is that if the "condition" before the -> succeeds, then the goal after the -> is invoked; otherwise the third goal is invoked. Any of the goals can themselves be Prolog goals. The conditional works exactly as if it were defined in DECsystem-10 Prolog as follows:

```
?- op(1050,xfy,->).
?- op(1100,xfy,';').

(X -> Y; Z) :- call(X), !, call(Y).
(X -> Y; Z) :- call(Z).
```

An *"indexed" database*. This allows you to associate information in the database with particular values, rather than having to use the standard Prolog retrieval mechanisms. For instance, if you wanted to store information about the ages of hundreds of people, the standard technique would be to have hundreds of clauses for a predicate like age. But then when you wanted to find out a particular person's age, Prolog would have to search through all of these until it found the right one. The trouble is that information is normally associated with predicates, and so there can be a lot of search when a predicate has many clauses. The indexed database would allow you to associate information in a more direct way with particular names.

The ability to access ancestors. We discussed the notion of ancestor goals in the chapter on debugging. DECsystem-10 Prolog provides built-in predicates that allow you to access ancestors from within a Prolog program.

Statistical information. DECsystem-10 Prolog provides built-in predicates that enable you to find out how fast your program is running and how much space it occupies.

Debugging Facilities

DECsystem-10 Prolog provides debugging facilities along the lines we have described in the book. In addition to the built-in predicates mentioned, there is a predicate that enables you to affect which ports are leashed during tracing.

References

DECsystem-10 Prolog User's Manual, Department of Artificial Intelligence, University of Edinburgh, Edinburgh, Scotland.

C-Prolog User's Manual, CAAD Studio, Department of Architecture, University of Edinburgh, Edinburgh, Scotland. Documents a system which runs under UNIX.

Prolog-1 User's Manual, Expert Systems Ltd, 9 West Way, Oxford, England. Documents a system which runs on a variety of computers ranging from a Z-80 under CP/M to a VAX under VMS.

APPENDIX E. micro-Prolog

We shall now describe some of the features of the micro-Prolog system developed for Z80-based microcomputers running under the CP/M operating system. micro-Prolog is also available for other microcomputers, and most of the comments below will apply to the other systems.

Example Session

All of our examples of micro-Prolog will make use of the "basic syntax". Other syntaxes, including one compatible with Edinburgh Prolog, can be loaded into memory if required.

Here is what might appear on your terminal in a typical micro-Prolog session. First of all, we instruct CP/M to run Prolog:

```
A>PROLOG
Micro-Prolog 3.00  S/N
(C) 1982 Logic Programming Associates Ltd.
9999 Bytes Free
&.?((likes x y))
Clause error at (likes x y)
```

The characters &. were printed by micro-Prolog as a prompt. This tells us that it expects us to type a command. The ? symbol means that we want to ask a question. What comes after it is a sequence of goals (to be taken as a conjunction) enclosed in round brackets. Each goal is itself given as a sequence inside brackets, with the predicate coming first and the arguments after it. Variables are signified by words beginning with x, y, z, X, Y, Z, and can be followed by numbers. In the goal given above, we ask whether anybody likes anybody. Since we as yet have no clauses for likes, micro-Prolog signals an error.

```
&.LOAD TEST
```

Another important command is LOAD. This is followed by the name of a file. Issuing this command causes the clauses in the file TEST.LOG to be read in, augmenting the database in the same way as consult does. We can now ask questions:

```
&.?((likes john bertrand))
?
&.?((likes john alfred))
&.
```

Notice that micro-Prolog signals the fact that a question has failed by typing a "?", and the fact that a question has succeeded by just printing a prompt again. To find out which clauses we have got for likes, we issue the LIST command. We can ask for a listing of the whole program, or of just the clauses for some set of predicates. Let's see what we have for likes:

```
&.LIST (likes)
((likes john alfred))
((likes alfred john))
((likes bertrand john))
((likes david bertrand))
((likes john x)
        (likes x bertrand))
```

To get some answers printed out for a question, we make use of built-in predicates. The predicate PP causes its arguments to be printed on the terminal, and the predicate FAIL fails.

```
&.?((likes john x) (PP x) (FAIL))
alfred
david
?
```

Here there were two solutions to the question "Who does John like?".

If we wish to add some new clauses to the database from the terminal, we don't have to use a special command — we can just type the clauses straight in. We discuss the micro-Prolog syntax for clauses in the next section.

```
&.((likes timothy bertrand))
&.?((likes john x) (PP x) (FAIL))
alfred
david
timothy
?
```

To leave micro-Prolog and return to CP/M, we give the QT command followed by a dot:

```
&.QT.
A>
```

Syntax

The syntax of micro-Prolog is quite different to what we have seen in this book, but it shouldn't take very long to get used to it. The basic idea is there is only one kind of term: the list. If we wish to construct the "term" with functor f and four arguments, we actually use a list of five elements, with f appearing as the head, and the four arguments appearing successively as the remaining elements. Thus, what in the core syntax would be written as

```
f(a,g(2,3),c)
```

would be written in micro-Prolog as:

```
(f (g 2 3) c)
```

Here we see the different syntax for lists as well, in which lists are enclosed in round brackets, with elements separated by spaces.

Clauses are represented as a list of terms, where the first is the head of the clause, and the rest are the goals, which taken as a conjunction, form the body. Here is a more complicated clause than that shown in the example session above:

```
((alter (z1|z2) (x|y)) (change z1 x) (alter z2 y) )
```

This is the second clause for alter of Section 3.4. Note that the vertical bar means the same as in the core syntax.

Arbitrary Bounds

micro-Prolog can handle floating point numbers with up to eight digits of precision and a (base 10) exponent in the range -127 to 127. Atom names (called "constants" in micro-Prolog) can have at most 60 characters, and a term cannot contain more than 64 variables. These restrictions are not a problem in practice.

Environmental

micro-Prolog provides a variety of facilities to aid the development of programs at the terminal. Built-in predicates LOAD and SAVE enable programs to be read in from and written out to disc files. A sophisticated line editor and program structure editor enable changes to an existing program to be made without the necessity of leaving the Prolog system. A running micro-Prolog program can be interrupted by typing control-C .

Particular Built-In Predicates

The names and purposes of built-in predicates vary considerably from those discussed in this book. Here is a brief summary of some of the facilities offered.

The type of a term can be tested using NUM, CON, and VAR, which succeed for numbers, constants (atoms), and variables respectively. In addition SYS tests whether a constant is the name of a built-in predicate, and INT tests for a whole number.

Predicates to manipulate the database are ADDCL (similar to assert), CL (similar to clause) and DELCL (similar to retract). These predicates can be provided with an extra integer argument, so that the Nth clause in a procedure can be easily manipulated.

Since the only kind of term in micro-Prolog is the list, a predicate like "=.." is unnecessary. The predicate STRING allows the programmer to create new atoms and to access the internal structure of atom names, in a way similar to name.

Compound goals can be constructed in micro-Prolog by using the built-in predicates OR, NOT, and IF. The predicate FAIL causes an immediate failure, and the "cut" also appears, represented by "/".

Arithmetic is provided through a number of predicates, instead of through a single predicate like is. The arithmetic predicates have been designed to be as "reversible" as possible, so that, for example, the goal

(SUM x y z)

causes z to be matched with the sum of y and x if x and y are both instantiated. On the other hand, if initially y and z are instantiated but x is not, then x will become instantiated to the difference z - y.

File operations in micro-Prolog are similar in spirit to the core Prolog, except that there is no notion of current input or output stream. Instead, output to a file and input from a file proceed through the use of predicates (WRITE and READ respectively) that require to be given the name of the file each time. Special predicates are provided so that input/output via the user's terminal is convenient.

micro-Prolog allows the programmer to develop programs in chunks called modules. This facility minimises the possibility of accidental name clashes in programs, and facilitates the exchange of programs between different programmers.

Debugging Facilities

A program tracing facility is provided with micro-Prolog, but has to be LOADed specially before it can be used. It provides information on the progress of all goals that do not involve built-in predicates. Messages are printed at that CALL, EXIT, and FAIL ports (called ENTER, FINISH, and FAIL, respectively). The user is allowed to interact at CALL ports, and can specify CONTINUE (carry on with traced execution), SKIP (discontinue tracing until the current goal is finished, FINISH (cause the current goal to immediately succeed), and FAIL (cause the current goal to immediately fail).

References

micro-PROLOG: Programming in Logic, by K.L. Clark and F.G. McCabe, Prentice-Hall, 1984.

INDEX